C000301779

Praise for

When Prime Brokers Fail

The Unheeded Risk to Hedge Funds, Banks, and the Financial Industry

"*When Prime Brokers Fail* is an excellent primer on the new landscape of leading prime brokers that emerged from the credit crisis. Jonathan Aikman has accurately captured the massive shift in the prime brokerage industry that occurred as a result of the need for banks within an increasingly global and complex hedge fund industry."

—JONATHAN HITCHON
Co-Head of Global Prime Finance, Deutsche Bank

"As someone who has worked on both sides of the street over the past fourteen years this is the first time I have seen such a succinct layout of the way things really are. Whether you have been in the business for twenty years or are just interested in how the machine really works, this is a must-read."

—STEPHEN BURNS
Director of Electronic Equity Trading, Wellington West Capital Markets

"Jon Aikman's book provides a great review of the world of prime finance and its interaction with hedge funds. It is an essential guide to understanding why so many hedge funds failed during the 2008 crash, and why so many will continue to fail in the future."

—FRANÇOIS LHABITANT, PhD
Chief Investment Officer, Kedge Capital
Professor of Finance, EDHEC Business School

"Aikman does a masterful job of examining and explaining the intricacies and interdependencies of prime brokerages and the role that these operations play in our increasingly complex financial system. In providing this thorough analysis, Aikman lends valuable insights into how the financial crisis, hedge funds, and regulations have impacted the area of prime finance and the broader banking and investing market. This book will be a valuable tool for students of finance, regulators, and practitioners from novice to veteran for years to come."

—PETER J. SHIPPEN, CFA, CAIA
President, Redwood Asset Management Inc.

"This is a must-read text for every hedge fund manager, investment banking executive, and prime brokerage professional. Our team searches daily for new great resources on prime brokerage to help build our web site on the topic, and this is hands down the #1 most educational resource on the challenges, trends, and risks within the prime brokerage space that we have ever come across—well over $10,000 worth of advice and valuable explanations contained here."

—RICHARD WILSON
Founder of Prime Brokerage Association and
PrimeBrokerageGuide.com

When Prime Brokers Fail

When Prime Brokers Fail

The Unheeded Risk to Hedge Funds, Banks, and the Financial Industry

J. S. AIKMAN

BLOOMBERG PRESS
An Imprint of

Copyright © 2010 by J. S. Aikman. All rights reserved.

Published by John Wiley & Sons, Inc., Hoboken, New Jersey.
Published simultaneously in Canada.

No part of this publication may be reproduced, stored in a retrieval system, or transmitted in any form or by any means, electronic, mechanical, photocopying, recording, scanning, or otherwise, except as permitted under Section 107 or 108 of the 1976 United States Copyright Act, without either the prior written permission of the Publisher, or authorization through payment of the appropriate per-copy fee to the Copyright Clearance Center, Inc., 222 Rosewood Drive, Danvers, MA 01923, (978) 750-8400, fax (978) 646-8600, or on the web at www.copyright.com. Requests to the Publisher for permission should be addressed to the Permissions Department, John Wiley & Sons, Inc., 111 River Street, Hoboken, NJ 07030, (201) 748-6011, fax (201) 748-6008, or online at http://www.wiley.com/go/permissions.

Limit of Liability/Disclaimer of Warranty: While the publisher and author have used their best efforts in preparing this book, they make no representations or warranties with respect to the accuracy or completeness of the contents of this book and specifically disclaim any implied warranties of merchantability or fitness for a particular purpose. No warranty may be created or extended by sales representatives or written sales materials. The advice and strategies contained herein may not be suitable for your situation. You should consult with a professional where appropriate. Neither the publisher nor author shall be liable for any loss of profit or any other commercial damages, including but not limited to special, incidental, consequential, or other damages.

For general information on our other products and services or for technical support, please contact our Customer Care Department within the United States at (800) 762-2974, outside the United States at (317) 572-3993 or fax (317) 572-4002.

Wiley also publishes its books in a variety of electronic formats. Some content that appears in print may not be available in electronic books. For more information about Wiley products, visit our web site at www.wiley.com.

Library of Congress Cataloging-in-Publication Data:
Aikman, J. S. (Jonathan S.)
When prime brokers fail : the unheeded risk to hedge funds, banks, and the financial industry / J.S. Aikman. – 1st ed.
p. cm.
Includes bibliographical references and index.
ISBN 978-1-57660-355-0
1. Hedge funds. 2. Brokers. 3. Investment banking. 4. Investment advisors. 5. Financial services industry. 6. Financial risk. I. Title.
HG4530.A395 2010
332.64'5—dc22
2009053602

Printed in the United States of America.
10 9 8 7 6 5 4 3 2 1

For Penny Aikman-Freedom:

"To strive, to seek, to find, and not to yield."
Lord Tennyson, Ulysses

Contents

Acknowledgments

This work is an initial effort to explore one of the most complex, obscure, and increasingly important parts of international finance. As the Chinese proverb states, "It is better to light a candle than to curse the darkness." I have been fortunate to stand on the shoulders of giants in completing this work, but all errors, omissions, and shortcomings are my own.

Thanks to the various individuals who assisted my understanding with their experience, intelligent discussion, insightful comments, and relevant criticisms. A special thanks to Jonathan Hitchon and Barry Bausano, Co-Heads of Global Prime Finance at Deutsche Bank, and many others from Deutsche Bank. Eric Sprott of Sprott Asset Management provided invaluable insights into the markets, derivatives, and its financial institutions. Special thanks to Stanley Hartt, Chairman of Macquarie Capital Markets Canada Ltd. for his astute analysis of the markets and the challenges for the future. Thanks to Steven Lofchie, partner at Cadwalader, Wickersham & Taft LLP for his profound insights and his invaluable work *Guide to Broker Dealer Regulation*; and thanks to the many other managers and professionals at BONY Mellon, JPMorgan Chase, and other leading firms. I wish to express my profound thanks to the many top managers and professionals in international and domestic prime finance and executing brokerage services that I have had the pleasure to know and learn from, including Nick Rowe, Neil Swinburne, Christopher Monnery, Jeanne Campanelli, Matthew Brace, Timothy Wilkinson, John Quaile, Jonathan Asher, and the inimitable James K. Cunningham.

I would like to acknowledge and thank my editor, Evan Burton, and other professionals at Bloomberg Press. Evan's expertise, diligence, and judgment improved the book immeasurably, and I am very grateful for his efforts. Also, thanks to Kevin Commins, Mary Daniello, and the other professionals at John Wiley & Sons. There are a host of others whose courteous assistance and intelligence assisted with this work, including Nabil Meralli, Chris Fearn, Stephen Burns of Wellington West Capital Markets Inc., Peter Shippen of Redwood Capital and Ark Fund Management Ltd., Bill Fearn, Stacey-Parker Yull, Allan Vlah, Thomas Sarantos, and Victoria Ho, and many others. Also, this work required a significant amount of research from both international and U.S. resources. Matthew Anderson was a diligent researcher for many daunting tasks.

There are many other friends, family, intellectuals, professors, and organizations that also deserve my gratitude for their influence and support, including Oxford University, the Saïd Business School, Brasenose College, Queen's University, the University of Toronto, Rotman School of Management, Bloomberg Press, the Chartered Alternative Investment Association, Canadian Hedge Watch, Professor Mark Ventresca, Professor Chris McKenna, Dr. Michael Ruse, Dr. Richard Spratley, and finally my friend and mentor, Dr. Robert M. Freedom.

When Prime Brokers Fail

PART I

The Business

1 Extraordinary Markets

The euphoria of the equity and debt markets that caused investment banks like Bear Stearns, Merrill Lynch, and others to take massive proprietary and operational risks is gone. These risky assets were taken on leverage and as a result, the five major independent investment banks have been transformed, bankrupted, or acquired. Lehman Brothers went bankrupt. Merrill Lynch and Bear Stearns have been acquired by Bank of America and JPMorgan Chase respectively. The premier remaining prime finance firms, Goldman Sachs and Morgan Stanley, are no longer independent. The capital base of the investment banks was risked and lost. The critics and risk managers who warned of the hazards of mixing leverage with speculative investments were terminated, excluded, and vilified prior to the global financial crisis.

The euphoria of the markets, or euphoric episode, has historical precedence. Speculation has been here before and undoubtedly shall return again, whether it is "tulips in Holland, gold in Louisiana, real estate in Florida . . ."[1] Once the pendulum of diligence and risk management has swung in favor of a new technology, commodities, or new "riskless" financial instruments

[1] Galbraith, p. 2.

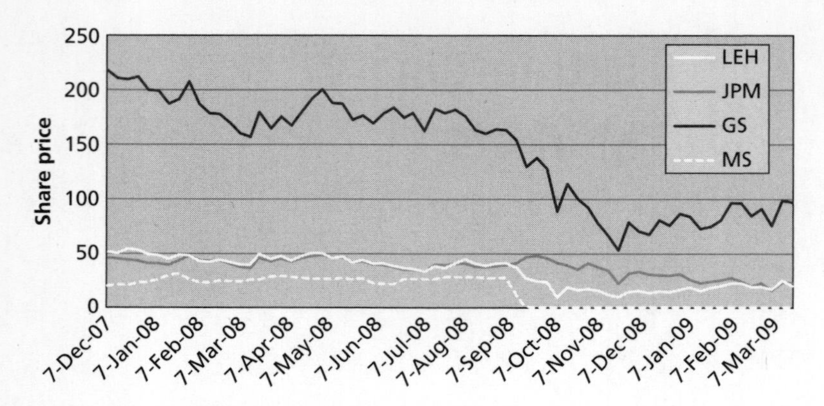

Figure 1.1 Leading Prime Brokers and Lehman

that offer easy wealth, then greed will undoubtedly rise in some new, unanticipated form. After all, the financial markets are driven by individuals with a vested interest in their success.

As the economist John Kenneth Galbraith noted, after the Great Depression, "the euphoric episode is protected and sustained by the will of those who are involved, in order to justify the circumstances that are making them rich. And it is equally protected by the will to ignore, exorcise or condemn those who express doubts."[2]

However, to blame any one party for the global crisis is overly simplistic, and fails to identify the underlying factors and causes of the current financial crisis. It also fails to yield an understanding of how to reduce the probability of a recurrence or an even worse scenario. The speculation, leverage, and vulnerability of investment banks and financial firms was exposed by the crisis.[3] The consequences of highly improbable scenarios were felt by all investment banks, prime brokers, and hedge funds in some form (see **Figure 1.1**).

---

[2] Galbraith, p. 11.

[3] See Baquero & Verbeek, 2005.

Lessons Learned

Today the international economic environment of euphoria has been punctured. Investor and public confidence and trust in the financial system have eroded considerably. That is hopefully a polite way of saying that the bubble has burst, and we are left with the sober task of reviewing the lessons to avoid yet another crisis. A variety of different reports have reviewed the causes, factors, and effects of the financial crisis.[4] In the financial crisis, we learned that:

- Investment banks can and do fail.
- The failure of investment banks, and prime brokers, threatens risks to hedge funds, investors, banks, and ultimately systemic failure.
- Hedge funds provide diversification (and some spectacular results), but do not provide absolute returns in bull and bear markets.
- Hedge fund and broker-dealer managers have been responsible for simplistic frauds on sophisticated clients and advisers.
- Ratings agencies have been unable or unwilling to assess risk accurately.
- Banking and securities regulators were not able to protect the public, investors, or the financial system even with extraordinary regulatory actions.
- Leveraged financing and a massive derivatives market pose a danger to the stability of major banks, financial institutions, insurance companies, pension funds, and even governments.
- Financial innovation and leverage are both important sources of financing but may pose individual, firm, and systemic risks.

---

[4] Various international reports examined the causes and impact of the financial crisis, including *The Turner Review* (Turner, 2009) at Chapter 1, the various G-20 reports that attempt to address the multiple layers of the financial crisis including G-20, 2009a, 2009b, and 2009d; FSA discussion paper (FSA, 2009); A World Economic Forum Report, 2009.

- The assessment of risk has been misguided and systemic risks created by interlinkages have not been transparent or understood.

There was a slow chain of antecedents and consequents, causes and effects that impacted the global financial system. The financial reckoning took some time to arrive, but like a tsunami, it was foreseeable to those who looked for the signs, or had an interest in its arrival.[5] The global economy has now contracted broadly and deeply. The current crisis in the global economy, financial markets, and international banking system is profound, with no simple solution.

Euphoria and Crisis

The euphoria of private equity, leveraged buyouts, and massive mergers and acquisitions which drove the capital markets into 2007 has disappeared. The bubble in the U.S and U.K housing markets, consumer spending, and easy access to credit fueled the subprime crisis, which brought about catastrophic contractions in liquidity and financing in the debt markets starting in the summer of 2007.

The result in the markets was a massive shift away from mortgage-backed and asset-backed securities and their derivatives. Those individuals and institutions left holding subprime securities had a new name for them: "toxic waste." The mortgage market downturn in the United States and increasing default rates led to the credit crunch, which in turn led to other consequences, particularly for prime brokers and hedge funds.

In early 2008, Bear Stearns was a leading prime broker. In attempting to catch a falling knife, Bear Stearns's hedge funds tried to call the bottom of the market. Bear Stearns was hit broadside by the subprime blow-ups of its proprietary hedge

---

[5] For an interesting prediction of the fall of the equity markets and the U.S. real estate market meltdown, see Farber, 2005.

funds and other mortgage-backed securities. Their distress caused many financial firms to reduce or eliminate counterparty risks. Prime broker clients removed significant assets from Bear Stearns, fearing that bankruptcy would impact their collateral assets. The impact of the toxic assets on its balance sheet, and a declining prime broker business, made the discount acquisition by JPMorgan Chase, with the support and financing of the U.S. federal government, the only reasonable option other than bankruptcy.

On May 30, 2008, Bear Stearns was acquired by JPMorgan Chase.[6] Bear's toxic assets were subsumed into JPMorgan Chase's balance sheet with assistance and guarantees from the federal government.[7] The Bear Stearns prime broker business continued on under JPMorgan Chase, and hedge funds soon returned their business. The prime finance market continued with business as usual until September 2008.

On September 7, 2008, two of the most significant financial events in modern history occurred. The public did not seem to focus on Fannie Mae and Freddie Mac possibly because of their status as semigovernmental organizations. Their distress and conservatorship did not immediately signal the crisis that was to follow. However, for the balance sheet of the U.S. federal government, whether one cuts a check (decreases assets) or assumes the liabilities of an organization (increase liabilities), the financial impact is the same. The sudden conservatorship of Fannie Mae and Freddie Mac were truly colossal financial and political events. With combined liabilities of approximately 6 trillion dollars, the financial risks of these entities were shifted to the U.S. federal government. The federal government's action prevented a total collapse of the housing, mortgage and debt markets, but their efforts would not prevent collateral damage

[6] JPMorgan Chase Bank (formerly known as Chase Mankattan Bank) et al. v. Springwell Navigation Corp., 2008.

[7] For the G-20 government considerations for removing toxic assets from banks' balance sheets, see Perkins, 2009.

to investment banks, financial firms, capital markets, and the OTC derivatives market.

Lehman Brothers

Lehman Brothers was considered by many to be the most vulnerable of the major bulge bracket investment banks. The concern for the future of the bank was public and widely discussed in the media given its public failures to raise capital or find a suitable partner.[8] Yet many observers remained optimistic to the end that Lehman Brothers would find a partner. There was no white knight to save the struggling investment bank, however, as there had been for Bear Stearns and would be for Merrill Lynch.

At close of business on September 12, 2008, Lehman Brothers Holding Inc. (LEH) ended trading at $3.65. On that day, Lehman Brothers international operations took extraordinary steps to rehypothecate customer collateral assets and utilized them for financing with a series of stock loan and repo transactions. This is not surprising as the investment bank was struggling for financing. Lehman Brothers did not receive a bailout from the federal government. At the end of the day, the international prime broker, Lehman Brothers (International) Europe, transferred approximately $8 billion from London to the parent holding corporation in New York. The cash swept out of the United Kingdom and other international locations was not returned. Hedge funds assets and other clients had their assets rehypothecated, liquidated, and the cash sent out of the jurisdiction. This was reportedly a normal sweep of cash and securities back to New York in extraordinary times. However, it effectively wiped out the international investment bank and its international clients, some of which were banks, financial firms, and hedge funds.

The Lehman Brothers parent holding corporation had the power to decide which of its hundreds of discrete subsidiaries

[8] http://www.smartmoney.com/investing/economy/september-12-2008-friday-will-lehman-find-a-buyer-how-harvard-s-endowment-did/.

would receive financing. On Monday morning Lehman Brothers Holding Inc. (LEH) started trading at $0.26, down approximately 93 percent. Some Lehman Brothers entities would receive financing to continue active operations at least for a limited period, while other entities were forced into bankruptcy immediately. The return of the collateral assets remains the source of contentious litigation as the clients and creditors to the international investment bank were effectively left with unsecured claims against a bankrupt firm with minimal assets and extensive liabilities. The battle to return collateral has been further fueled by the rather awkward disclosure that the discount acquisition by Barclays Capital of Lehman Brother's U.S. brokerage operations resulted in a reported windfall profit of $3.47 billion.[9]

The long, slow path of Lehman Brothers to bankruptcy pointed out the frailty of unfavored independent broker-dealers and the effects of imposing market discipline over systemic risks. It also exposed the vulnerability of the independent investment banks which were not deemed to pose systemic risk. Not since the junk bond kings, Drexel Burnham Lambert had a major broker-dealer become bankrupt. The Lehman Brothers bankruptcy appeared to be justified in order to restore market discipline leading up to the event and even at the time of the initial bankruptcy filing on September 15, 2008. The potential for systemic failure and contagion was not immediately clear.

Further, the experience of Bear Stearns may have made investors, financial firms, and hedge funds complacent that a government bailout or eleventh hour acquisition was forthcoming. A variety of investors had started negotiations with Lehman Brothers, but for one reason or another, had passed on direct assumption of the business. In light of the massive liabilities to the derivatives and debt markets, potential suitors preferred to scavenge the remaining assets (including many skilled Lehman Brothers' employees) rather than acquiring a

[9] Scinta & Sandler, 2009.

distressed business poisoned with toxic assets and a troubled business model.[10]

Lehman Brothers' market capitalization and businesses dropped rapidly prior to its bankruptcy. Ultimately, Lehman Brothers revealed how interconnected the banks, financial institutions, and hedge funds had become. The Lehman Brothers bankruptcy had a catastrophic effect on prime broker clients, stock lending funds, and money market funds which provided liquidity to the markets and were significant holders of ultrasecure short-term U.S. government debt. Lehman Brothers' bankruptcy created broad trading and massive derivative exposures for many of its counterparties. Similarly, credit default swaps on Lehman Brothers created huge gains for some hedge funds and created corresponding liabilities for less fortunate counterparties, such as AIG.

After Lehman Brothers' collapse, brokers and banks stopped trusting each other. Hedge funds stopped trusting the investment banks and their prime brokers. No hedge fund, prime broker, or investment bank wanted exposure to any other party. Hedge funds reduced their leverage significantly, and the deleveraging cycle of the investment banks and other firms continued. Investment banks reduced lending and the leverage available to clients, and banks ceased lending and borrowing from each other.[11] Normal financing transactions ground to a halt after September 16, 2008.

The Run on Money Market Funds

When the damage was revealed the markets panicked. There was a flight to safety. Investors sought only the safest investments; traditionally short-term U.S. government debt was such a safe

[10] For a review of the lead-up to Lehman's bankruptcy see Sender, Guerrera, Larsen, & Silverman, 2008. Also, many parts of Lehman were subsequently parceled out to a variety of investors, including a variety of asset management arms; Reuters, 2008 and Grene, 2008.

[11] The record spreads of LIBOR-OIS demonstrated the breadth of the problem in the financing markets post-Lehman,

haven. Money market mutual funds are huge purchasers of U.S. short-term debt, and on September 16, 2008, the Reserve Primary Fund, the oldest money market mutual fund, reported substantial exposures to Lehman Brothers. These exposures to Lehman Brothers reduced the money market mutual fund's net asset value (NAV) to approximately $0.97. By dipping below a NAV of $1.00, the Reserve Primary Fund had "broken the buck." Although this is only a small loss, it is an extremely rare occurrence, and it had a massive impact on already nervous and falling markets. If the most liquid and safe investments could lose money, then was any investment safe? Other money market mutual funds soon came under similar pressure from investor redemptions. The run on money market mutual funds and securities lending funds had begun and involved some of the most systemically important firms, including the Bank of New York Mellon.[12] U.S. money market funds were redeemed at a record pace. The run on money market mutual funds contracted liquidity and threatened to cause the liquidation of other funds such as the Putnam Investments Prime Money Market Fund.[13]

The money market funds are important sources of liquidity for the international markets and especially for broker-dealers. The run on money market mutual funds resulted in massive contractions in liquidity as redemptions threatened to swallow up available cash reserves. Updates and assurances from money market mutual funds attempted to allay concerns, including statements of exposures to various notable market counterparties, such as AIG, Morgan Stanley, Goldman Sachs, and Washington Mutual.[14] Notwithstanding these assurances, institutional investors continued redemptions as the shocking revelation that U.S. money market mutual fund investments were potentially worth less than

---

[12] The Bank of New York Mellon's security lending fund also "broke the buck" due to exposures to Lehman Brothers.

[13] The Putnam Investments Prime Money Market Fund held over $15 billion, and other leading money market mutual funds cumulatively held assets in excess of $600 Billion.

[14] See Management, 2008.

holding cash set in.[15] The money market mutual funds reported that initial waves of redemptions came from institutional investors. Due to the mechanics of their redemption waiting periods, redemptions from retail investors had not even been processed but loomed in the following week.

In response, the U.S Department of Treasury announced an emergency program to insure the holdings of any eligible money market fund to guarantee that if the fund dropped below a NAV of $1.00, it would be restored to $1.00.[16] The run on the money market mutual funds was stemmed by the insurance program, as the Treasury guarantee of the money market funds was effectively a guarantee that the fund would always be as good as holding cash. Thus institutional and retail investors ceased redeeming money market investments. This was a particularly important step for the U.S. government as the liquidation of the U.S. money market funds would have dumped significant amounts of U.S. short-term debt on the international market. The run had the potential to cause a total collapse of the U.S. debt market and may have resulted in a run on treasuries and ultimately the U.S. dollar if the money market funds were liquidated and contagion spread. This in turn would have posed systemic risk by preventing the government from financing multitrillion-dollar bailouts and stimulus packages, potentially leading to the collapse of the international reserve currency.

A run of a different kind occurred with prime brokers. The remaining two elite prime brokers—Morgan Stanley and Goldman Sachs—had massive collateral holdings in their prime finance businesses. Their clients, the hedge funds and other investment funds, reduced leverage, sold out of their positions, and withdrew collateral at alarming rates. This was an indirect run on the prime brokers, who were forced to return cash and collateral that had previously been used for financing them. The run on

[15] The money market investment managers continued to assure investors with updates, including Federated Money Market Fund (Federated, 2008), UBS (Management, 2008), and other major funds.

[16] The insurance program was supported by the Exchange Stabilization Fund.

the free-standing investment banks saw clients move assets to perceived safe havens, including custodians and universal banks. The universal banks that benefited were able to offer security, transparency, and the potential for support from governments in the United States and internationally.

Many U.S. financial firms had reportedly been targeted by short sellers. In some cases, the significant drop in the value of financial firms was attributed to abusive short sales, while in other cases it was merely investors liquidating long positions, and falling equities markets globally. On September 19, 2008, the SEC issued the first short-selling ban for an expanding list of U.S. securities firms, banks, and other financial institutions. The various regulators around the world followed suit in a haphazard cascade of similar, but distinct, short-selling restrictions. The short-selling ban was designed to limit the pernicious acts of abusive short sellers who were pounding falling financial stocks with additional short positions, and even naked short sales. The result was a spiraling decrease in the value of the bank and financial stocks around the globe. The short sellers were not stopped from creating short positions, which had a variety of other structures, derivatives, and financial instruments to achieve their investment goals. However, the short-selling restrictions did impact the financing of the broker-dealers. Broker-dealers were unable to utilize stock loan and repo transactions to finance operations on the stocks, and this further limited the available financing at just the time when they could afford it least. The result of a run on the prime brokers by clients removing collateral and their inability to finance with remaining stocks deprived the independent investment banks of necessary sources of financing.

There was pervasive confusion and fear throughout the international financial system and markets in September 2008. Of particular concern to hedge funds were the solvency, security, and transparency of Goldman Sachs and Morgan Stanley. One week after the largest bankruptcy in U.S. history, Lehman Brothers' $683 billion in assets, both Goldman Sachs and Morgan Stanley were registered as bank holding companies. Why was the transformation to deposit-taking financial institutions necessary? The structural changes were required in part for financing. It was necessary as hedge funds, investment banks, and other counterparties stopped lending and borrowing from these independent investment banks. The hedge funds continued to withdraw their collateral assets as they had with Lehman Brothers and Bear Stearns, and institutional counterparties restricted or eliminated exposures. A combination of concerns captured investors, and forced hedge funds into a prisoner's dilemma. The fear of a deep-freeze of collateral assets similar to what happened at Lehman Brothers, hedge fund manager's concerns about fiduciary duties to their investors, and ongoing efforts to mitigate and diversify risks against prime brokers all led to removal of collateral assets and a run on the prime brokers. The removal of collateral assets is critical for prime brokers as fees, expenses, and financing are derived from these collateral assets. The other banks, hedge funds, corporations, and institutions stopped lending and borrowing as liquidity evaporated and counterparty default concerns became pervasive and paramount. Deleveraging of the banks and prime brokers and the removal of hedge funds' collateral assets increased in this tumultuous period.[17] After the dust settled, we have some insight as to where the hedge fund assets, cash and securities, were transferred. Notable beneficiaries of the change in the prime finance market were large universal banks, and significant amounts of the business transferred to the perceived safety of European banks with U.S. affiliates.[18]

In the extreme liquidity crisis after Lehman Brothers' bankruptcy, the financing model of the independent U.S. investment banks failed. The only remaining lender was the lender of last resort, the Federal Reserve. However, only banks with secured financing such as triparty repo agreements may have

[17] Avery, 2008.

[18] Reportedly, some beneficiaries include Credit Suisse, Deutsche Bank, BNP Paribas, and JPMorgan Chase, which is now the largest prime broker.

access to the Federal Reserve window. On September 21, 2008, the elite prime brokers, Goldman Sachs and Morgan Stanley, were transformed into bank holding companies, a previously unthinkable option. This last registration, while apparently minor, was a significant event in that it changed the investment bank's regulatory regime and allowed for direct financing by the Federal Reserve.

The important lesson Lehman Brothers revealed was that independent investment banks were highly leveraged and vulnerable to liquidity shocks. Hedge funds were exposed to significant counterparty risk to their prime broker, particularly in the international sphere where domestic protections were absent. Hedge funds liquidated positions, reduced leverage, and withdrew collateral and funds from the remaining independent investment banks.[19] The concern for clients' collateral spiraled into a category five securities run. By the end of October 2008, all the free-standing investment banks were extinct and hedge funds were sitting on record amounts of cash.

The Lehman Brothers bankruptcy was a catalyst for the financial crisis in the fall of 2008. The crisis precipitated catastrophic effects for prime brokers, investment banks, financial institutions, and the international equity and credit markets. Other victims of the financial carnage included MBIA, Wachovia, and Washington Mutual, and many smaller banks. There were just as many near misses as well. Many other firms and banks were financed only by the grace of the Federal Reserve, FDIC, and U.S. federal government initiatives such as the Troubled Asset Relief Program (TARP). These firms include AIG, Chrysler, General Motors, GMAC, American Express, and many others.[20] The other aspects of the bailout were financed by raising more debt. Thus without stemming the run on major money market

[19] The withdrawals from Morgan Stanley and Goldman Sachs were significant in 2008; see Terzo, 2008b.

[20] For an interesting review of the markets and accidents along the way, see Lewis & Einhorn, 2009.

funds and other systemically important banks and firms, the entire U.S. financial system would have been placed in jeopardy.

Broker-dealers, investment banks, and universal banks were challenged in 2008. Many hedge funds were totally annihilated in the crisis. The breadth and number of hedge funds that became distressed, redeemed, voluntarily closed, or blew up was unprecedented. There were legal, operational, and investment pitfalls. Some funds made catastrophic investment decisions to remain highly levered in volatile markets. Others managed to navigate the storm in the markets, to avoid failures of prime brokers, and rejected investments in toxic assets were still redeemed by nervous investors. Institutional investors pulled more and more capital from the alternative investment asset class in both struggling and successful funds. The fear of complete global meltdown, coupled with frauds and failing trust, became pervasive in the financial industry. It did not help that, on average, the hedge fund industry lost capital. While there were notable exceptions of superior management and exceptional returns, the poor industry average performance and egregious cases of fraud led to record redemptions. The myth that hedge funds perform well in both bull and bear markets was dispelled. However, it is important to note that hedge funds did not precipitate, nor were they central to, the crisis.

Many institutional investors redeemed hedge fund investments across the board. Nowhere were the strains or implications of unprecedented markets felt more than in the area of prime finance. Although it is not a cause of the crisis, prime finance is the intersection of investment banks and hedge funds, and their investors. Prime finance is the axis point of many important actors on the world financial stage. Prime brokers are primarily responsible for leverage and may provide liquidity to the individual investors, hedge funds, and markets. The complexity of the relationship should reveal that the prime brokerage model is largely a safe and preferable form of secured financing. In fact, the prime finance model is designed to protect prime brokers and the larger financial industry from failing hedge funds. Although the hedge funds borrow from prime brokers, they also provide important sources of financing for them in the form of cash and collateral securities posted with the prime broker. The interrelationship and complexities of the services provided are among the most complicated in international finance.

The effects of a prime broker failure require a detailed examination of the fallout from Lehman Brothers. The Lehman Brothers bankruptcy was an international failure. It revealed the complexity of the prime finance market and the need for clarity, transparency, and security over assets held with prime brokers. Major hedge funds with billions in assets were caught wrong-footed and had their assets frozen with Lehman Brothers in the United States and internationally.

An International Crisis

The Lehman Brothers bankruptcy was an international failure that continues today. The parent holding company, Lehman Brother Holdings Inc. (LBHI), took only days to fail, but the cascade of effects will take years to come to completion.[21] Lehman Brothers Inc. (LBI) was a subsidiary of LBHI. LBI was the primary trading vehicle in the United States and stood as one of the largest broker-dealers in the world. The European broker-dealer, Lehman Brothers (International) Europe (LBIE) was brought down early while the U.S. prime finance operations continued for a number of days. LBIE is a U.K. limited liability company largely responsible for trading and financing activities in Europe and internationally.

When LBHI declared bankruptcy in the United States on September 15, 2008, under Chapter 11 of the U.S. Bankruptcy Code, a huge range of other subsidiaries and Lehman Brothers' vehicles were drawn into the bankruptcy.[22] The many other vehicles relied upon the parent holding company for daily financing. LBIE relied on LBHI for funding. LBHI had regular

[21] See MacIntosh, 2008.

[22] See In re Lehman Brothers Holdings Inc., et al., Debtors, 2008, and In re Lehman Brothers Holding Inc., Debtors, 2008.

sweeps of cash to and from the parent company in the United States. The collapse into bankruptcy of LBHI had the effect that all the other Lehman entities that relied upon LBHI for funding were forced into insolvency with it.

Many of the more than one thousand hedge funds which held collateral assets within Lehman Brothers were prime broker clients. The effect of the bankruptcy has been catastrophic for many funds which have been forced to liquidate remaining assets and terminate operations.[23] Some funds tried lobbying governments and exigent litigation to free their collateral assets from the bankruptcy.[24] It was estimated that approximately $40 to $65 billion in collateral assets were frozen and may be unrecoverable in the LBIE bankruptcy.[25]

Many of these hedge funds had relationships with both LBI, the U.S. broker-dealer, and LBIE, the non-U.S. international broker-dealer. There were prime broker and margin lending agreements in place with many of these funds. In some cases, under the prime broker agreements, LBI maintained the Prime Broker Account and LBIE maintained the Margin Lending Account. LBI in turn transferred the collateral securities to LBIE, which was authorized to make loans and provide other ancillary services. The collateral assets posted with LBIE served as collateral to secure any obligations from lending or the provision of services. Like other prime brokers, the Margin Lending Agreement provided that LBIE was authorized to lend the securities to itself or others, to pledge, repledge, hypothecate, and rehypothecate the collateral assets. The power to do so was largely unrestricted except as contractually agreed. However, LBIE was required to

---

[23] Mackintosh, 2008; Larsen, 2008; Gangahar, 2008.

[24] Reuters, 2008; Giles & Mackintosh, 2008; and Hughes, Mackintosh, & Murphy, 2008.

[25] The delay is accessing an estimated $65 billion in collateral assets that were "calling into question the future of the UK prime broker market" in a letter to Mervyn King, the Governor of the Bank of England (Giles & Mackintosh, 2008, p. 15). However, others estimated the prime broker collateral assets at approximately $40 billion (Hughes, 2008).

pass through any payments, distributions, or dividends paid on the collateral assets.

The administrators of LBIE in the United Kingdom were faced with the overwhelming task of overseeing the bankruptcy administration of a multibillion-dollar international trading company, making Lehman Brothers the largest and most complex bankruptcy in history.[26] When the U.K. administrator in bankruptcy applied for directions on amounts held on trust or any proprietary claims to the bankruptcy court, the bankruptcy court ordered the trust and proprietary amounts held to be identified and separated from the property of the bankrupt. However, this was a more difficult task than originally anticipated.

When the U.S. and U.K. bankruptcies occurred, many were surprised by the complexity and differences in the two regimes. One of the challenges was to manage expectations of the creditors in fundamentally different systems. In the U.S. bankruptcy regime, there is a generally accepted predisposition to allow reorganization of a business as a "going concern." Lawyers lead efforts to restructure the business in the United States. In the United Kingdom, the administration is dealt with by accountants and the majority of bankruptcies result in liquidation.

Hedge funds were facing devastating markets and broad redemptions. There were delays and confusion resulting from the Lehman Brothers collapse. Four investment funds sought the assistance of the bankruptcy administrator in the United Kingdom and asked the bankruptcy court to return their collateral. The bankruptcy effectively froze the positions of the hedge funds indefinitely. Several hedge funds with assets located at Lehman Brothers attempted to compel the bankruptcy administrator to return collateral assets on an expedited schedule while their identities remained strictly confidential.[27] It was feared that if their

[26] Hughes, 2008.

[27] RAB's attempt to have $50 million in collateral assets returned, in RAB Capital, PLC v. Lehman Brothers International (Europe), 2008, and also the confidential efforts of certain funds' failed effort to return collateral, in Four Private Investment Funds v. Lomas et al., 2008.

identities were revealed, investors would immediately redeem their investments and hedge funds business would be finished. The initial expedited efforts to return assets were unsuccessful. The administrator pointed out that LBIE had more than one thousand prime brokerage clients that had assets frozen in the bankruptcy administration. The hedge funds that attempted to have the assets returned on a priority basis were rejected. They stood in a similar position to other creditors, and their collateral securities had been utilized by Lehman Brothers prior to the bankruptcy.

The difficulty for the administrator of the bankruptcy is that all the prime broker clients, hedge funds, and others stand in a similar position. The bankruptcy judge reiterated the detailed due diligence on Lehman Brothers' books:

> [The administrators] say that in order to determine whether to accede to a client request for the re-delivery of securities and monies provided by way of collateral, they must carry out a variety of tasks:
>
> (1) Investigate and obtain definitive information on closing, reversing, unwinding or otherwise dealing with any unsettled trades which may affect the client's account, (2) ascertain the client's holding of securities and monies in accordance with the LBIE database once it has been fully updated, (3) conduct a reconciliation of LBIE data and records held by LBIE's custodians and resolve any difference or disparities, (4) establish whether and how securities may have been reused, (5) establish whether and how monies provided by way of collateral are held, (6) determine the extent of any indebtedness of the client to LBIE and any other Lehman Group entity and whether there are other reasons for the exercise of LBIE's lien over the securities, and (7) establish whether other clients had interests in the stocklines of the securities held in each custodian account in case there should be a competing claim to the securities in the event of a shortfall.[28]

[28] Four Private Investment Funds v. Lomas et al., 2008, para 19, p. 9.

This detailed analysis is required to ensure that competing claims are recognized and that creditors are dealt with fairly and equally. One problem with immediately returning securities is that the LBIE books were a moving target, with assets and liabilities constantly changing. For example, there were more than 140,000 failed trades as a result of the bankruptcy, which resulted in additional claims for and against LBIE.

Also, the actions of LBIE prior to the bankruptcy effectively moved all assets, rehypothecating and lending out securities and utilizing them for financing transactions. The resulting cash from financing securities was transferred to the U.S. parent company at the end of September 12, 2008, leaving nominal assets in LBIE. The problem for the prime brokerage clients was in the location of securities and details of related transactions. The bankruptcy judge outlined the problem for applicants in seeking to have their assets returned immediately.

> [The Administrators] state that, like many other LBIE prime brokerage clients, the applicants held long and short market positions, had borrowed securities to cover short positions and had long assets which were re-hypothecated. They explain that, under the contractual arrangements entered into with the applicants, LBIE was entitled to use the applicant's assets as collateral for loans to its clients, to lend securities to cover the settlement of short sale transactions, to pledge securities to market counterparties in order to collateralize obligations and to lend the securities to other market counterparties. They state that from the data available it would appear that as of 12 September 2008, being the last available date at which information from the LBIE database is available, LBIE had extensively exercised its right to re-use collateral securities that the applicants had provided and that, from enquiries made, some of those securities may have been transferred to LBI with whom the applicants had their main prime broking relationship and that other securities may have been provided to other third parties as collateral for other transactions. They also explain that LBIE holds, in segregated client accounts with third party custodians, securities which have been provided

> to it by way of collateral and that the client account in question is simply a pooled fund of assets which may belong to a number of different clients. They explain that it is segregated only in that it contains assets beneficially owned by clients rather than LBIE itself.[29]

The collateral assets which were extensively reused as collateral for other financing transactions were now the property of the counterparty. The bankruptcy of Lehman Brothers was an event of default. The event of default crystallized financing and made the collateral the property of the other party which could not be claimed back. With a significant amount of collateral being extensively utilized immediately prior to bankruptcy, the terms and good faith of the transactions will be questioned in future litigation, but these actions moved collateral assets with LBIE to other counterparties, including LBI. Finally, there were difficulties in how the collateral assets were held with Lehman Brothers. Efforts to segregate client accounts that end up in pooled client accounts are of limited value.

> [The administrators] are not able to say with certainty whether securities can be returned in full to any given client or whether a shortfall exists which must be shared pro rata across all client holdings. . . . They explain that until the reconciliation of each stockline or each custodian-held client account is carried out, a process which they say will take a long time, it will not be possible for [the administrators] to return assets to clients.[30]

The collateral assets were held with third-party custodians. Client assets were segregated from proprietary firm assets. However, client assets were allegedly lumped together in a pool of clients' assets or pooled client accounts. The value of a segregated account is diminished and undermined if the client assets are not clearly separated and distinguishable from other client

[29] Four Private Investment Funds v. Lomas et al., 2008, para. 20, p. 9.
[30] Four Private Investment Funds v. Lomas et al., 2008, para. 23, p. 10.

assets. The segregated client accounts may ultimately prove to have sufficient assets; however, it is possible that due to the extensive rehypothecation and utilization of client assets, along with transfers to the other Lehman Brothers entities, recovery will not be possible.

There is also a jurisdictional challenge for the clients who hold accounts from both LBIE and LBHI. The jurisdiction of the collateral holding may fall to either the English regime (which dictates that PRIMA prevails) or the American regime in which the explicit agreement in the Account Agreement governs the assets, subject to U.S. law and the dictates of The Hague Securities Convention.

The Lehman Brothers bankruptcy has led to massive changes in the prime broker market and counterparty risk assessments. Lehman Brothers' default stands as an important example of the challenges in addressing multinational issues in prime brokers in the future.

Lehman Brothers also changed the way the parties to prime finance assess risks. Traditionally, prime brokers have been concerned about hedge funds blowing up, not the other way around. From LTCM's blow-up in 1998, to Bear Stearns' distress in the spring of 2008, systemically important firms were not allowed to fail. A major bulge bracket investment bank has long been considered "too big to fail." The failure of Lehman Brothers and its prime brokerage business led to a paradigm shift.

The unthinkable scenario of a leading prime broker failure quickly became a stunning reality on September 15, 2008. Suddenly, hedge funds that ignored the lessons of failures like Refco and Bear Stearns were finally forced to ask primary questions about prime brokers and to differentiate between the creditworthiness of prime broker counterparties, that is, between independent prime brokers and universal banks. What is the probability of the credit default of the prime broker? What transparency is there into the prime broker entity? What is the governing regulatory regime? And how are the various assets held by a prime broker differentiated, segregated, and accounted for? Prior to Lehman

Brothers, all prime broker counterparties were thought of as the same. Suddenly, it was critical to differentiate between prime brokers and establish clear and unambiguous answers for worst case scenarios.

Lehman Brothers, in both the United States and internationally, showed the importance of understanding the vulnerability of the prime broker counterparty. A great deal of the credit exposures for hedge funds were related to international transactions and financing arrangements. LBIE was the actual international counterparty in many cases. LBIE was a severely subordinated vehicle. LBIE was responsible for a great deal of the leverage supplied to the hedge funds. The actions of LBIE prior to the bankruptcy to rehypothecate assets, utilize them for financing, and transfer remaining cash and securities to the U.S. parent corporation effectively liquidated client assets. It was critical to establish with detailed specificity which regulatory regime would apply to the variety of assets held by the prime broker, including client's cash, fully paid securities, encumbered securities, and rehypothecated securities.

Understanding Prime Finance

In the public press there has been great interest in finding the culprits, vilifying the wrongdoers. Who betrayed us? Who stole our money? In isolated cases the answer is that fraudulent fund managers were to blame.[31] But in the majority of the cases, there is no one to fault. There was a combination of compounding errors in assessing and understanding risk (epistemology), errors in understanding the nature of the financial products and investment vehicles (ontology), and grave lapses where self-interest and inappropriate incentives lead to excessive risk taking for princely rewards (ethics). These international institutions were highly levered with risky assets, and the models employed to assess risk

[31] A notorious example is the Ponzi scheme allegedly perpetrated by Bernard Madoff.

were inaccurate and sometimes flawed. The combination of high leverage, unprecedented illiquidity, toxic assets, and unpredictable low frequency, high severity events was a lethal combination of factors. The result was a broad based, international loss of capital. The international system has been structured to employ offshore unregulated vehicles, and these same vehicles are important sources of capital for the leading banks. The following chapters will examine hedge fund and prime finance markets, the parties to prime finance, and their transactions, risks, and regulations. Finally, we shall look to the future of hedge funds, executing brokers and prime brokers.

When attempting to understand and prevent a recurrence of the global financial crisis, the first step is to ask primary questions to understand the nature of the organizations and transactions that stand at the intersection of investment vehicles, leverage, financing, and financial products. The area of prime finance and hedge funds is among the most complicated areas of international law and finance. It is critical to know the parties involved in order to understand and address systemic risk, avoid market abuses, and protect both individual and institutional investors, sometimes even from themselves. Once the basics are reviewed, then the more significant task of regulating and potentially reforming the vehicles of international finance will be addressed. The first step to understanding hedge funds and prime finance is to understand the primary customer, hedge funds, and to examine their anatomy, structures, objectives, and strategies.

2 Fundamentals of Prime Finance

The prime finance area operates by providing full-service trading, securities lending, and other services for hedge funds. Investors provide initial capital to hedge funds. Prime brokers provide additional leverage and comprehensive services to hedge funds. The executing broker effects trades for hedge funds. There are brokers who work together to provide the single conduit for multiple products, including:

- Prime Brokerage
- Stock Loan
- Repo (Finance)
- Derivatives and other products
- Executing Brokerage
- Commission Sharing

The hedge funds utilize the prime brokers for a variety of services from leverage to market access and capital raising. Many have described the relationship as similar to a partnership. It is likely that a partnership or fiduciary relationship is explicitly denied in the relevant agreements and account documents. The contractual relationship with a prime broker is a critical component for operating a hedge fund particularly when investment strategies employ significant leverage. The relationship between

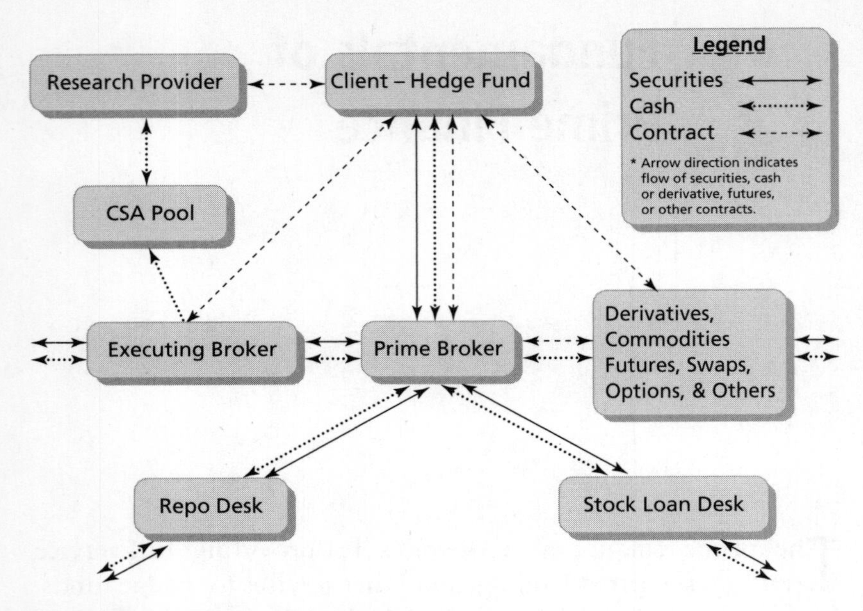

Figure 2.1 Prime Finance Relationships

the hedge fund and prime broker, and related functions of the investment bank, is invariably a complex and complicated affair (**Figure 2.1**).

At its core, the hedge fund takes principal risk for its investments, and investors expect principal rewards to go to the hedge fund. The prime broker will seek fees for services but will not engage in principal risk, except in extraordinary scenarios.[1] The multifaceted relationship between the prime broker and hedge fund may include custodian–beneficiary, lender–borrower, stock lending–stock borrowing, seed capital investor or capital raiser, assistant in capital introduction or client, and even landlord–tenant, consultant–principal, and staff utilization relationships. The prime broker services the various needs of the hedge fund clients and arranges for other ancillary financial services, such as execution, derivatives, and research. The prime broker's primary

[1] Such as where the prime broker also arranges to provide seed capital in the hedge fund, and has a direct stake in the hedge fund's performance.

contractual obligations are with the hedge fund itself, as directed by the hedge fund manager.

Lending and Borrowing

In the normal course, the traditional primary relationship between hedge funds (borrower) and prime brokers (lender) is related to lending and borrowing cash and securities. Lenders are primarily concerned about the collateral provided by borrowers and their solvency. Borrowers are primarily concerned with the terms of financing, and risks in the event of a default.

The standard roles played by prime brokers and hedge funds may be reversed in certain cases. In the standard scenario, the broker-dealer acting as a prime broker lends securities, cash, and financial instruments to hedge funds, which seek to implement strategies and gain benefit from increased leverage. Recently, hedge funds have become a valuable source of liquidity for prime brokers and other market participants. With hedge funds holding record amounts of cash, and liquid government and corporate securities, some hedge funds have reversed traditional roles and acted as lenders to prime brokers and the investment banks.[2]

A prime broker, in theory, stands market neutral and charges fees to clients for services, exposed to neither the upside nor downside of the market except as incidental to providing services, to clients. The actual position of a prime broker may have a long or short net position. Hedge funds lend securities and cash to prime brokers. Hedge funds provide capital to prime brokers in the form of collateral, which is used for the prime broker's own financing. However, in addition to financing from collateral deposited with the prime broker, hedge funds may also utilize additional contracts for financing at preferred rates.[3]

[2] See Sender, 2008.

[3] Many hedge funds that deleveraged prior to the fall of 2008 were holding cash and treasuries. The hedge funds became a valuable source of capital for the investment banks in addition to posted collateral.

The intersection of the prime broker and hedge funds in international finance is a particularly opaque world.[4] The international investment banks have quietly been operating in the area for decades. Whether the historical practices of lending and massive leverage will continue is a question for the respective national regulators and the governments. Many prime brokers and investment banks have requested huge sums of financing from governments around the world, either directly in the form of loans or equity investments, or by governmental guarantees of debt.[5] Consequently, it is necessary to provide some transparency into the business of international finance and how bailout funds have been utilized.

The prime finance area includes a variety of services and transactions for hedge funds, investment funds, sovereign wealth funds, pension funds, and others. The prime broker lends cash and securities, and the hedge funds borrow. The prime broker stands at the forefront of the execution of an investment fund's strategy.

In the most fundamental relationship, the hedge fund stores its cash, financial instruments, or securities with the prime broker as collateral. The effect of storing the collateral with the prime broker is to place the securities or cash on the books of the prime broker. The crux of the relationship is to deposit collateral amounts with the prime broker. The prime broker will have benefit of the stocks and may rehypothecate the stock deposited as collateral.

The leverage offered by a prime broker depends largely on its registration and the jurisdiction and management of the hedge fund. Where a fund is located (incorporated), its management, advisors, investors, and the location of investment decisions are

[4] The Financial Industry Regulatory Authority (FINRA) has proposed guidance regarding International Prime Brokerage Practices business as a result of findings that industry practices varied considerably between international firms, as opposed to domestic brokers as outlined in the SEC's 1994 No Action Letter (SEC, 1994). The result was an ongoing effort to solicit comments from member firms and harmonize industry practices internationally; see FINRA, 2007.

[5] It is notable that certain leading prime brokers, such as Deutsche Bank, have not received government financing.

factors of the relevant legislation and jurisdiction. The largest market for prime finance is the United States. The implications of falling under U.S. regulations are many and pose complicated issues for U.S. and non-U.S. prime brokers with issues around registration, custody, settlement, trade execution, reporting, margin lending, and access to securities offerings.[6]

Prime Finance Services

The fundamental areas of prime finance include prime brokerage, stock loan, financing (repo), and derivatives. Many prime brokers who are part of major investment banks also offer execution brokerage services as well, including a variety of services related to trade execution, transition management, commission sharing arrangements, direct market access (DMA), and research. To understand the various areas of prime finance and their interrelationship, each component will be reviewed. The central relationship is the prime broker agreement.

The Current Market

Recently, the prime broker market has seen unprecedented change. In the global financial crisis, turmoil in the financial markets created massive changes, opportunities, and challenges for both domestic and international prime finance. As John Hitchon, Global Co-Head of Prime Services of Deutsche Bank, noted: "For most of the last 17 years of prime finance, moving a 1 percent share of the prime broker market has been trench warfare. We are currently in a period of fluidity which is rapidly closing."[7] The performance of hedge funds, prime brokers, investment

[6] See McMillan & Bergmann, 2007, for a detailed examination of the various requirements under U.S. regulations. For issues related to prime brokers which may offer access to initial offerings of securities, subject to the National Association of Securities Dealers, Inc. (NASD), see www.nasd.org.

[7] Hitchon & Bausano, 2009; this sentiment is shared by other leading prime broker executives; see Reuters, 2008.

banks, and the financial services industry were challenged and in some cases competitive advantages were increased, while in other areas barriers to entry disappeared. While some experienced devastating losses, others emerged as the new elite in the industry.

Leading Prime Brokers

This has reflected a fundamental change in the prime finance market and the allocation of assets among the elite and leading prime brokers. While there is a large list of prime brokers, there are generally regarded to be three tiers[8]: The prime broker market includes a handful of elite prime brokers,[9] several leading prime brokers and many tertiary regional and smaller niche prime brokers.

Historically, the prime finance market was an oligopoly, dominated by three major elite U.S. investment banks: Goldman Sachs, Morgan Stanley, and Bear Stearns (now JPMorgan Chase). Within the larger prime broker market, there were several leading prime brokers that shared a smaller remainder of prime broker services. The leading prime brokers included Merrill Lynch, Credit Suisse, Lehman Brothers, Bank of America, BNP Paribas, UBS, Deutsche Bank, Citigroup, and others. Other tertiary prime brokers filled in niche gaps and regional prime broker services.

Mini-Prime Brokers

Prime Brokers are split into small independent prime brokers (sometime referred to as "mini-primes") and full-service prime brokers associated with large investment banks and universal banks. The independent prime brokers are normally linked to larger broker-dealers but often service smaller niche hedge funds with fewer assets under management or that focus on specific trading strategies that are better served by mini-primes.

---

[8] See List of Prime Brokers in Appendix A.

[9] Prior to the financial crisis some regarded the prime finance market as a "duopoly" rather than an oligopology due to the public distress of Bear Stearns.

The Changing Global Prime Broker Market

March 2007	July 2009
1. Morgan Stanley Prime Brokerage	1. Credit Suisse
2. Deutsche Bank	2. Deutsche Bank
3. Bear Stearns	3. Citi Prime Finance
4. UBS	4. JP Morgan Chase
5. Lehman Brothers	5. Barclays Capital Prime Services
6. Merrill Lynch	6. Bank of America Merrill Lynch
7. Goldman Sachs	7. Goldman Sachs
8. Credit Suisse	8. Morgan Stanley Prime Brokerag
9. Barclays Capital	9. UBS
10. Citigroup	10. Newedge
	11. RBC Capital Markets
Top Global Prime Brokers, Global Custodian Survey, March 21, 2007	Top Global Prime Brokers Global Custodian Survey, July 1, 2009

Figure 2.2 Prime Broker Market

Due to the apparent distress and implosion of Bear Stearns, bankruptcy of Lehman Brothers, and the threat to the remaining prime brokers, the prime finance market has altered dramatically (**Figure 2.2**). The prime broker market has shifted massive amounts of hedge fund assets to prime brokers that can offer security, including:

- Size
- Balance sheet
- Credit quality
- Reduced default risk
- Transparency
- Legal certainty
- Security of assets

The paradigm shift in the oligopoly created opportunities for leading prime brokers. Certain of the leading firms had developed their capabilities, service, and product offering to become indiscernible from the elite offering. In the market distress, many hedge funds were searching for additional prime brokers offering reduced counterparty risk, increased transparency, and a sound regulatory environment, in addition to the similar service they received with the old elite firms. The major gains were made by a few leading firms from late 2008 into 2009 when all hedge funds, broker-dealers, and investment banks were concerned about minimizing counterparty risk. Gains were made from leading and tertiary prime brokers that were able to offer excellent service, reduced counterparty risk, and simple transparent structures. Notable entrants to the elite tier of prime brokers included Deutsche Banks, Credit Suisse, and JPMorgan Chase.

Ancillary to the market movements in prime brokers, hedge funds increasingly employed financing models utilizing custodians. Custodian models increased due to the pervasive fear in the markets. In the bull markets leading up to the crisis in September 2008, access to leverage was preferred to safety and security of assets. During the crisis, hedge funds fearing another broker-dealer bankruptcy allocated assets to leading custodians. In order to limit risk to unencumbered cash and other collateral, many prime brokers saw part of their assets move to the major custodians, including BONY Mellon, State Street, and Northern Trust.

Also, new entrants have made significant gains into the niche prime broker market. For example, Shoreline Trading Group was ranked ahead of Morgan Stanley and Goldman Sachs to top the rankings of prime brokers.[10] The changes to the market created opportunities and lowered long-standing barriers to entry. A variety of firms have benefited from the disorder in the market and the distress of the elite market leaders.

Events in Prime Finance

Massive amounts of capital have shifted within the prime broker market as a result of the downfall of Lehman Brothers and acquisition of Bear Stearns. Bear Stearns imploded due to massive

[10] Merlin Securities was the best hedge fund service provider according to *Alpha* magazine. The top four included Shoreline Trading Group, Morgan Stanley, Goldman Sachs, respectively. For more see Wall Street Newsletter, 2008.

losses of capital related to subprime and other exposures, high leverage, and transfers of collateral assets elsewhere. The collateral assets that shifted away from Bear Stearns have reportedly been returning to JPMorgan Chase as a consequence of the market volatility. Market events and shifting collateral assets have made JPMorgan the largest prime broker. Foreign prime brokers were primary beneficiaries in the shift in collateral assets, including Credit Suisse, UBS, BNP Paribas, and Deutsche Bank.

The Lehman bankruptcy painfully demonstrated that a bulge bracket broker-dealer is not "too big to fail."[11] The exodus of assets out of Lehman Brothers, due to a failing business model and the inability to finance from street counterparties and hedge funds, all compounded to form the perfect storm for Lehman Brothers. In contrast to Bear Stearns, other counterparties did not believe that Lehman Brothers was a business worth saving, but the value of the investment bank was in acquiring individual business units and the top staff. Head-hunters and competitors swarmed the firm before and after the bankruptcy. The apparent view was that it was preferable to let Lehman fail and scavenge the remaining assets for anything of value. Many of the valuable parts of Lehman Brothers were purchased and continued operations, including the North American brokerage operations.[12]

If Bear Stearns was a warning shot, Lehman Brothers was a direct hit. The result was extreme concern over the huge consolidation of assets in the remaining two premier prime brokers, Goldman Sachs and Morgan Stanley. After all, the history of the

[11] In the fallout from Lehman Brothers, many U.S. government officials have taken significant steps to address systemic risk including the involvement of the Board of Governors of the Federal Reserve, U.S. Treasury Department, Commodity Futures Trading Commission, Securities and Exchange Commission, and Securities Investor Protection Corporation. The federal legislation provides for the key objective of orderly liquidation of systemically important firms as set out in the Resolution Authority for Systemically Significant Financial Companies Act of 2009.

[12] The assets management arm and various other entities were purchased by competitors and continue operations.

Great Depression demonstrates that even Goldman Sachs is not immune from bankruptcy in the most extreme markets.[13] The Lehman Brothers bankruptcy "led many hedge funds to flee the two largest prime brokers, Morgan Stanley and Goldman Sachs, to the perceived safety of universal banks."[14] The pressure on the remaining independent investment banks, which were then not associated with commercial or retail banking arms, created a shift in the business model to sudden perceived stability of the universal bank model. The only option to allay concerns and restart the financing model was to register as bank holding companies. Both Goldman Sachs and Morgan Stanley registered as bank holding companies on September 21, 2008. The risk associated with an independent prime broker default was revealed in the long shadow of Lehman Brothers.

The result of these extraordinary events was a run on prime brokers. It was not a run on cash holdings, such as a bank run, but a run on securities held with prime brokers. The collateral securities were an important source of financing of the investment banks. The flood of collateral leaving the investment banks effectively limited their financing options to only one, the Federal Reserve. The securities run on the remaining independent investment banks also caused a fragmentation of the prime broker market. A significant number of new prime broker relationships were created, and a reprioritization occurred. Hedge funds diversified risk against their prime brokers by various methods. Whereas previously many hedge funds were reliant on one or two prime brokers, now hedge funds were moving toward diversification in prime brokers both domestically and internationally. The concern for counterparty risk also had the effect of causing some fund managers to adjust the priority of prime brokers to spread risk. Indirectly, reductions in settlement flow and

[13] See Chapter IV, In Goldman, Sachs We Trust, for the tale of the meteoric rise and fall of Goldman Sachs Trading Company, in Galbraith, 1954, pp. 69–90.

[14] Fletcher, Dmitracova, & Dealtalks, 2009.

reduced collateral held with a prime broker reduces risk to hedge funds to counterparty default.

Both the supply and demand for prime broker financing decreased in 2008. Hedge funds reduced leverage in many markets, and there was a concomitant reduction in the supply of leverage as banks entered deleveraging cycles to increase regulatory capital. While hedge funds owned 4.5 percent of U.S. equities in June, they owned only 3.5 percent by September 2008.[15] However, the need for leverage has not been universally reduced. Certain funds that rely on leverage for specific strategies still require leverage and some have had record years, including many global macro and short-bias funds. Notwithstanding notable exceptions, hedge funds have greatly reduced exposure to long positions in U.S., European, and Asian markets.

The hedge funds that did not reduce leverage to long positions have largely suffered significant reverses.[16] The unprecedented market volatility has forced many funds to reduce leverage and risk significantly. The actual leverage statistics are not publicly available. The FSA's biannual survey of hedge funds revealed an apparent reduction in borrowing from 1.92 times geared in October 2007 to 1.45 times geared in April 2008.[17] The reduction in supply and demand for borrowing may continue to fall in the private sector. The reduction in funds seeking leverage has been met with reduction in the availability of leverage and increased costs for borrowing. There has been a reduction in the supply (or availability) of leverage and a reduction in the demand from funds seeking leverage and the size of those positions. Deleveraging of both prime brokers and hedge funds ultimately leads to a shrinking prime finance

[15] Mackintosh J., 2008a.

[16] The VIX index has hit records in the fourth quarter of 2008; see the CBOE volatility Index (WCB).

[17] These statistics are likely conservative and understated for the discretionary reporting to the Financial Services Authority, and are undoubtedly a limited definition of what constitutes "leverage."

market; however, there will be increased competition for the remaining market.

Many of the larger investment banks and other financial institutions have undergone dramatic changes to deleverage, in order to reduce risk and protect core regulatory capital. Fundamentally, the investment banks are regulated and full-service banks have capital requirements and leverage restrictions for regulatory purposes. The prime broker, and associated investment bank, may be concerned about its balance sheet and thus unable to offer financing. The result is that banks and other lending institutions have been shoring up capital, reducing risks that are driven by concerns about counterparty and default risks. The impact of the deleveraging cycle has been significant. The decreased lending appetites for prime brokers and banks—decreased need to borrow for hedge funds in general—has caused a dramatic decrease in the availability of financing and a corresponding increase in the cost of borrowing.

Customer Satisfaction

The customers of prime finance are the broad range of hedge funds, investment funds, and managers with particular needs. The prime finance clients have reported decreased satisfaction with their prime brokers and almost one-third were considering changing their prime brokers recently.[18]

Prime Finance Market

The confluence of a radically altered market, with heightened counterparty risk, decreasing returns for hedge funds, dissatisfied clients, and a broad range of prime brokers to choose from, has left significant questions unanswered about the future of the prime finance market. The big winners have been full-service investment banks with a secure capital base, notably Credit Suisse, Deutsche Bank, BNP Paribas, and a few others. However, shifting

[18] Finalternatives.com produced a survey that was based on results from 120 hedge funds and CTA managers.

allegiances and collateral assets of hedge funds have not settled. The market will likely continue to see decreased leverage, and fewer remaining hedge funds, being shared amongst more prime brokers. Also, the tertiary prime brokers have been successful in attracting new business when focused on niche services for successful hedge fund clients and specific niche strategies.

3 Strategy and Opportunity

To effectively analyze the prime finance industry, it is critical to analyze both corporate strategy (whether to enter an industry) and business strategy (how prime brokers compete with each other in the industry). First, we will examine the industry attractiveness and assess the market, and then we will examine the available opportunities and how firms compete for customers.

The prime finance industry is in the middle of a major transition as significant competition has arisen for a diminishing client base; see **Figure 3.1**. There are new entrants making gains into the market, increasing the number and likelihood of substitutes for leading prime brokers. There is also an increasing recognition by hedge fund managers of the power that successful hedge fund clients have over prime brokers. This will likely be met with strategies by prime brokers to increase market share with these hedge funds, either by building business internally (an organic strategy) or by mergers and acquisitions of competitiors (an inorganic strategy). New, smaller prime brokers will likely play an increasingly significant role for small and start-up hedge funds. Many larger prime brokers are limited from making acquisitions as a result of restrictions related to government bailouts and equity financing. However, the leading prime brokers, which have thrived in the market following Lehman Brothers due to their

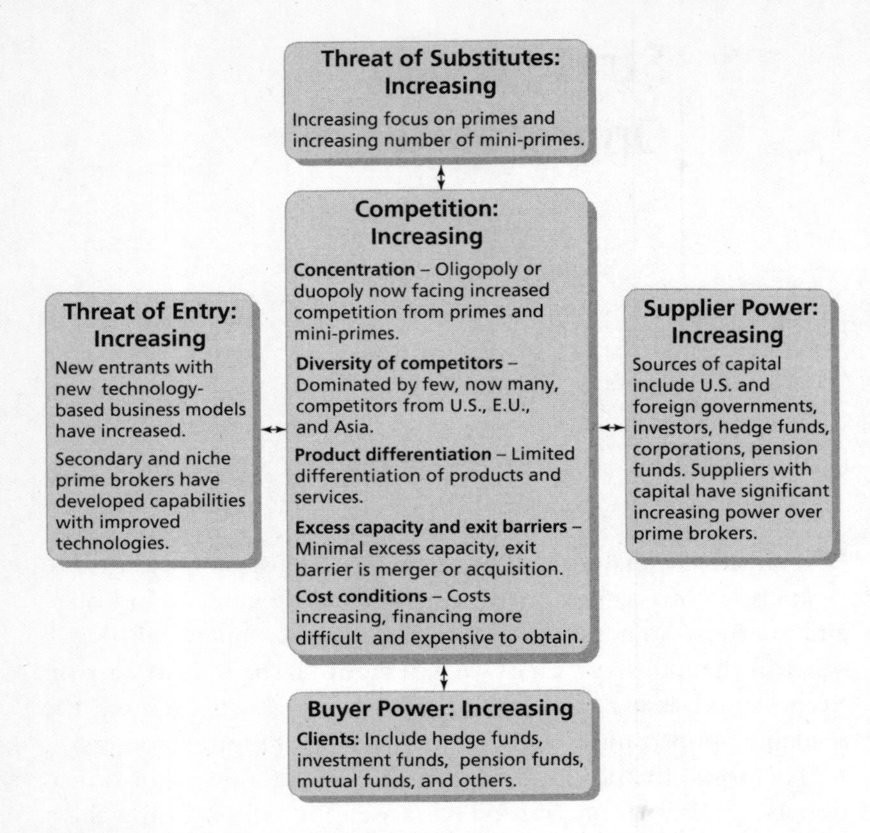

Figure 3.1 Prime Finance-Industry Analysis

security, broad offering, transparency, and service, will likely continue to consolidate market share.[1]

Corporate Strategy

Investment bank leaders have stated that they will invest more capital into the prime finance area. Due to an infusion of capital

[1] Certain leading firms, such as Morgan Stanley and Goldman Sachs, have seen increased regulatory oversight. This oversight has extended to limitations on acquisitions and compensation. By comparison, other elite prime brokers, such as Deutsche Bank, are not restricted as such. Deutsche Bank has not accepted government support and has always been subject to stringent banking regulations.

and internal allocations to prime finance, the market has opened to new entrants fueled by allocations in the developing prime finance market. The buyer of services (the fund) is also the supplier of capital in the form of collateral. Collateral is normally in the form of liquid securities such as equities, bonds, and government debt, but may include other securities, derivatives, commodities, or financial products. So while hedge funds are financed by prime brokers, prime brokers are increasingly financed through collateral posted by hedge funds. This is the reason that withdrawals of collateral from prime brokers are effectively a run on the assets of a prime broker, and creates a financing problem for the prime broker.

The Five Forces of Prime Finance (**Figure 3.2**) reveals how the market is changing through competitive pressures, the threat of new entrants, the changing dynamics of supplier and buyer power, and the availability of substitutes.[2]

Competition Goldman Sachs, Morgan Stanley, and Bear Stearns dominated the majority of the prime finance industry for many years. That era is now over. With the entrance of a few top tier investment banks and smaller firms, the diversity and composition of the market has fragmented. With the fragmentation of traditional market share dominance by a few elite firms, competition is increasing for the remaining market.

Threat of Entry The likelihood of new entrants is high. Many firms have the capital requirements to enter this market and have indicated that capital allocations to challenge incumbents are available. Indeed, the entrance and success of such start-ups as Bank of New York Mellon's Pershing unit and Shoreline Capital Group suggests that more new entrants will follow. The market disruption also continues to incite collateral asset movement to prime brokers with minimal risk and competitive lending rates.

[2] Porter, 1980.

Competition

Concentration – Oligopoly (or duopoly) now faces increased competition
Diversity of competitors – Dominated by few now many
Product differentiation – Limited differentiation
Excess capacity and exit barriers – Minimal excess capacity
Cost conditions – Costs increasing, financing more difficult

Threat of Entry

Economies of scale – Large economies of scale
Absolute cost advantages – Large players have advantage
Capital requirements – Significant capital required
Product differentiation – Ability to provide universal prime services is an advantage, as is global reach
Access to distribution channels – Limited distribution channels
Government and legal barriers – Registration requirements and increased government oversight expected

Threat of Substitutes

Buyer propensity to substitute – Typical to have back-up prime brokers, which provides many substitutes
Relative prices and performance – Ability to compare is increased, with additional secondary, tertiary prime brokers
Substitutes – Broad availability of substitutes for both major and mini-prime brokers

Supplier Power (Sources of Capital: Government, Investors, Hedge Funds)

1) PRICE SENSITIVITY
Cost of product – Cost of financing increasing for many primes
Product differentiation – Minimal product differentiation
Competition between suppliers – Minimal competition

2) BARGAINING POWER
Size and concentration of buyers relative to producers – The market for investors has altered dramatically and their power has increased
Buyers switching costs – There are reputational and legal issues to consider
Buyer's information – Limited view into complex organizations

Buyer Power (Clients: Hedge Funds, Investment Funds)

1) PRICE SENSITIVITY
Cost of product – The easy availability of comparable financing forced prime brokers to provide lock-ups, guaranteed financing rates, and low fees
Product differentiation – There is competition in the bulge bracket primes, but more differentiation in the smaller primes
Competition between buyers – HFs compete to reduce their

2) BARGAINING POWER
Size and concentration of buyers relative to producers – 6,000–10,000
Buyer's switching costs – Legal fees, transactions, portfolio transition effects
Buyer's information – Limited disclosures have restricted buyer information

Figure 3.2 The Five Forces of Prime Finance

Supplier and Buyer Power The relationship between supplier power and buyer power is extremely complicated in the prime finance industry. The power of successful hedge funds has increased with significant choice among various prime brokers. However, supplier power is also high, with restrictions on leverage available, compensation, and regulatory oversight. The combination of supplier power and increasing substitutes, new entrants, and risk mitigation from hedge funds has squeezed prime brokers from all sides. The sources of financing for the prime brokers are common shareholders, institutional investors, and, increasingly, governments. The benefits and problems associated with accepting government financing are complex. The benefit is that the liquidity and solvency of prime brokers may be recapitalized with equity investments and government financing.[3] However, the regulatory oversight for such banks is heightened with restrictions on everything from board composition, strategy decisions, compensation, to mergers and acquisition, which has led some investment banks and prime brokers to attempt to repay government support as soon as possible.[4]

The complexity of the relationship between buyers (hedge funds) and suppliers (prime brokers) is difficult to underestimate. The increasing government support for investment banks and their prime finance divisions has spawned relief for hedge funds with collateral assets held at struggling brokers. The U.S. government investments and financing after the failure of Bear Stearns was a pivotal reason for the acquisition by JPMorgan Chase. In contrast, this support, when it causes the dissolution of investors' common equity, has a negative impact on the firm's ability to raise other forms of capital.

---

[3] Triparty repo financing with asset managers, corporates, and government entities, including the Federal Reserve, has been a critical source of financing for many U.S. investment banks.

[4] Goldman Sachs and others have paid back or are attempting to pay back TARP and other government financing as quickly as possible in part to alleviate oversight, allow for acquisitions, to finesse government restrictions on remuneration, and the potential for voiding contracts.

Threat of Substitutes Hedge funds have minimal switching costs, and there are ready substitutes for many hedge fund clients. The combination of increased counterparty risk and additional measures to mitigate risk has created a number of new, smaller firms that have gained significant assets.

The result is fierce new competition that is increasing as the normal barriers to entry have been removed, albeit temporarily.[5] The efforts to secure hedge fund clients has led to offering lock-up agreements and other financing with significant proprietary risk to prime brokers. Some industry experts suggested that price competition was already growing increasingly untenable prior to the financial crisis. Legacy financing agreements may yet threaten firms that provided such long-term lock-up agreements and other enticements to hedge fund clients. The shake-up of the industry has created an unprecedented opportunity for new entrants and incumbents with stable balance sheets to increase market share. The result of the increased competition and dispersion of the collateral assets of the hedge fund industry suggest that there will be continuing efforts to capture market share before the liquid market returns to a fixed state. This may be in the form of both organic and inorganic efforts to increase market share in a declining market. Ultimately the combination of increasing competition, comparable services, and a declining market may result in further prime brokers experiencing distress. Consequently the market dynamics and competitive pressures may increase the probability that another prime broker will experience distress, bankruptcy, or be acquired as the prime finance market continues to mature.

Business Strategy

The strategic outlook for the prime finance market indicates that prime brokers' corporate strategy may include increased asset

[5] Some prime finance executives have called for corrective action to be taken as "a rush of prime brokers into the market had caused aggressive margin pricing"; see Mackintosh, 2008a.

allocation and introducing new entrants into the prime finance market. There will be opportunities for the old elite prime brokers to recapture market share, provided the innovative services and proprietary technologies that created competitive advantages for the elite prime brokers can be established once again. However, there are significant questions unanswered about the future market and how to go about capturing the market opportunity:

- What kind of clients to target?
- What products and services to offer?
- How to compete with other prime finance firms? Price? Differentiation?

The business strategy can only be set with an understanding of the current internal capabilities of the prime broker and an understanding of external factors at play.

Strategy Pyramid

The Strategy Pyramid is a useful prime finance metaphor, at least in terms of business strategy (**Figure 3.3**). The Strategy Pyramid allows the internal capabilities of firms to be matched with the external environment. The external environment has seen unprecedented change and movement in hedge fund assets. Hedge fund clients suffered massive losses, and the debt and equity markets have experienced record volatility. Some industry observers expect a consolidation in the market to ultimately eliminate 10 to 60 percent of hedge funds. Prime brokers are reassessing their competitive strategy in light of changes to the market and the new opportunities.

Similarly, the internal abilities of prime brokers are changing. With increased pressure on some of the elite prime finance firms, there are opportunities for other leading prime brokers and mini-primes to fill the market gaps. The consolidation of hedge funds suggests that prime brokers will attempt to focus on funds that have solid potential, fit with their risk profile, and have weathered the economic storm to date.

From the perspective of the hedge fund, it is critical to match the prime broker's capabilities with the hedge fund's investment

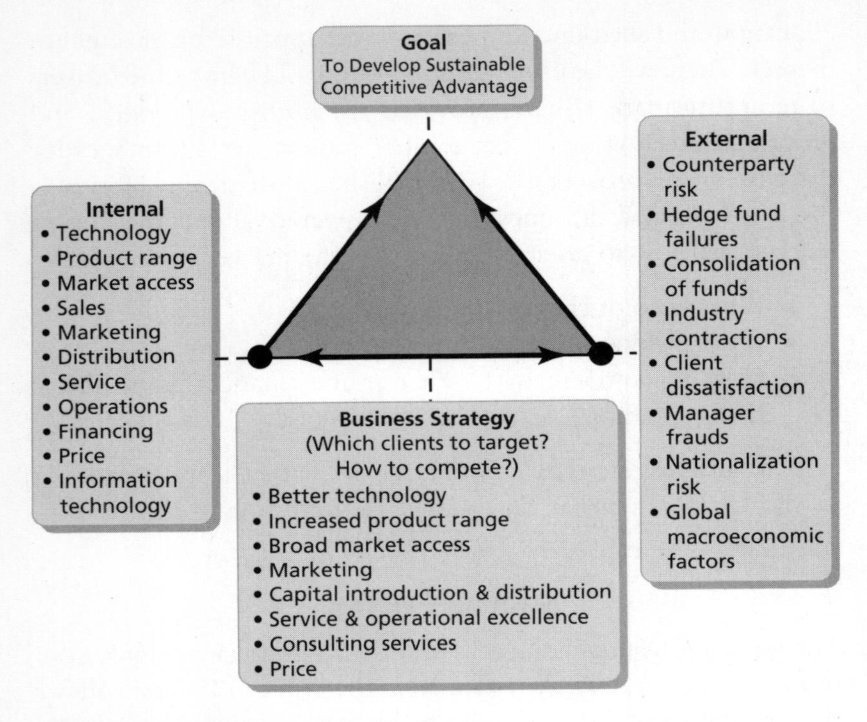

Figure 3.3 Prime Finance Strategy Pyramid[6]

strategies and tactics. Matching investment strategies to prime broker offerings is a critical consideration in selecting a prime broker. The prime broker may also captures economies of scale and scope by matching with appropriate hedge fund clients. Decisions in the past have been made on the availability of initial seed investment, capital raising, and marketing. These services, however, will not be sufficient to attract and retain new hedge fund clients for prime brokers.

The internal workings of hedge funds require a number of products and services. Common hedge fund needs include:

- Technology
- Product range

[6] Concept adapted from Grant, 2005, pp. 75–80.

- Market access
- Marketing
- Distribution
- Service
- Price
- Information technology

The primary goal of the hedge fund should be to match its internal needs with the external offering of the prime broker to operate effectively in the markets.

Prime Broker Due Diligence

Prime brokers may be simple vehicles or structures, or they may be part of large universal bank groups with several thousand legal entities. As a result, due diligence may be dauntingly complex, where counterparty risk is a paramount consideration against the most complicated financial organizations in existence. In assessing a prime broker, the hedge fund should assess both the risks and potential rewards. The prime broker is often the focal point of prime finance services in general. A prime broker may simply offer minimal brokerage and margin services. However, often there is a list of relevant factors for individual funds.[7] The prime finance offering must be complementary to the strategies, tactics and objectives of the hedge fund (**Figure 3.4**).

The underlying portfolio of clients with a particular prime broker is often overlooked. The attractiveness of the prime broker will depend on the match between the underlying portfolio of the hedge fund and the portfolio of clients of the prime broker.

Large hedge funds with a global macro strategy may benefit from the large leading prime brokers. Smaller funds with more limited technical or niche strategies would be better served and may receive better financing from prime brokers with focused operations. There are economies of scale and economies of scope that impact both the prime broker and the underlying hedge fund client.

[7] See Appendix C: Due Diligence on Prime Brokers.

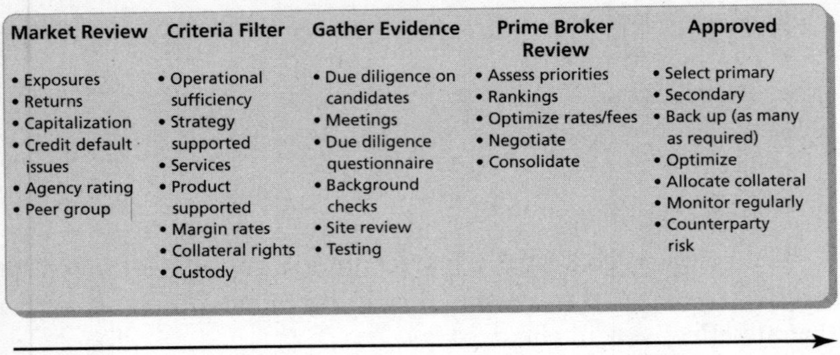

Market Review	Criteria Filter	Gather Evidence	Prime Broker Review	Approved
• Exposures • Returns • Capitalization • Credit default issues • Agency rating • Peer group	• Operational sufficiency • Strategy supported • Services • Product supported • Margin rates • Collateral rights • Custody	• Due diligence on candidates • Meetings • Due diligence questionnaire • Background checks • Site review • Testing	• Assess priorities • Rankings • Optimize rates/fees • Negotiate • Consolidate	• Select primary • Secondary • Back up (as many as required) • Optimize • Allocate collateral • Monitor regularly • Counterparty risk

Figure 3.4 In-Depth Due Diligence on Prime Broker

The prime broker ideally stands between two or more buy-side clients. The position of the prime broker in such circumstances generates economies of scale and scope, particularly when cross-selling can be facilitated. For the hedge fund, it is economical and useful to match with other hedge funds with the same prime broker. The economies of scale may avoid the interposition of two prime brokers' fees and market costs detracting from the efficiency of transactions. One hedge fund may want to have long-term holdings of a security, and another may want to borrow those securities. If the prime broker needs to service both transactions with street counterparties, there will be significant costs on both transactions. If the prime broker can interpose services between internal clients, there are clear advantages and economies of scope and scale.

Goal

The goal of the prime broker should be to develop sustainable competitive advantages over other service providers.[8] If innovation is not fostered within an organization, the strategy for diversification is to develop a comprehensive acquisition strategy.

Prime brokers may follow one or more of two fundamental strategies to compete in the current market: differentiation or price.

[8] For information on strategy for creating corporate advantage see Prahalad & Hamel, 1990; Collis & Montgomery, 1998; and Powell, 1995.

A trading market requires inefficiency for market participants to profit. The sources of the inefficiency in trading markets include:

- Imperfect information
- Transaction costs—benefit to the lowest cost provider
- Infrastructure
- Systemic behavioral trends

Imperfect information has created greater need for both timely market information and accurate research. Thus, prime brokers with advanced information or risk management software may have a competitive advantage over their competitors.

Competition on transaction costs may ultimately reduce profits for brokers to the point of nominal returns. The majority of prime brokers and executing brokers competing on cost will ultimately feel the squeeze from decreasing returns as markets continue to mature. The systemic behavioral trends may be the increasing need for transparency, certainly with hedge funds and their prime brokers. The global financial crisis has decreased the value of financial services firms and will increase the likelihood of major acquisitions of prime brokers, as well as complementary services within prime brokers. New entrants, elite, leading, and tertiary prime broker firms may attempt to wait for stabilization in the global financial markets to do so. However, international competitors are clearly watching the area closely, and when prime finance opportunities appear they may be addressed quickly. The development in the market has been a decided shift from U.S. banks to a more internationally diversified market. In the future, there may be additional efforts to globalize the prime broker market with international treaties and multilateral regulatory objectives.[9] In such a scenario, the harmonization will require additional services and products to sustain competitive advantages and to provide certainty for market participants.

---

[9] Paul Volcker, a former Federal Reserve chairman and chairman of the Trustees of the G-30, is working on suggestions for increasing regulations and altering capital limits for banks, as well as tightening regulation on proprietary trading and co-mingling bank assets with hedge funds and private equity units.

PART II

The Players

4 Hedge Funds

The hedge fund market is conservatively estimated at $1.5 to $1.9 trillion, but with leverage the market impact is undoubtedly much larger.[1] Accurate data is notoriously difficult to ascertain for proprietary business—managers closely guard their numbers—and for political reasons—prime brokers seek to position themselves as leaders, and the battle for market share is highly competitive. What is not in doubt is that the hedge fund industry is currently in transition. Broad estimates of total market redemption rates predict that approximately $1 trillion may have been redeemed in 2009 alone.[2] This is an estimate of the redemption rate for hedge funds alone. Undoubtedly, the broad range of investment funds experienced massive changes during the financial crisis, but the focus of this book is on hedge funds and their relationship to brokers (see **Figure 4.1**).[3]

Hedge funds are among the largest investment funds in the world. Hedge funds' economic strength has toppled corporate

[1] The Universe on which the RBC Index is based currently consists of 5,926 hedge funds (excluding funds of hedge funds) which has aggregated assets under management estimated at $1.471 trillion.

[2] Anonymous, 2008d.

[3] For an overview of investment funds, see Chatfeild-Roberts, 2006.

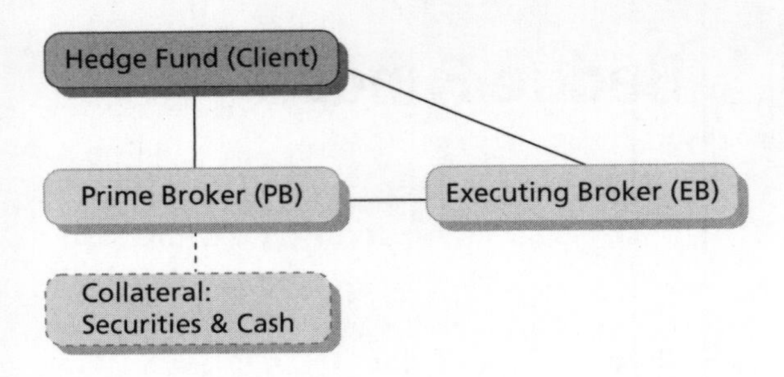

Figure 4.1 The Hedge Fund and Brokers

boards and even impacted global currencies.[4] The total number of hedge funds is roughly estimated at approximately 10,000. Hedge funds are not directly regulated in many jurisdictions. The majority are lightly regulated with assets under $100 million USD. There are many other investment funds, corporations, institutions, trusts, pension funds, and family offices that utilize prime finance services.

Hedge funds are typically smaller than massive sovereign wealth funds, which may run into several hundred billion dollars in assets.[5] Hedge funds encompass a range of fund sizes, including micro hedge funds with assets of less than $100,000. Bulge bracket prime brokers and their associated investment banks tend to focus on the larger investment funds with assets of at least $100 to $300 million.[6] These mega-funds are smaller in number but more lucrative in terms of long-term fees to justify the expenditures to provide services. They also typically have a longer track record with reputable, established managers.

---

[4] Certain hedge funds, including the legendary philanthropist and hedge fund manager, George Soros, recognized the inaccuracy and executed short strategies on an overvalued British pound. The British government and the Bank of England were forced to withdraw from the European Exchange Rate Mechanism and the Pound Sterling devalued accordingly.

[5] Sovereign wealth funds (SWFs) may, at times, utilize hedge fund strategies and have hundreds of billions of dollars in assets under management, such as the SWFs of China, Qatar, Abu Dhabi, Singapore, Brunei, and Kuwait.

[6] There are approximately thirty leading prime brokers, and many hundreds of other smaller mini-prime and regional prime brokers.

The ambit of alternative investments, including hedge funds, private equity funds, sovereign wealth funds, pension funds, national and multinational corporations, investment companies, and others, all utilize prime finance services. The prime broker's primary client base is the hedge fund industry. Understanding hedge funds is a complex and challenging undertaking. A hedge fund is a nebulous concept to define. Understanding the variety of hedge funds' activities and strategies is a daunting task, as there is considerable diversity in the spectrum of hedge funds. Our analysis begins where hedge funds began.

Original Hedge Fund

It is commonly accepted that the original hedge fund was created by Alfred Winslow Jones.[7] His original idea, from investigating investment funds as a journalist, was to create a limited partnership with a few investors and try to privately invest in certain stocks that were predicted to outperform the market, while shorting other stocks that were expected to underperform the market.[8] With his own money, and some investors, the first double alpha hedge fund was launched. Jones's fund quietly continued consistent risk-adjusted performance, beating the Standard & Poor's 500 Index for many years.[9]

However, judging a hedge fund by comparison to a traditional market standard, like the S&P 500, DJIU, or DAX, belies the fundamental goal of hedge funds. The original promise of the hedge fund was to provide absolute returns in either bull or bear markets. One hedge fund manager described the objective of hedge funds, "to provide the returns of equities with the risk of bonds."

[7] A variety of authors have reported on the story and success of Alfred Winslow Jones; see Lhabitant, 2004.

[8] The relevant market for performance measurement (or beta) depends upon the objectives of the hedge fund. An absolute return strategy fund should not be judged as compared to an index, but it may be appropriate to compare hedge funds with other hedge funds with similar strategies, such as global macro or statistical arbitrage; see Hedge Fund Index.

[9] See Anson, 2006.

Hedge funds were to focus on absolute returns rather than judging their performance related to an index or other asset class. For relative returns of many mutual funds, results of –25 percent when the market dropped –50 percent would be considered to have beaten the benchmark by 100 percent. However, this is unacceptable if the results are judged on an absolute basis. Ultimately one needs to understand what a hedge fund is in order to assess both potential returns and risks.

Hedge Funds: Definition

Lhabitant provided a useful, pragmatic definition of hedge funds:

"Hedge funds are privately organized, loosely regulated and professionally managed pools of capital not widely available to the public."[10]

While this is a useful start, it is so broad that almost any private investment fund may be considered a hedge fund. This poses particular problems for investors attempting to understand and analyze the risks and rewards associated with a particular fund.[11] Investors and prime brokers both need to have a detailed understanding of the structure, objectives, tactics and strategy of the hedge fund.[12]

Any definition of a hedge fund is ambiguous, in part because defining a hedge fund is the first step to regulation. Hedge fund entities were designed to be private and efficient with minimal regulatory oversight. The reporting, auditing, legal, and compliance requirements and associated infrastructure on regulated funds, such as mutual funds, are far too onerous for many hedge funds to sustain. If hedge funds became regulated like mutual

[10] Lhabitant, 2004, p. 4.

[11] For a review of the investor's considerations see Nicholas, 2005; Kirschner, Mayer, & Kessler, 2006; Boucher, 1998; Burton, 2007.

[12] Minimal basic information from "know-your-client" and anti-money laundering, to legal, and business requirements need to be satisfied. Also, details on domicile, incorporation, directors, investor eligibility, disclosure obligations, distribution, and product regulations will need to be addressed with the prime broker, particularly where marketing or capital raising is conducted in conjunction with prime finance sales staff.

funds, some hedge funds' strategies would become ineffective, and hedge funds would either cease operations or relocate to more hospitable jurisdictions. These are highly mobile, well-capitalized, lean, and sophisticated organizations. Many have core investment staff which are internationally mobile and have largely outsourced operations and ancillary services. Hedge fund managers and staff have an elevated sensitivity to regulatory oversight and a proclivity for privacy and remaining out of the public eye.[13] However, some managers have reduced sensitivity to regulatory oversight with the *proviso* that their proprietary trading strategies and current portfolio positions remain private and confidential.

The United States dominates the hedge fund market, with a majority of hedge fund managers and investors domiciled in the United States. The result of sweeping U.S. domestic, regional, and international regulation may not have the desired effect to control and regulate the hedge fund industry. To regulate and bring the hedge funds themselves under direct scrutiny may ultimately relocate the hedge fund industry to another, less operationally onerous, more efficient regulatory environment.

In order to stop the hedge fund industry relocating offshore to avoid competitive disadvantages, regulators have been content to impose indirect regulation on hedge funds. The typical hedge fund itself is not regulated directly. The prime broker, executing broker, investment manager, and adviser are regulated, and the hedge fund investors are screened for financial and other qualifications. In this way, the Securities and Exchange Commission (SEC), Financial Services Authority (FSA), and other regulators within the G-20 indirectly monitor the activities of hedge funds by imposing regulations on investment managers and broker-dealers who execute trading strategies for hedge funds.

Although the concise definition of a hedge fund is not possible, they do share certain characteristics. The first step to understanding these characteristics is to review their objectives.

---

[13] For a review of some of the personalities in the hedge fund industry see Chapter 2, The Players, in Coggan, 2008.

The Anatomy of Hedge Funds

Hedge funds:

- Have an objective of absolute returns (or returns relative to an index)
- Are singular or multiple legal entity structures
- Are structured under limited or effectively no regulation
- Attempt to generate trading income rather than investment income
- Have private investment strategies
- Have complex and diverse investment strategies
- May utilize both long positions and short positions
- Attempt to achieve tax efficiency
- Are only offered to special investors and are not available to the general public
- Are illiquid investments which may only be redeemed intermittently
- Incentivize managers to create wealth for investors and for the managers themselves

Objective: Absolute or Relative

The ambit of hedge funds ranges from sophisticated financial institutions with thousands of employees and over $100 billion in assets executing complex investment strategies to nascent start-up funds reliant on one prime broker with two traders and a dog. Understanding hedge funds requires understanding what they are after.

Alpha and Beta

Hedge funds seek to profit from investment strategies that rely on maximizing two different measurements: alpha and beta.

Beta: Market Risk

The standard way to make money in the financial markets is to take on systemic risk, which is known as *beta*. The beta coefficient is the covariance of a stock or portfolio in relation to the rest of the market. For example, if the market is the Financial Times–Stock Exchange 100 Index (FTSE 100) or Dow Jones Industrial Index (DJIU), the beta of a stock or portfolio is the relationship of that stock or portfolio to the relevant market. A perfect correlation would total one. Stocks often rise or fall disproportionately in relation to the market.[14]

There is nothing extraordinary about achieving results equal to the beta of the market. This can be achieved by mutual funds or exchange traded funds (ETFs) which parallel the volatility (at least in theory) or the underlying market. The real objective of hedge funds is to capture the elusive alpha.

Alpha: Non-Market Risk

Alpha is defined as:

> The coefficient measuring the portion of an investment's return arising from a specific (nonmarket) risk. In other words, *alpha* is a mathematical estimate of the amount of return expected from an investment's inherent values, such as rate of growth in earnings per share . . . and can be viewed as a measure of the value added by a manager.[15]

The other way to make money in the financial markets is by taking it away from other market participants. Only investors who are smarter than the market and able to implement their strategies will be able to provide alpha on a consistent, reliable basis.[16] Returns related to alpha are not correlated to the market. The fact that a manager recognizes that a particular security is undervalued in the market and invests in it, or that a security is overvalued and shorts it, is uncorrelated to the larger market. A manager who profits from accurately valuing securities by identifying and utilizing strategies

[14] For example, technology stocks, for example Google (GOOG), have significantly higher correlations to their index (in this case NASDAQ), whereas other defensive stocks, such as utilities, will not be as exposed to market risk.

[15] Downes & Goodman, 2006, p. 23.

[16] Jenson & Rotenberg, 2004.

to exploit their mispricings, excluding or reducing exposure to market risk, will generate results unrelated to market risk.

Where a manager recognizes alpha and executes trades that profit the hedge fund irrespective of market risk, the manager has captured alpha. This is often likened to the ability to spot mistakes of others and capitalize on them. The errors may be conceptual, financial, or philosophical and based upon accounting, economics, mathematics, psychology, behavioral or statistical errors.

Locusts and Efficient Markets

In different jurisdictions the perception of hedge funds ranges from a valuable part of the alternative investment community to pernicious pests.[17] Even within the EU there is a broad range of opinion on the value of hedge funds. Franz Müntefering, a former official in the German government, repeatedly compared hedge funds and other investment funds to locusts.[18]

Other areas of the EU hold strikingly divergent, and more enlightened views. By contrast, Hector Sants, Chief Executive of the FSA, has defended hedge funds as important market participants:

> There is a lot of pressure for more regulation at the moment, given the recent events, however, you can be assured, [The FSA] intend to stick to our guiding principles of proportionality, and outcome-focused regulation.
>
> Regardless of the current climate and all that has happened we still believe the [hedge fund] sector is positive for capital markets, with the community as a whole continuing to provide liquidity to a market in which it has been severely lacking.[19]

---

[17] German regulators and officials have made numerous negative political statements about hedge funds.

[18] When asked how he feels about the metaphor, the man who was then Germany's vice-chancellor grabbed a metal grasshopper from a shelf and borrowed from singer Edith Piaf. "I have no regret whatsoever," he said, speaking from his office in the labour ministry. "It is a nice image, locusts that move into a field, eat it to the ground, and move on to the next without looking back. I think it was quite apt" (Benoit, 2007).

[19] See *Speech*, 2008.

The conflict over hedge funds is largely political rhetoric, but it will be important for the future regulation and location of the industry. There is some public and government sentiment against hedge funds which purportedly caused short pressure on certain financial stocks.[20]

There are many beneficial aspects of the hedge fund's activities and many criticisms are unjustified. In defense of the hedge funds, regulators and market professionals have stated that hedge funds are important market participants and counterparties who create liquidity, help with price discovery, and create more efficient markets. If hedge funds did not search for mispricings, true values would not be made apparent. Consequently, hedge funds improve the operational efficiency and integrity of markets.

Without hedge funds and short-sellers, there are few who would be looking for overvalued stocks or checking the integrity of financial statements. The result is that industry players would only benefit from rising prices, which would undoubtedly lead to even greater asset bubbles and ultimately would likely create capital markets with greater volatility and systemic risk and reduced integrity. Hedge funds have been instrumental in increasing price discovery, increasing liquidity, and improving the efficiency of markets.

Hedge Fund Performance

According to CS Tremont, the average results for hedge funds in 2008 were –18 percent. Clearly a result of –18 percent is much preferable to the staggering –38 percent decline for the S&P Index. In terms of absolute returns, the hedge funds myth has been shown false.[21] However, there are brilliant exceptions to the negative industry average from certain hedge fund managers. The awe-inspiring results of top performing hedge fund managers reveals

---

[20] This concern in the United States has led legislators to reinstate the up-tick rule, which requires a stock to move up before a short may be effected.

[21] See Molinski, 2008.

just how important manager selection is to hedge fund performance.[22] Nonetheless, the justification for hedge fund investments in providing diversification from traditional markets and investments remains sound, though the myth of absolute returns in both bull or bear markets by all managers has been dispelled.

By comparison to global equity markets, hedge funds and hedge fund indices performed significantly better. Indeed, many hedge funds and strategies performed exceptionally well before, during, and after the financial crisis. Short-bias funds returned positive results with an average of positive 20 percent returns.[23]

One fundamental question is whether these returns are superior to simple passive replications of indices on a risk adjusted basis. A simple unleveraged short derivative contract or ETF on the S&P 500 would have yielded positive 38 percent. If double leverage were employed, the results would have been approximately 75 percent. Given that many of the short hedge funds produced lower returns but had higher leverage, the question is why invest in hedge funds if the risk adjusted returns are less than simple, more liquid, and more transparent financial products. There are some who question the whole investment process in hedge funds and funds of hedge funds. Warren Buffett has reportedly bet a prominent fund of funds manager $1,000,000 that a low cost-index fund would beat the fund of funds' performance over a decade.[24]

The question from a due diligence perspective is whether the active management is actually generating superior risk-adjusted returns or whether the actively managed funds are charging exorbitant fees for underperforming passive index funds. Due diligence in the future will likely focus on risk adjusted performance, transparency (over strategies, trading, and assets), and discerning the differences between managers' risk adjusted returns.

---

[22] Top hedge fund managers, including Paulson & Co., Greenlight Capital, and many others, have earned billions for their clients in the financial crisis.

[23] See Appendix D: Useful Links for More Hedge Fund Information.

[24] Buffett estimates that his odds of winning are 60 percent. See Anonymous, 2008c.

Hedge Fund Structures

Hedge funds may be structured to be either single entity or multiple entity vehicles. The structure is guided by the specific needs of investors and the investment manager. In the single entity structure, the hedge fund is composed of the hedge fund vehicle and the directors. The directors sit and direct the activities of the hedge fund broadly but do not take responsibility for day-to-day operations. They appoint an investment manager to enter into primary agreements, control operations, and effect strategies. The directors often have individual liability and fiduciary obligations to the underlying investors. An example of a single-entity hedge fund with an onshore manager is set out in **Figure 4.2**.

In the single entity structure, the investors may be pooled together and directly invest in the hedge fund vehicle, receiving shares or limited partnership credits. The undifferentiated investment approach may create difficulties for investors and managers in the event that investments trigger fiduciary or other legal requirements in certain jurisdictions. Similarly, there may be implications for the investor being pooled into the same vehicle from a risk perspective.

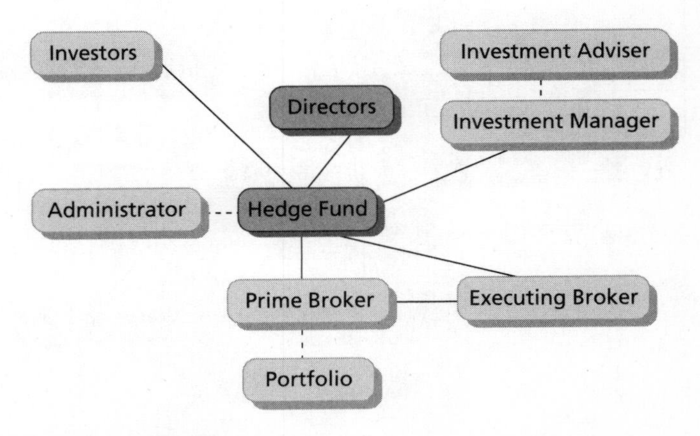

Figure 4.2 Single-Entity Hedge Fund

The multiple entity structure is more common with investors from various jurisdictions. An example of a multiple vehicle master-feeder hedge fund is set out in **Figure 4.3**. The master-feeder structure is employed in order to meet regulatory require-ments in investors' respective jurisdictions. Each regulator and tax authority may have different views of the taxable nature of the feeder vehicle or regulatory obligations that may be imposed. Accordingly, it is common to split investors into various feeder structures to ensure tax efficiency or to finesse any regulatory issues for particular investors. Certain issues may arise if different investors are placed into the same pooled feeder vehicle or directly into the master fund.

The variety of legal entities used by hedge funds is broad, complex, and international. The structure of hedge funds is guided by considerations of the purpose of the fund, operational and regulatory efficiency for the manager, and tax and regulatory efficiency for the various investors. In a typical example, a hedge fund may be set up as a Cayman Island incorporated investment company with a manager in the United Kingdom, an investment adviser in Connecticut, and investors from around the globe. Where there are investors from a variety of jurisdictions,

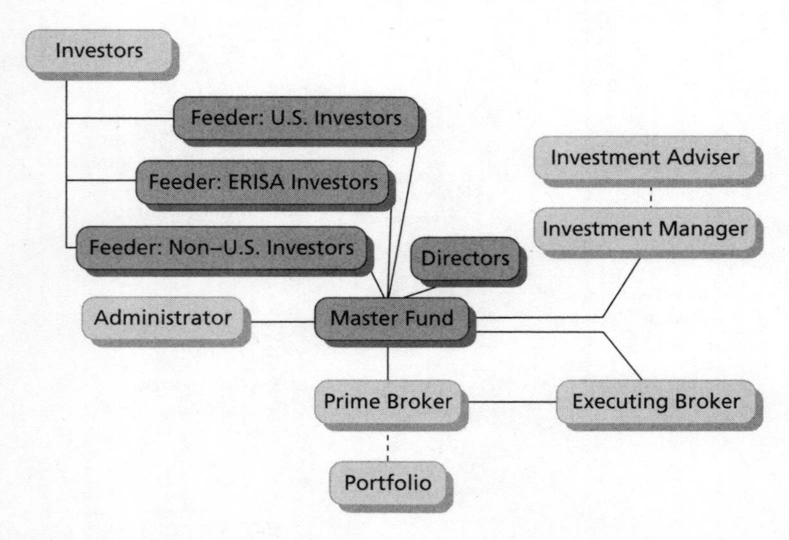

Figure 4.3 Master-Feeder Hedge Fund

the complexity of regulations may require a variety of feeder funds to meet the requirements of investors, and for operational and tax efficiency considerations. The requirements of investors or managers may result in bespoke multiple structure vehicles being utilized and legal and tax advice sought in the relevant jurisdictions as a part of the due diligence process.

Limited Direct Regulation

There has been limited regulatory oversight on hedge fund vehicles in the past. The regulatory considerations have been dictated by the location of incorporation, domicile, structure, and registration of the investment manager or investment adviser and investors.

The hedge fund itself is typically not regulated except for minimal account opening and anti-money laundering provisions. For example, the primary regulations upon a Cayman hedge fund are complying with anti-money laundering (AML) provisions for registration with the local regulator and any applicable listing obligations. Many funds have standard "know-your-client" (KYC) operations in place, and there will be various requirements in the event that that fund is listed on an exchange such as Cayman Islands Market Authority (CIMA). Also, the basics of account opening, KYC, and AML may be delegated to an external administrator.

Given that the hedge fund vehicles have minimal regulatory obligations, it falls to the individual investment adviser or investor to ensure basic due diligence is completed. From an investor's viewpoint, due diligence should be focused on the effect the legal entities have on the investor and the corresponding impact on the manager's fiduciary or investment duties to the investor.

- What are the tax implications of investing in the hedge fund?
- What regulatory protections does an investment have in the hedge fund?
- Are there applicable "client money rules" or other protections?

- What is the maximum potential loss?
- What reporting and transparency can be expected from the hedge fund?
- How can the investor be assured that the fund is acting (trading, reporting, borrowing) as originally described in the offering materials?
- Are investment gains, losses, redemption rights, and fees shared equally, or are certain investors in a privileged position?

The prime broker and executing broker will normally require full disclosure of incorporating documents, relevant agreements, signing authorities, and other ancillary documents. With this information the brokers will perform KYC, AML, and credit risk on the hedge fund. It should be noted that the regulatory oversight imposed directly on hedge funds is minimal, whereas indirectly there are business, operational, and regulatory disclosures required by prime brokers and executing brokers.

Income: Trading vs. Investment

There is a significant difference between traditional long-term investment funds and hedge funds. The standard hedge fund's goal is to generate income from short-term trading profits.[25] The investment is structured to provide for relatively frequent NAV calculations (daily, monthly, or quarterly) to allow for redemptions, fee calculations, and active management.

Two significant differences exist between the investment objectives of hedge funds as opposed to other types of alternative investments, such as private equity. The differences are the time horizon and ultimate goal of the investments. Private equity fund investments have an expected duration of several years (often six to ten years) with the objective to create capital gains for investors. Hedge funds, by contrast, are normally subject to shorter time horizons for investments and have their fees calculated in accordance with monthly NAVs, allowing for more periodic redemptions.

[25] Elder, 1993.

This time horizon creates trading profits rather than capital gains. Trading profits often have differential tax treatment. The trade off is that frequent trading should increase liquidity of the underlying portfolio and access to capital. Whether the portfolio is actually focused on liquid investments or illiquid positions is a matter of due diligence on the underlying portfolio.[26] Also, in order to finesse regulatory requirements, certain funds have shifting, transferring, and folding vehicles. The transitional nature of hedge fund entities requires ongoing due diligence to ensure that the entities and structures of the hedge fund are current and due regard is given to the relevant regulatory requirements.

Private Investment Strategies and Transparency

There is a profound tension between privacy over the manager's proprietary trading strategies and current positions versus disclosure and transparency of risks to investors. Undoubtedly, it is important for hedge funds to protect the confidentiality and privacy over their portfolios and strategies. Often strategies are not scalable, and investors may be competitors. It is also critical for investors to understand the portfolio in which they are investing and to be able to conduct due diligence on investments.[27] Proper due diligence requires the ability to look through to the assets being traded, how they are traded, and how they are financed.

Regulated mutual funds for retail investors must disclose their holdings. Mutual fund strategies are published publicly in offering memoranda. By contrast, hedge funds will not divulge their current holdings or trades that would prejudice their results or expose any vulnerability. In disclosing current portfolio positions there are two major risks. First, the fund may be vulnerable in the event that positions are made public and expose the fund to trading risks, such as short squeezes. Second, there is a potential that

[26] The Manhattan Investment Fund provides an example of a departure from the standard trading strategies of a hedge fund. The manager effectively concentrated the entire fund into an illiquid position which resulted in the fund's blow up.

[27] Chandler, 2002.

others will copy their positions or strategy, and this will dilute the opportunities of the manager's trading strategy. The collapse of trading opportunities requires the hedge fund manager to search for new, untapped sources of trading profit or alpha. Whether transparency would give others access to proprietary information and eliminate opportunities or the disclosure would potentially threaten the funds' positions or existence is irrelevant. They are both justifiable and legitimate reasons for restricting access to and transparency over the current investment portfolio.

When the hedge fund manager refuses to provide transparency in the portfolio due to fraud or refuses to provide accurate details of the investor's account, it is clearly not justifiable or to be condoned. The difference between legitimate reasons and illegitimate reasons for nondisclosure is critical for an investor to understand.

While the specifics of current portfolio positions may not be disclosed, the general details should be available from the manager. This includes reports on:

- Investment style
- Kind of investment securities
- Breadth: number of positions
- Direction of positions (long or short)
- Size of positions
- Risk of positions
- Industries targeted
- Markets traded[28]
- Leverage employed (how much is borrowed)
- Liquidity of the positions and portfolio
- Management fees
- Performance fees
- Calculation of performance

The purpose of advanced due diligence is to look beyond the basic structure of the hedge fund. The primary concern is what

---

[28] For a general review of the major markets see Levinson, 2006; for a review of the idiosyncratic issues related to emerging markets see Pacek & Thorniley, 2007.

the hedge fund and manager are doing with the investor's money. In essence, what are the trading strategies and operational tactics of the hedge fund? How is the hedge fund utilizing the investor's capital to generate revenues above the costs of capital? What are the associated market and nonmarket risks associated with the hedge fund? An investor, and sometimes the public in general, have an interest in the strategy of funds, assets invested in, and the leverage utilized by hedge funds.

So what do hedge funds do? There are many different trading strategies.[29] The investor may have access to reports from the investment manager, or through administrator reports, and the prime broker has direct knowledge over their portion of the hedge fund's portfolio. It is understood industry practice that the manager will not disclose the current portfolio positions that may prejudice the hedge fund. There may be indirect ways to ascertain risks without direct, real-time views into the portfolio. The administrator and prime broker will have insight into the manager's trading activities and the holdings of the hedge fund. The prime broker may have insight into whether a particular strategy is followed. This may be for the period of trading or only upon valuation dates. In complex funds with a multi-prime broker model, no particular prime broker may have sufficient information to recognize that the manager is not acting in accordance with its prospectus or offering documents.

There are limits to what may be expected from a prime broker. The prime broker has no obligation to the investors directly.[30] The investor should request that the hedge fund itself provide this information (or confirmation) from an independent administrator or from the prime brokers. There is no perfect due diligence which can prevent or protect against all potential manager misrepresentations or fraud. In the event that the reports of the manager are fraudulent, the investor will seek direct relief from the manager and the hedge fund, but alternatively investors may seek remedies

[29] See Beck & Nagy, 2005.
[30] Eurycleia Partners LP et al. v. UBS Securities, LLC, 2008.

against the administrator, auditors, and prime brokers.[31] Advanced due diligence assists in avoiding allocation to underperforming funds and detecting fraud. Administrators, auditors, and prime brokers have insight into the holding and trading of the hedge fund. Thus, investors may gain some level of transparency indirectly through these service providers.

Investment Strategies

There is a diverse range and variety of investment strategies that hedge funds utilize. Hedge funds may look for various kinds of arbitrage opportunities or may take direct market risk.[32] An arbitrage is defined as "the simultaneous purchase and sale of securities to take advantage of pricing differential created by market conditions."[33] Hedge funds may typically seek out investment opportunities in or between inefficient markets to exploit arbitrage opportunities. The mispricing of assets may allow for arbitrage between different assets or jurisdictions. For example, incorrect calculations of values between an index and the underlying stocks may provide for inefficient pricing of the underlying assets or index. Ultimately, certain hedge funds' focus on exploiting inefficiencies is a valuable service that enhances market efficiency and liquidity and improves price discovery.

While arbitrage is one kind of strategy, there is a broad range of hedge fund investment strategies.[34] The various strategies may involve investments in debt or equity securities, convertible bonds, futures contracts or derivative products, options, warrants, and commodities contracts.[35] Each kind of strategy requires specific skill sets. These skills sets may or may not be transferable between

[31] Beacon Hill provided significant insight into the handling of the fraudulent reporting of a fund manager.

[32] For more on arbitrage see Billingsley, 2005.

[33] Calamos, 2003.

[34] See Billingsley, 2005, and a broad review of strategies in Beck & Nagy, 2005 and Kirschner, Mayer, & Kessler, 2006.

[35] See Diamond & Kollar, 1989.

strategies which depend upon their analysis of opportunities. The manager's investment analysis may be either top-down or bottom-up, or some combination of both. The difference in the view of the manager and their focus on investments may indicate sources of alpha or error. Bottom-up analysis focuses on individual securities in detail and later considers how the security will fit into the larger economic picture. Hedge fund managers who employed bottom-up analysis were focused too closely on the value within MBS, ABS, or real estate investments in the United States and ignored the larger macroeconomic factors that led to massive changes in valuations and volatility. Similarly, top-down analysis may result in a focus on larger macroeconomic factors that may be irrelevant for many strategies that rely on small mispricings of similar securities. The style of the manager and their process for selecting investments and identifying risks are critical concerns for investors. It is important to understand the hedge fund's objectives, strategies and tactics. The strategies may be promising, but tactical execution may not be possible with volatile markets, competition or operational limitations. Arbitrage opportunities may exist for a short period (from days to microseconds) and may collapse when a hedge fund (or several funds) attempts to capitalize on the inefficiency.

Investment Strategy and Tactics

The strategy of a fund is the overarching plan. The fund's tactics involve how the manager and fund actually go about implementing the strategy. Two funds may be attempting to effect the same strategy but go about effecting that strategy in completely different ways, and there will be different risks associated with each. To understand the tactical risks involved in implementing a hedge fund strategy, a number of factors are relevant, including:

- Percentage of capital risked per trade
- Trade size
- Trading commissions and fees
- Payoff ratio

- Average win
- Average loss
- Hit rate
- Maximum loss tolerated
- Loss rate
- Leverage utilized and financing charges
- Number of counterparties
- Expenses from service providers (e.g. prime brokers, lawyers, accountants)
- Operational risk: independent administrator
- Regulatory risks: fines or regulatory issues (e.g., short selling)
- Business risks: redemptions

A fund that has one or two trades that risk the entire capital of the fund will have tactical risks, although the underlying strategy appears to be promising. It is important to have a view into the positions of the fund to allow both qualitative and quantitative analysis of the hedge fund's specific risks. If the actual positions are not clear, an accurate view of the tactical positions will yield important information about both potential risks and returns.

Hedge Fund Taxonomy

Common hedge fund strategies include:

- Long/short equity
- Event driven
  a. Merger arbitrage
  b. Bankruptcy and distressed debt
  c. Divestiture
- Equity market neutral
  a. Pairs trading
  b. Dividend capture
  c. Index arbitrage
- Convertible arbitrage
- Fixed income arbitrage

- Relative value
- Mortgage/asset backed arbitrage
- Credit
- Global macro
- Managed futures
- Multistrategy

Listing the taxonomy of hedge fund strategies is not enlightening unless one looks through to understand the business of the fund.[36] The business of the fund is how investments are selected, traded, and financed. The investor should have an understanding of the flows of capital and securities. While many investors have focused on promising strategies, expected returns, and looked no further, this will likely not be sufficient for future hedge fund investments. The ultimate aim of a hedge fund is to beat the cost of capital and generate returns for the investor and manager on a risk adjusted basis. A review of a few of the major strategies will illustrate the anticipated returns and risks posed by certain strategies.

Long/Short Equity

A long/short equity strategy will hold long and short positions in equities. Often long/short funds have a long bias to reflect a directional (market) component, such as 130-30 funds. The manager of long/short funds may utilize technical and fundamental analysis in the selection of positions. Technical analysis may be sufficient for many hedge fund managers, but often fundamental analysis of the underlying securities must be evaluated. An example of a long/short trade with General Motors and Toyota is set out in **Figure 4.4**.

What is important for the long/short strategy is the relative position of the two equities. The two positions are immune from

[36] For a review of the different styles and an entertaining view into the management and personalities behind hedge funds, see Coggan, 2008.

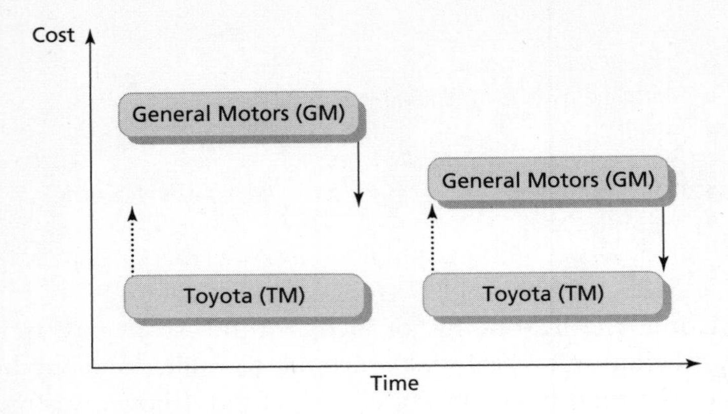

Figure 4.4 Equity Long/Short

the changes of the larger market. What is relevant to the hedge fund manager is the relative positions of the equities and the costs of funding the short position and any leverage utilized.

Managers with long/short strategy may be restricted to investments in a particular geographical area, industry, or sector. If there is no restriction on the ambit of the investments or strategies of the fund, long/short equity may be global. In such circumstances, the top-down manager may have additional skill in locating opportunities, whereas bottom-up analysts will likely prefer to stick to industries and sectors the manager understands well.

Event Driven

Event driven hedge funds invest in strategies that seek to profit from a variety of events. These may be regulatory changes, corporate actions, mergers, bankruptcies, or divestitures. The most commonly known form of event driven arbitrage is merger arbitrage (risk arbitrage).

The traditional strategy of an event driven, risk arbitrage fund in its simplest form is to profit from the merger of two entities, the acquirer and the target (**Figure 4.5**). The manager will make an investment in the target, short the acquirer, and wait for the convergence of the two securities, which creates a premium on the target's securities and loss in value for the acquirer.

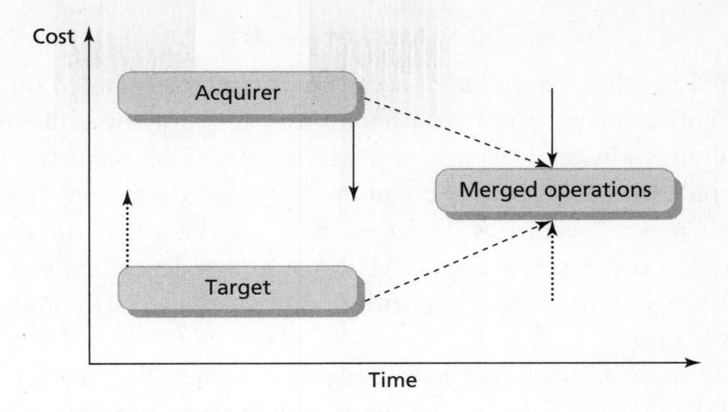

Figure 4.5 Merger Arbitrage Tactics

Fund managers attempt to estimate the probability of mergers from a detailed understanding of the industries, companies, regulatory restrictions, and even personalities of the management of the target and acquirer companies. In the event that the merger fails to complete, both target and acquirer may experience losses. The losses from event driven funds may be significant, and particular attention should be given to the skill of the manager and the potential opportunities in the market or sector focus of the fund.[37]

In the present context, there may be a variety of mergers and acquisitions in the fallout after the financial crisis. The merger and acquisition activity may yield returns for event driven funds in the consolidation of various industries. However, recently the market for merger arbitrage has been limited, and what would have previously been merger arbitrage is now repackaged as distressed debt. Given the particularly sensitive nature of event driven funds to material nonpublic information, there have been notorious examples of fund managers who utilized illegal insider information to secure returns.[38]

[37] There have been several high-profile and notorious managers who attempted to enhance their understanding of mergers and acquisitions through material nonpublic information, which led to SEC investigations, fines, and imprisonment in some cases.

[38] For more information, see Stewart, 1991.

Equity Market Neutral

Statistical arbitrage strategies focus on differences between similar or identical shares listed on different exchanges or the differences between individual securities and indices. The securities are referred to as pairs, and the pairs trading rely upon convergence between the securities.[39] There may be securities listed in American depositary receipts (ADRs) or global depositary receipts (GDRs), or the actual securities may be located in another jurisdiction.

Ultimately, the equity market neutral strategy will attempt to capitalize on inefficiencies between exchanges or indices without taking on direct market risk. This can be difficult to evaluate as the differences in the valuation of securities may result from different concerns about a particular jurisdiction and what appears to be an inefficiency is actually a different risk. This may be systemic, national, or currency risk, built into the valuation of one security and not another. There is often extensive leverage used in equity neutral strategies. To exploit small differences or inefficiencies in related securities may require substantial leverage. When price differentials are small, leverage is utilized to enhance returns. The level of leverage for all strategies is a critical consideration, as trading losses and associated risks are compounded by leverage. Thus risk of ruin calculations, scenario analysis, and stress testing are necessary to fully assess the potential risks of strategies and portfolios. This is particularly acute where extensive leverage is utilized.

Global Macro Strategy

Global macro strategies invest in currencies, bonds, stocks, indices, and derivatives based upon macroeconomic analysis.[40] The global macro hedge fund managers are typically in charge of very large hedge funds that may have a significant impact on

[39] Ehrman, 2006.

[40] For more on global macro strategies see Chandler, 2002 and Lederman & Klein, 1995.

various markets, currencies, and securities. The investment managers of the large global macro hedge funds include famous figures in the hedge fund industry.[41] The combination of complexity and reputation makes due diligence investigations particularly daunting for individual investors. As a result, many investors have turned over due diligence to investment advisers, funds of hedge funds, and investment consultants.[42]

The global macro fund manager often takes a global view and utilizes a variety of scenario analyses to identify opportunities from a top-down perspective. The hedge fund's positions are designed to exploit market opportunities when the scenario or market conditions come to reflect their view of the global economies. One such trade is the purchase of long positions in certain commodities, such as gold, and short positions in common shares of financial or real estate firms. Some of the largest names in alternative investments have managed global macro funds.

Multi-Strategy Funds

In analyzing funds, the multi-strategy fund is a combination of one or more investment strategies. This strategy is difficult to quantify and assess for risks to the investor as the manager often has almost unfettered discretion. This discretion is subject only to the offering memorandum or fund prospectus, which are typically vague for multi-strategy funds. For due diligence, multi-strategy funds often pose significant challenges, as past performances and investment strategies may not be reflected in current fund investments or trading strategies. Underlying the ambiguity and vagueness around hedge fund strategies and tactics is a fundamental problem. Multi-strategy hedge fund managers are self-defining and may not follow past strategies.

---

[41] Famous hedge global macro fund managers include Julian Robertson, Paul Tudor Jones, Bruce Krovner, and George Soros.

[42] Investment consultants were successful in avoiding certain fraudulent fund managers such as the Madoff fraud but have not been successful in all cases; see the Westridge fraud in Weisenthal, 2009.

Investment Style: Broad Definition

To some extent, naming a style belies the ignorance over what a fund is actually doing. A hedge fund may state that it invests in a multi-strategy style in diversified European equities in high growth industries. After due diligence, it may surprise investors to find that the hedge fund is actually only invested in a few illiquid investments in Russia leveraged one hundred times.

Another problem with broad definition of the fund can be "strategy drift." Studies of hedge funds have shown considerable correlation between hedge funds and may have a form of groupthink.[43] Hedge fund managers tend to look for the same opportunities and may therefore be exposed to the same risks. When a specific fund is searching for new sources of alpha there may be a tendency to stray from areas of core competence to new areas that appear to offer opportunities; however, the risks may not be fully understood. If the strategy is not disclosed or is misrepresented to investors, the manager may exceed the proper sphere of his trading jurisdiction, which may lead to redemptions, fines, criminal and civil litigation, and even incarceration.

A fund may experience strategy drift secretly and slowly. This change in strategy may lead to positive or negative results, but the investors may find that the hedge fund does not offer the diversification anticipated. Consequently, one of the major reasons and justifications for the hedge fund investment has disappeared. Strategy drift is a particularly significant risk where the manager has a broadly defined investment style and strategy. Investors may have very little information on the portfolio or investment strategies, such as those that may be employed in multi-strategy or global macro funds. The result is that investors have little transparency or knowledge over the risks or potential returns.

[43] Groupthink is a type of thought pattern whereby individuals with similar backgrounds, education, and personal characteristics view problems and opportunities in a similar manner. This may lead the group behavior to focus on a consensus opinion regarding a particular problem or course of action and may ignore, omit, or discourage alternative ideas or options.

Some level of due diligence must be allowed on the tactics of the fund to provide transparency into risks and to protect investors' interests, while simultaneously protecting the integrity and security of the investment portfolio. Some experts suggest that the fund manager should be able to provide examples of the trades it has made or anticipates it will enter into.[44] Given that the investors in hedge funds are particularly sophisticated individuals, entities, and organizations, it may be the case that investors will try to discern the exact strategies so that side investments may be made. Similarly, a fund manager will have to be limited in terms of side activities and other investments.

Key Man Provisions

Investors should ensure that sufficient time and resources are focused on the day-to-day operations of their particular hedge fund investment. This risk may be particularly acute where a star investment manager is involved, but may be dealt with key man provisions in a side letter or subscription agreements. In the event a key man departs a hedge fund manager or adviser, investors will want the ability to redeem their investment on an expedited basis. Similarly, the investment universe of the fund should be carefully considered, for the larger the definition of suitable investment, the more limited side investments will be possible for an investment manager. Where investors provide significant remuneration for managers, it should be expected that investments within the scope of the fund should be made to the benefit of the hedge fund and its investors.

The nature, diversification, and leverage of the portfolio must be consistent with the objectives and the declared strategies and tactics of the hedge fund. While the current positions of the hedge fund are private and guarded, it may be appropriate in the future for funds to provide ongoing due diligence by accountants, auditors, and consultants under confidentiality. These professionals may provide confirmation to investors that the declared investment

[44] Lhabitant, 2004.

portfolio, strategies, and tactics are being followed. This will normally be conducted by auditors of funds who will certify that the financial statements of the fund are materially correct. In addition to assuring the "material correctness" of the hedge funds, the material risks need to be disclosed and examined. This may be achieved with the assurances of the prime brokers and fund administrators, subject to the consent of the fund managers and hedge fund directors. The intersection between the hedge fund and prime brokers has been explored in certain litigation.[45] The result is that hedge funds and prime brokers have a contractual relationship. Investors in hedge funds have no standing to make a claim against the prime broker, except in exceptional circumstances.

The intersection between the investors, hedge funds, and prime brokers is the prime brokers' awareness and participation with funds that are not trading in a manner consistent with their stated objectives, strategy, and tactics. However, the limitations of the prime broker agreement have left investors with limited rights to sue the prime broker directly. In *Euryclea Partners, LP, et al. v. UBS Securities, LLC ("UBS")*, the New York State Supreme Court dismissed the complaint against UBS. The UBS case centered on the prime broker's alleged acknowledgment that a fund manager was acting in a fraudulent manner. The manager, John Whittier and Wood River Partners L.P., had effectively concentrated the entire fund's assets into Endwave stock. The plaintiffs claimed that the prime broker had inappropriately made the Endwave positions available to borrow by short sellers in order to generate stock loan fees, shorted Endwave itself, and had leaked information about selling Wood River's position in Endwave. The complaint alleged fraud, constructive fraud, breach of fiduciary duty, aiding and abetting, gross negligence, tortuous interference with contract, and unjust enrichment.

The court dismissed all claims against UBS as the investors had no standing to bring an action against the prime broker. Fundamental was the court's finding that the prime brokerage

[45] See Eurycleia Partners LP et al. v. UBS Securities, LLC, 2008.

agreement had a specific disavowal of any fiduciary obligations to the fund. The fund's investors were unsuccessful in their claim against the prime broker due to the limitations of the contractual relationship. The case may have been decided differently if the hedge fund manager and hedge fund had taken the action against the prime broker directly. Ultimately, the matter was decided on technical grounds, but future cases will likely return to this issue.

Long or Short Positions

Hedge funds are not limited to investing in securities that are expected to rise in value, such as traditional mutual funds. Hedge funds also take short positions that benefit from reductions in the value of securities.[46] The majority of hedge funds have a slightly long bias. Given the favorable returns in equity markets over the last two decades, it is not surprising that some correlation with the beta of the markets will yield higher returns. It was this combination of net long positions that left many hedge funds open to the financial crisis in 2008.

Short-bias funds suffered generally poor returns relative to other strategies for many years in the bull markets. Many hedge fund managers and experts viewed short-bias funds as a tool for reduction of risk in bear markets, but not as a means to increase portfolio values.[47] Recently, bear markets have vindicated the short-bias strategy and provided significant returns for short-bias funds and managers. Short-bias funds prospered by taking short positions in mortgage-backed securities, asset backed securities, financial stocks, and major indices. Even short-bias funds may have been negatively impacted when sudden market regulations shocked the markets. Provided the level of leverage utilized by short-bias funds was not negatively impacted by the extreme volatility in the markets, and they were not caught wrong footed

[46] Examples of short-bias funds include Einhorn's firm, Greenlight Capital; see Einhorn, 2008.

[47] Anson, 2006.

by the changing regulations, substantial gains were made in the global financial crisis.

Long and Short

What is a long position? The long position is created in the normal way of trading. For example, anyone who invests in a security (financial instrument, commodity, derivative) is said to be "long" the particular stock. The investor will gain when the markets or stock increases in value and will lose when the stock falls. The potential for losses in the long position is limited to the value of the securities. However, slightly more complicated is the short position, where there is unlimited downside potential.[48]

Short positions (or "shorts"), by contrast, provide economic benefit to the holder of the short position when the security falls, or reduces in value. The short position creates potentially unlimited liability in the event that the securities increase in value. The short position is not necessarily a free-standing short exposure, but may be a way for investors to hedge their long positions (or reduce exposure to markets or specific securities).[49] As such, short positions are a critical component of many *bona fide* investment strategies. Hedge funds, and other market participants utilize short positions to effectively manage risk.

Creating a Short Position

There are several ways to create a "short" economic exposure, including securities, exchange traded funds, derivatives, or by other financial products. Derivative contracts (such as buying put options) are a commonly employed way to create short exposures. These instruments may be traded on exchange (exchange traded) with a central counterparty or may be made privately between two entities, termed Over-The-Counter (OTC). The standard way to generate a short position with securities involves stock lending.

---

[48] See Anson, 2006, pp. 44–45.
[49] See for example, Calamos, 2003 and Kirschner, Mayer, & Kessler, 2005.

A typical equity short position is created by borrowing a security and then selling it into the market. In the case of market timing, the borrower typically sells the borrowed securities into the market when he expects that the borrowed stock will fall in value. When the stock does fall in value, the short position may be closed by buying the stock back and redelivering the stock to the lender. It is important to note that the obligation to the lender is to redeliver equivalent securities, not the same securities or at a particular value.[50] The basic transaction is set out in **Figure 4.6**.

The result of the short sale is two-fold. The short sale creates a specific economic risk inversely related to the change in value of the security which has been shorted. A short sale is a financing event that creates liquidity for the short seller. The financing aspect of shorts is an important transaction for both hedge funds and financial institutions, as it drives many of the financings for a variety of strategies. The short positions may finance other long positions.

In general, short positions create an economic exposure inversely related to the change in value of a loaned security. Short positions allow for hedge funds to profit from short positions or to finance long positions. The combination of long and short

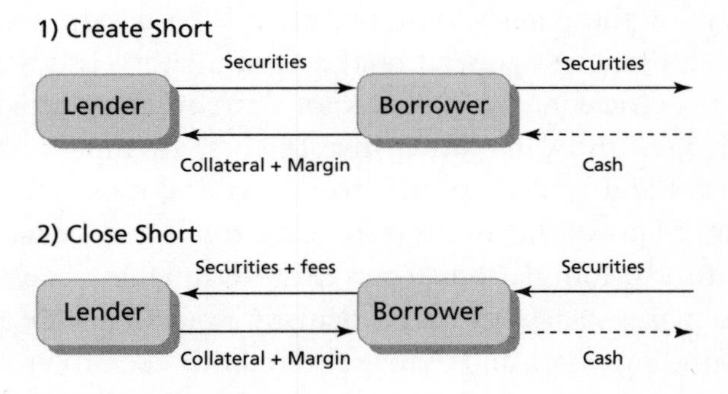

Figure 4.6 Short Sale Mechanics

[50] For a very useful introduction to securities lending in the United Kingdom, see Faulkner, 2004.

positions is critical for hedge funds to exploit inefficiencies between securities that are overvalued and those that are undervalued. Short positions are also an important source of financing for both hedge funds and their prime brokers.

There are other occasions where stock loans are not used for the purpose of short selling but rather for other reasons. This may be to cover certain positions or to exercise certain rights associated with a particular security.[51] An important distinction between long positions and short positions is the maximum potential loss. The risk to the fund in a long position is limited to the value of the investment. The risk of exposure for a short position is unlimited. There is no limit to how high certain stocks may go, with the added responsibility to pay for any dividends that are received on the borrowed security. The result is that short-sellers may be liable for losses in excess of the value of the securities. Hedge funds utilize long positions and short positions for a variety of strategic and financing objectives. Another important consideration in any alternative investment is tax efficiency.

Tax Efficiency

A core objective of structuring the hedge fund is to provide tax efficiency for the parties. The objective is to design a structure that finesses strategic, operational and regulatory issues and still remains tax efficient. There is no motive to evade or avoid proper taxes. Hedge funds, like other investments, attempt to structure investments and trading profits to receive the most efficient tax treatment. Many of the investors in hedge funds may be tax exempt pension funds, foundations, or even governments. Their unique tax status makes such investors particularly aware of double taxation. Hedge fund investors and managers are both keen to ensure that profits are passed through to investors without unnecessary taxation on investment vehicles.

---

[51] Calamos, 2003.

The tax payable in an offshore jurisdiction of a hedge fund is typically nil.[52] Individual investors will have tax liabilities associated with their individual characteristics and residency.[53] Thus tax efficiency is achieved by structuring the hedge fund to pay taxes on gains by delivering investment profits to individual investors.

Structuring investments for tax efficiency is a legitimate business practice. It does not mean attempting to pervert proper tax remittances or taxable income reporting. It is merely an important factor in structuring investments and transactions to avoid double or unnecessary tax liabilities for investors. It is critical to efficiency and competitiveness in international finance and the international investment banks, hedge funds, and other parties. Hedge funds are structured to be tax efficient as this is vital for investors. Individual investors, family offices, pension funds, trusts, and local and national governments seek to pay tax in their home jurisdiction at the rate and amount legally required.[54] If there were additional layers of taxation, this may make certain alternative investments uncompetitive to other options. This would require a reassessment of hedge fund investments, or a change in structure, domicile, and jurisdiction of the hedge funds to fall outside overarching regulations.

With the new developments in international markets, there may be additional changes to the structure and domicile of hedge funds. However, international attempts to increase transparency, tax reporting and remove bank secrecy are ongoing,

---

[52] In certain offshore jurisdictions, such as the Cayman Islands or Bermuda, there are no income tax obligations and yet other jurisdictions offer other reduced tax. However, the tax implications of different jurisdictions and the various treaty rights are among the most complex areas of investment, tax, and legal practice.

[53] U.S. investors pay tax in their particular state according to their particular tax status. Other jurisdictions ascribe tax liabilities according to residency and citizenship with respect to taxation. It is common to require U.S. regulations declarations, such as non-Regulation X declarations, for investors in international investment funds.

[54] Many large institutional investors, such as pension funds or insurance companies, pay no taxes due to their particular regulatory framework or location of incorporation.

particularly in light of recent G-20 developments.[55] Whether international efforts to limit tax havens, and increase remittances to tax-paying jurisdictions will ultimately succeed is questionable.[56]

Special Investors

There is a broad range of investors who may consider investments in hedge funds. Regulators in the United States and European Union have limited access to hedge funds and other private investments from many retail investors. In the international sphere, there is a complex mosaic of regulatory and legal regimes regarding the total number of investors, domicile, citizenship, residency requirements, minimum income, and other limits on marketing to certain investors. Due diligence must be undertaken in each jurisdiction, as there is no common regulatory framework, and each jurisdiction may impose its own requirements.

Ongoing due diligence is required in each jurisdiction where funds anticipate marketing to investors. The investors who may invest in hedge funds in many jurisdictions are limited to financial institutions and high-net-worth individuals ("HNWIs").[57] HNWIs qualify for investments in hedge funds based upon the restrictions imposed on the investment manager. In many cases, the hedge fund manager will avoid taking investments from

---

[55] The developments in international cooperation and regulation indicate there will be continuing efforts to limit bank secrecy and improve tax reporting. In their final report, the G-20 urged acceptance of OECD standards; Group, 2009, pp. 35–36.

[56] Although the G-20 have stated broad principles to increase transparency and reporting, the reach of the G-20 leaves many important jurisdictions outside their scope and authority.

[57] Regulators often consider wealthy individuals and financial institutions as requiring less regulation, the purpose of the legislation being to protect the individual retail investor from being taken advantage of by unscrupulous professionals. The regulations in the United States defined "qualified" investors as those with income higher than $200,000 or assets in excess of $1,000,000.

small, retail investors, as this may trigger a variety of regulatory oversight, operational, and disclosure requirements.

In the United States, investors are required to be "qualified" investors, so as to not attract regulation.[58] Access to hedge funds has not been extremely restrictive, as the obligation is on the investor to declare that they are in fact a "qualified investor." Managers (or administrators where delegated) have been obligated to perform rudimentary due diligence on this representation, including minimal KYC and AML requirements.

The hedge fund investors have developed from largely wealthy individual investors to include financial institutions, family offices, pension funds, governments, and foundations.[59] The size of the capital allocated to hedge funds in 2008 stands at an estimated $1.9 trillion by HFR group.[60] The financial crisis of 2008 has led many observers to conclude that there will be both broad redemptions and increased allocations as the hedge fund market transitions. Some analysts have questioned the growth prospects for the entire alternative investment industry. Some investors have withdrawn funds from the asset class while others have increased their allocations due to the relatively positive results of hedge funds.[61]

Illiquid Investments and Control

The hedge funds have traditionally focused on trading strategies where control over portfolio companies is not an objective. These are distinguished from other alternative investments, which utilize illiquid investment strategies and seek control over portfolio companies, such as is common in private equity. It should be noted that the lines between hedge funds and private equity have been blurred with the development of activist hedge funds and

---

[58] See Regulations X, and for more detail see Lofchie, 2005.
[59] Baquero & Verbeek, 2005.
[60] Reuters, 2008.
[61] Gangahar, 2008a.

hybrid funds. Hybrid funds sit somewhere between hedge funds and private equity and although structured as hedge funds, may pursue activist strategies.

The liquidity of hedge fund investments relates to the investment horizon of the hedge fund and the ability of investors to access their investment capital. The liquidity of the investments in alternative investments ranges from days or months for hedge funds to six or ten years for private equity, infrastructure, and mezzanine funds.

The liquidity of an investor's investments into hedge funds is limited. Investors' redemption rights are subject to offering documents and other bespoke contractual restrictions. In the normal course, it may take between one and three months for an investor to redeem shares in a hedge fund. However, certain funds may be considerably longer.[62] With the surge of redemptions in the financial crisis, certain funds have invoked limits or restricted redemptions entirely. This drastic step has been criticized, but managers have attempted to justify this position in order to avoid total liquidation, forcing them to sell illiquid portfolio assets at massive discounts.

The investment in a hedge fund may be structured as securities in an open-ended investment company or limited partnership units, or another suitable structure. The ontological specifics of the securities or financial product investment needs to be clarified and understood with legal and financial due diligence. One of the complexities arises when a manager has a number of different vintages of funds or investors invest at different times in an open ended fund. In order to finesse problems of investors investing at different times, a manager will often utilize accounting methods to show that older investors are not financing newer investors, and investors are treated equally with regard to incentives for the manager.

Free Riders and Equalization Payments

There is a well-documented concern that late investors may benefit and pay lower fees than earlier investors, known as the "free

[62] Redemptions may be extended for months; see Anson, 2006, p. 124.

rider syndrome."[63] The free rider syndrome may occur where a fund has a down month and new investors enter the fund. The fund will not pay out performance fees until the high water mark of the fund is surpassed. That is, where the AUM of the fund drops significantly, the manager will not get the benefit of the performance fees until the prior AUM is surpassed. Thus the structure of the investments should provide for mechanisms to address free rider problems, such as invest-ment corporations issuing additional securities, simple equalization payments, or awarding credits to earlier investors.[64] Investors moving into funds that have suffered significant losses will have to address the free rider syndrome with the fund manager.

Redemptions and the Return of Capital

The specifics and significance of redemptions for hedge funds should be carefully examined. While the hedge fund may invest in liquid investments and may enter and exit trades in less than a day, the investor's access to the hedge fund investment may be delayed significantly. Under the terms of the subscription agreement and the private placement memorandum, the contractual terms may specify various dates for redemptions and time delays for access to the investor's capital. These contractual provisions may delay the redemption for months or longer.[65]

The risk associated with such delays should not be underestimated.[66] Also, redemptions themselves may have a negative impact on the value of an investment. In cases where a hedge fund is a major participant in the market, invested in a few illiquid securities, the act of reducing leverage or selling positions may impact the market and the value of securities. In addition, the marking to market of the fund's holdings may lead to a

[63] Lhabitant, 2004, pp. 140–141.

[64] Lhabitant, 2004, pp. 140–144.

[65] The risks and delays associated with redemptions are set out in Lhabitant, 2002 and 2004, which demonstrate the significance and length of delays in relation to redemptions.

[66] Risk is the square root of time.

pernicious cycle of redemptions and falling values, where redemptions drive the falling market.[67] The value of a hedge fund unit may fall based upon the fear and decisions of investors. It is particularly important for investors to understand the impact of other investors, priority redemption positions, delays, timelines, and the managers' rights to restrict redemptions for redeeming capital from hedge funds.

Certain large hedge funds were oversubscribed and compelled investors to agree to significant restrictions on redemptions with extended lock-up provisions. While this is an added protection for the hedge fund that creates certainty that portfolio investments will not need to be put up in a fire sale, it also ensures that hedge fund managers will continue to receive management fees.

Side Pocket Investments

Investment managers may side-pocket certain investments. That is a special provision that allows greater rights for the investment manager to set certain assets outside the realm of redemptions, or to create other investments that are protected from redemptions. When a hybrid hedge fund intends to take effective control over portfolio companies, then there may be a *bona fide* reason for exercising side pocket investments; however, this substantially increases risks for prime brokers. The specifics of side pocket terms should be examined to avoid negative impact on an investor's ability to redeem shares or units of the hedge fund in a timely manner. Side pocket investments may significantly restrict investors' rights and should be carefully considered.

Side Letters

Side letters are another important area for both fund managers and investors. While side letters are standard in private equity

[67] However, the changes to FASB standards on the "mark to market" rule will give managers and banks greater latitude to assess illiquid investments on a more favorable basis.

funds and other investments, they are less so with hedge funds. Certain cornerstone investors or institutional investors subject to internal or external requirements on investments will request side letters. When a hedge fund has negotiated a side letter with an investor, the terms of the side letter are designed to supersede the limited partnership agreement or other governing documents.

When hedge funds revealed exposures to Lehman Brothers, many investors provided notice of their intention to redeem their investments. Some investors were surprised to find that others stood in a preferred position for redemptions as a result of undisclosed side letters. Investors should be clear to request transparency and may access the same terms as applicable to others through most-favored nation (MFN) provisions in side letters. The MFN side letter grants the recipient the benefit of any other side letter. The result is that these side letters may have the effect of creating two levels of investors.[68] This apparent difference in treatment has caused regulators to express concerns about side letters and differential treatment of investors.[69] However, not all aspects of side letters are disturbing for regulators. Particular concern has arisen over side letters that have granted preferential access to portfolio information and priority in redemptions.[70]

Incentives

Hedge fund managers benefit from one of the most lucrative incentive schemes in the world (**Figure 4.7**). In successful hedge funds, managers may earn billions of dollars in a single year. Unsuccessful managers may still make significant sums from management fees even where investors lose capital.

Hedge funds are different from other investment vehicles in that managers are incentivized to seek out investment opportunities

---

[68] See Spangler, 2007, p. 13.

[69] For the FSA's published position paper on side letters see FSA, 2006.

[70] The SEC position has been revealed through testimony before the U.S. Senate, specifically Wyderko, 2006.

Figure 4.7 Hedge Fund Manager Incentives[71]

Rank	Name	Firm Name	2008 Earnings
1	James Simons	Renaissance Technologies Corp	$2.5 billion
2	John Paulson	Paulson & Co.	$2 billion
3	John Arnold	Centaurus Energy	$1.5 billion
4	George Soros	Soros Fund Management	$1.1 billion
5	Raymond Dalio	Bridgewater Associates	$780 million
6	Bruce Kovner	Caxton Associates	$640 million
7	David Shaw	D.E.Shaw & Co.	$275 million
8	Stanley Druckenmiller	Duquesne Capital Management	$260 million
9(tie)	David Harding	Winton Capital Management	$250 million
9(tie)	Alan Howard	Brevan Howard Asset Management	$250 million
9(tie)	John Taylor Jr.	FX Concepts	$250 million

and profit with the underlying investors in proportion to gains. The hedge fund managers (or partners in the firm) charge incentive fees for both maintenance of the assets under management and a significant portion of the profits for the hedge fund (performance fees).

It is common for managers to charge 1 to 5 percent for maintenance of assets under management, and to take 10 to 48 percent of profits for performance fees. The market standard has rested on a 2 percent maintenance fee and 20 percent profit share. Given recent returns, this market standard is under increasing pressure. The alternative investment industry standards for incentives are coming under greater scrutiny as many hedge funds have suffered significant negative returns in the unprecedented global market

[71] See Alpha Magazine, 2009 for the full compensation report.

volatility. In effect, many long portfolios that were leveraged have been devastated. They have been or will be fully redeemed or terminated by the managers. Investors have been increasingly focused on incentives as a result of incentives for both successful managers and unsuccessful managers in **Figure 4.8**.

Investors have been prepared to accept significant manager incentives for superior performance. The incentives are justified to ensure that incentives between managers and investors are aligned. However, the chart demonstrates that the alignment is biased to the upside. Downside risk is born by investors. This bias toward upside returns without downside risk may have led hedge fund managers to utilize leverage without corresponding financial incentives to minimize the downside risk to investors. Similarly, prime brokers are predominantly concerned with covering their own exposures in relation to the hedge fund client. The investor is left with the ultimate loss in the event a hedge fund blows up.

In times when hedge fund managers are concerned about volatile markets, it may make them particularly sensitive to downward risk of loss and possible redemptions. When markets are extremely volatile, the manager may be perfectly satisfied to sit on investments

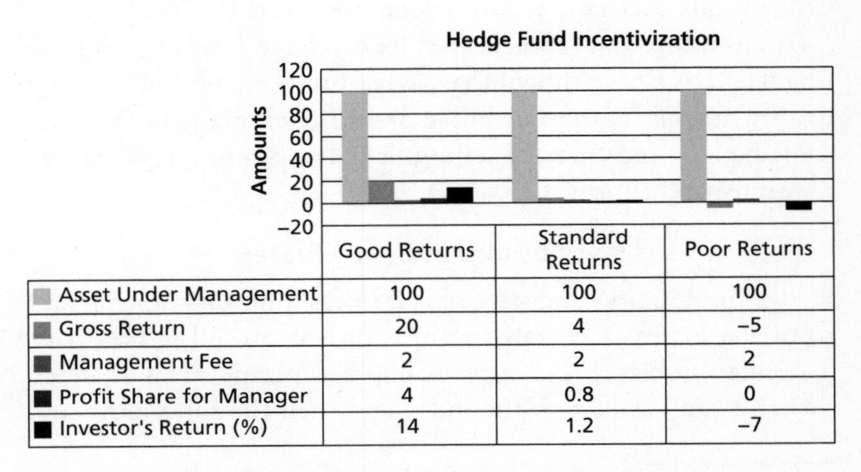

	Good Returns	Standard Returns	Poor Returns
Asset Under Management	100	100	100
Gross Return	20	4	–5
Management Fee	2	2	2
Profit Share for Manager	4	0.8	0
Investor's Return (%)	14	1.2	–7

Figure 4.8 Standard Hedge Fund Incentivization (Management fee 2% and Performance fee 20%)

in low interest cash arrangements to protect their management fees, forgoing possible performance fees. Hedge funds amassed an unprecedented amount of cash reserves in anticipation of redemptions during the financial crisis.[72]

The question remains whether this is what the managers should be doing. The promise of hedge funds was that the manager, through alpha, could profit in either bull or bear markets. Sitting out the volatility may be lost opportunities for greater returns. The manager may be concerned about redemptions and thus may wish to avoid any losses. Whether this is the new alpha, good risk management, or unnecessarily conservative measures by managers to preserve their assets under management remains an open question.

The performance fees and management fees seem to push managers in different directions, making them too aggressive in some scenarios and too conservative in others. Given the fees to be paid for poor performance, many investors will likely redeem investments unless the manager's incentives are properly aligned with investors' interests. If hedge fund returns are reduced to below the other outside options, including bonds or money market instruments with greater transparency and lower risks, hedge funds will have record redemptions in the future.

If anything, the reported results of hedge funds during the financial crisis have shown that hedge funds are not all immune to downturns in the current extraordinary markets. In fact, some hedge funds may be selling beta as alpha in a repackaged, nontransparent form.[73]

Hedge Fund Indices—Biases

Hedge fund indices and statistics all suffer from survivorship and reporting biases. The stated returns of hedge fund indices have particular problems. The survivorship bias occurs when an index carries a fund as part of the index and then the fund blows up.

---

[72] Hodson & Lim, 2008.

[73] Jenson & Rotenberg, 2004.

The index faces the problem of dealing with a bankruptcy and transitioning the index after the blow-up. Due to the survivorship bias, a hedge fund index, like any index, may be artificially inflated.[74] In effect, the index is more properly a measure of the surviving funds rather than all funds, as more and more funds either cease reporting or blow up entirely. The index is adjusted to reflect only the surviving funds.

Similarly, even though a fund may not totally blow up or be fully redeemed by investors, negative results are not necessarily disclosed. A hedge fund manager has no interest in making negative results available to the public in the event of a sharp drop in performance. Hedge fund results have been used as a marketing tool to show that a particular fund was superior to others, particularly for investors or funds of hedge funds, in order to attract additional asset allocations.

There may also be problems with late reporting of funds. When a manager delays in sending results to the index, the results cannot be included in indices for timely publication. Thus, hedge fund results and indices may be subject to biases and intentional or unintentional manipulation by managers for their own purposes. When accessing and utilizing hedge fund indices it is important to understand the biases that may skew results or may only represent a partial view of the market. Nonetheless, the hedge fund indices provide a useful benchmark, provided their limitations are recognized.

Conclusion

Hedge funds are private investment vehicles. Although there is no universally accepted definition, it is useful to examine the structures and objectives of hedge funds.[75] Hedge funds may

[74] See the detailed discussion of hedge fund indices in Lhabitant, 2004 and Anson, 2006.

[75] U.S. and international regulators may struggle with definitional issues or may take a pragmatic approach and declare regulatory oversight when financial institutions behave like hedge funds.

be singular or multiple-entity structures which attempt to create trading income in a tax-efficient manner. The goal of the hedge fund is to attempt to generate trading income, rather than investment income.

Often a hedge fund investment is limited to specially qualified investors and generally not marketed to or available to retail investors.[76] The traditional objective of the hedge fund is absolute returns in bull or bear markets. The returns of hedge funds have been on average superior to the international equity markets. However, the myth of absolute returns in both bull or bear markets has been dispelled. Hedge funds offer an important role in diversification for alternative investments and institutional investors, and certain superior managers have demonstrated stellar returns.

The initial failures of due diligence make it clear that additional due diligence is necessary for hedge fund investors and their advisers. As markets continue to be volatile, there will be pressure on underperforming managers to become more creative with accounting and NAV assessments. This is particularly true with regard to illiquid securities that are difficult to value.[77]

The hedge fund market has undergone a revolutionary transformation and is continuing to change. Asset allocations to hedge funds reduced significantly as a result of industry average returns and record redemptions. Ultimately, the future of the hedge fund industry will depend upon investor sentiment and regulatory changes—how the calls for transparency, rules, and ethics are met—and the ability of hedge fund managers to continue to outperform traditional markets or simply to provide valuable diversification for investors.

---

[76] Regulatory restrictions vary on the minimum educational or financial knowledge qualifications for individual and institutional investors in hedge funds or other investment funds.

[77] The new FASB rules on marking to market change NAV calculations for investment managers considerably.

5 Hedge Fund Managers and Investment Advisers

Investment advisers serve a variety of functions in the hedge fund industry. In prime finance, investment advisers fall into two basic functions: those who act as managers for hedge funds and those who act for investors to allocate assets into various hedge funds, including funds of hedge funds. **Figure 5.1**

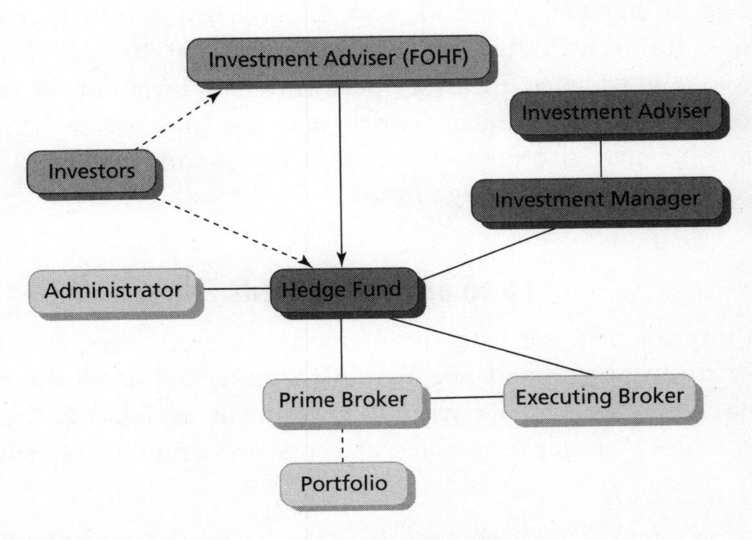

Figure 5.1 Hedge Fund Investment Advisers/Managers

depicts the relationships between advisers, managers, brokers, and the connections between other parties directly involved in the hedge fund.

In such cases where the investment adviser is managing or advising the fund directly, the adviser is contracted to take responsibility for the hedge fund's investments by the manager or the directors of the hedge fund, depending upon the structure of the hedge fund. This is typical where the investment manager has unlimited liability, similar to a general partner in a limited partnership. The investment manager will delegate investment authority to the investment adviser, who takes day-to-day control. While this contractual structure limits the manager's liability exposure, the investment manager still owes fiduciary and other duties to the hedge fund and its investors.[1]

The other major function of hedge fund investment advisers is to advise and act for investors. An investor has a choice of how to invest in hedge funds. Many institutional investors have established and developed sophisticated alternative investment programs to invest directly in hedge funds.[2] These institutional investors tend to manage their entire alternative investment portfolio, and directly invest into specific hedge funds or indirectly through funds of hedge funds. These sophisticated investors perform their own operational and strategic due diligence when investing directly in hedge funds but may also rely on a fund of hedge funds (FoHFs) to invest in a variety of hedge funds.

Fund of Hedge Funds

An investor may not have the financial resources, expertise, or time to investigate and negotiate with individual hedge funds. Thus, investors contract with an investment adviser who performs due diligence, investigates, and compares a number of hedge

[1] See Black, 2004 and Coggan, 2008.
[2] See Anson, 2006, Chapter 4.

funds. Investment advisers may either provide advice on which hedge funds to invest in directly or may have their own FoHF. Funds of hedge funds have the mandate to invest in hedge funds depending upon the manager's assessment of which funds or strategies have the greatest current profitability expectation.[3] For investors seeking exposure to the alternative investment asset class, investments in FoHFs are common. The manager establishes a fund, similar to a hedge fund; however, the assets the manager invests in are individual hedge funds, commodity funds, managed accounts, or private equity funds. Accordingly, FoHF investments may be illiquid and require longer holding and redemption timelines.

FoHFs typically allocate capital to a range of hedge funds, from five to twenty, and charge management and performance fees similar to hedge funds. In effect, investing in a number of hedge funds provides for diversification of risk. Asset allocation and spreading risk within hedge funds derives from the work of Markowitz and Modern Portfolio Theory.[4] It is presumed that FoHF managers have the ability to diversify risks; however, managers need the skill to select the best performing funds as any random selection of more than twenty hedge funds would likely provide some diversification. The skill of the FoHF manager is to be able to select the best hedge funds with the best managers, and greatest potential. Recently, empirical studies have questioned this assumption.[5] When investors have placed funds with FoHF to invest in hedge funds, the minimal expectation is to develop a system of due diligence for selection. In recent cases, in which investment advisory firms advised investors to invest, or actually invested through FoHFs, there may be liability for breach of fiduciary duty, negligence, fraud, or aiding and abetting fraud, or other sources of liability.[6]

---

[3] See Anson, 2006.

[4] See Markowitz, 1959.

[5] Anson finds a negative skew in distributions of funds of funds; see Anson, 2006, exhibit 6.16, pp. 161–162.

[6] See Reuters, 2008 and Weisenthal, 2009.

Hedge Fund Manager

From an investment manager's perspective, the hedge fund is constructed to allow operational and investment efficiency. The hedge fund's labor pool is largely outsourced.[7] The manager will seek to limit liability to itself and the employees or partners. This may be as a general partner in a limited partnership and be exposed to unlimited liability. In such circumstances, the manager will minimize liability by incorporating itself with the minimal required assets and may outsource responsibilities to an investment adviser to conduct day-to-day investment business and operations. The result is that the manager will be structured as a limited liability vehicle and insulated from unlimited liabilities. This will prevent the manager from having unlimited exposure to the investors and others in the event that the hedge fund, which may be one of many, fails. The liability of the manager will often be limited by a corporate vehicle and outsourcing of investment advisory and administration services. The investment adviser will normally have fiduciary obligations to investors but would not necessarily have unlimited liability to the investors or the fund in the absence of fraud. Notwithstanding this common structure to limit liability, managers will make all efforts to ensure competitive returns, operational and tax efficiency.

Hedge Fund Manager Regulation

Hedge fund managers typically have limited regulation applied to their activities. However, they are subject to regulation, statutory, and common law obligations depending upon the location and activities of the manager. These may be federal/national, state/provincial regulations and depend upon the registration, domicile, and operations of the hedge fund manager.

U.S. Hedge Fund Managers

U.S. managers are subject to both federal and state laws for investment advisers. U.S. managers are subject to the overarching

[7] Zola & Finkel, 2008.

federal regulations in the U.S. Investment Advisers Act of 1940 (the "Advisers Act"), which entails certain statutory duties for the manager. There are also broad obligations for managers arising from statute, regulation, criminal law, and common law tort and fiduciary obligations. Additional regulatory oversight and fiduciary requirements are triggered by accepting certain investments that trigger obligations under the *Employees Retirement Investment Security Act (ERISA).*[8]

In the normal course, hedge fund managers have been regulated in only one jurisdiction. Multiple jurisdiction registration is cumbersome and duplicative. The U.S. position by the SEC prior to the *Goldstein* decision was to take an overarching view of managers and require dual registration.[9] This is not required of investment managers; however, requiring dual registrations may return. The SEC's position and the U.S. regulatory regime for investment managers remain in transition.

International Regulation

Managers in other international jurisdictions face local, national, and regional regulations. For U.K. managers, the Financial Services Authority (FSA) regulates their activities in a more general sense by governing under stated principles and the more detailed Conduct of Business (COBs) rules, rather than a rules-based approach from the SEC, and various no-action letters.

Hedge fund managers are often lean organizations which seek to limit cumbersome financial and regulatory oversight that would otherwise increase the amount of capital necessary for start-ups and ongoing compliance. Direct regulation of the hedge fund, in the event the fund was to accept retail clients, would greatly increase ongoing due diligence, transparency, and

---

[8] *ERISA* is a particularly complicated and onerous statute, with punitive penalties for technical violations. The effect of regulation under *ERISA* entails a variety of compliance obligations. Many hedge fund and alternative investment managers will take steps to finesse *ERISA* obligations by limiting investors subject to *ERISA*.

[9] Goldstein v. SEC, 2006.

regulatory disclosures for the manager. These obligations in turn may effectively eliminate trading opportunities (or alpha) if publicly disclosed.

Due Diligence on Hedge Funds

Due diligence involves a range of legal, financial, commercial, operational, and strategic reviews. There are a variety of filters and screens, as demonstrated in **Figure 5.2**, that investors and professional advisers have employed to assess risk and select hedge fund managers.[10]

Due diligence often commences by assessing the results of managers, starting with a database review of reported returns, drawdowns, and volatility. Individual criteria filters will vary depending upon the comparable goal, that is, absolute returns or returns related to an index. Investors will need to then gather both quantitative and qualitative evidence about managers from meetings, questionnaires, background checks, and site visits. The managers examined and vetted will need to be compared against the relevant criteria and a selection of investments made from the approved manager list in accordance with the asset allocation parameters.

Due diligence on the manager should consider:

- What is the structure of the hedge fund manager?
- Where and how is the hedge fund manager regulated and what are the investor protections?
- What regulations, rules, laws, and fiduciary obligations apply to the fund manager?
- Are there restrictions on investing, amounts, or reporting requirements for the manager directly or through an administrator?
- What is the level of transparency into the hedge fund manager's activities, fundraising, strategies, and trades?
- Who is the manager? Is there a key man?

[10] See Horowitz, 2004.

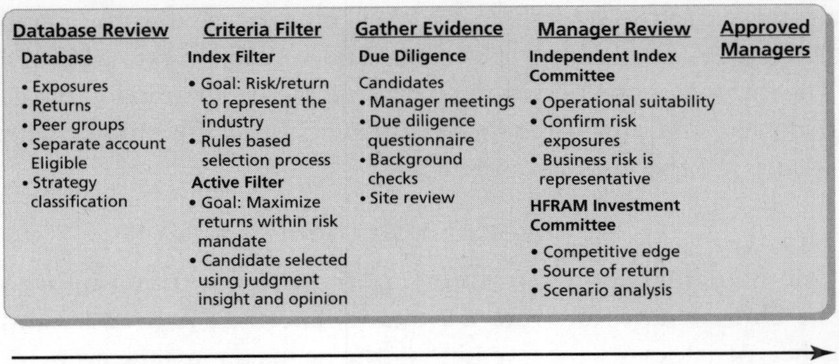

Database Review	Criteria Filter	Gather Evidence	Manager Review	Approved Managers
Database • Exposures • Returns • Peer groups • Separate account Eligible • Strategy classification	**Index Filter** • Goal: Risk/return to represent the industry • Rules based selection process **Active Filter** • Goal: Maximize returns within risk mandate • Candidate selected using judgment insight and opinion	**Due Diligence** Candidates • Manager meetings • Due diligence questionnaire • Background checks • Site review	**Independent Index Committee** • Operational suitability • Confirm risk exposures • Business risk is representative **HFRAM Investment Committee** • Competitive edge • Source of return • Scenario analysis	

* Modified from Hedge Fund Research (HFR).

Figure 5.2 Advanced Due Diligence and Manager Selection

- Does the manager have the right to extend the investment or delay redemptions?
- What happens if the fund or the fund manager becomes bankrupt? What is the manager obliged to do?
- What additional rights does the fund manager have? Side-pocket investments? Lock-ups? Key man provisions?
- Has the manager agreed to other side-letter arrangements that will place other investors in a preferred position (liquidity preference, preferred access to fund information, MFN provision)?

All these questions are related to understanding the nature of the investment and identifying risks associated with a particular fund manager and fund. A manager can state any target or expected return it deems appropriate, but the due diligence considerations for investors should discern the pitfalls and potentials in alternative investments. More than ever, investors should seek to stress test investments with best case, expected returns, and worst case scenarios.

Structure of the Hedge Fund Manager

The structure of the hedge fund manager must be understood. Claims against the manager may be judgment proof, if the manager itself is structured to hold minimal capital assets and delegate or contract out operational and strategic responsibilities. The investor protections will be defined by the jurisdiction of the manager, and applicable law, regulations, and the enforcement position of the respective regulator.

Investor Protections

One fundamental investor protection is best execution in both the United States and internationally. There are regulatory and other penalties in the event that the manager makes arrangements that fail to act in the best interest of investors, or directly siphons funds from investors for improper or clandestine purposes.[11] In the EU, the provisions of the Markets in Financial Instruments Directive (MiFID) provide that the professional client cannot waive the right to best execution.[12] Accordingly, investors in hedge funds should expect that the investment manager receives best execution on their behalf, and the hedge fund manager is unable to waive the best execution requirements. The definition of best execution is broad however. The application of best execution to particular transactions may be difficult to state unequivocally as there are a number of factors involved in best execution. The United States has similar rules regarding soft dollars and commission sharing and acceptable payments.[13]

In the United States and internationally, SRO regulations, rules, laws, and fiduciary obligations apply to the hedge fund manager. For English managers, the manager as an "authorized person" is subject to the obligations under Financial Services and Markets Act, 2000 (FSMA). As such, the manager and

[11] The hedge fund manager may have discretion over pools of capital and may make payments for inappropriate or illegal services or products for the benefit of the investment manager, such as vacations or luxury items. See the CSA model in Chapter 7.

[12] For more on MiFID, see Skinner, 2007.

[13] See SEC regulations on commission sharing.

prime brokers are subject to the FSA's Principles of Business, COBs, and broad principles, which include:

- Integrity: A firm must conduct its business with integrity.
- Skill, care, and diligence: A firm must conduct its business with due skill, care, and diligence.
- Customers' interests: A firm must pay due regard to the interests of its customers and treat them fairly.
- Clients' assets: A firm must arrange adequate protection for clients' assets when it is responsible for them.

The protections for investors may vary significantly depending upon the applicable regulation and SRO of the manager and how customer assets are held. In the event of a bankruptcy of the hedge fund manager, client assets may be structured as managed brokerage accounts or as investments into corporate vehicles or otherwise.[14] The various bankruptcy regimes will look to whether assets are pooled with assets of the manager and whether these may be traced to specific investors and segregated in deciding whether assets fall within the estate of the bankrupt manager or not.[15]

Investor Risks to Hedge Fund Manager

The hedge fund investor is exposed to the failure of the hedge fund vehicle, the conduct of its manager, the failure of prime broker, or losses caused by other service providers. Some investors in highly successful hedge funds that executed successful strategies, navigating difficult markets with solid operational due diligence and excellent business management, suffered

[14] In the United States, the Securities Investor Protection Act of 1970 (SIPA) may apply to redress limited investor losses from failed brokerage firms; see www.sipc.org.

[15] The Ontario Superior Court was able to exempt assets from the property of a bankrupt manager where the funds were traceable and held at a different financial institution segregated from the manager's assets; see Ontario (Securities Commission) v. Portus Alternative Asset Management Inc., 2006.

catastrophic losses and ultimately bankruptcy when their hedge fund manager placed collateral assets with a failing prime broker. The hedge fund manager is responsible for protecting the assets of the investor. The failure to exercise due diligence and monitor the solvency of the prime broker creates significant risk for investors.

The primary operational risks to the hedge fund investor include:[16]

- False or misleading investment valuations and pricing
- Technology, processes, or staff which are not able to competently handle operating volumes or the investments required
- Investments made outside the stated fund strategy without investor knowledge or approval
- Failure of manager to monitor or manage risk to counterparties or service providers
- Removal of money from fund either as outright theft or to hide trading losses

False or misleading investment valuations and pricing are particularly acute risks for investors. Experts routinely recommend that all positions should be independently priced by a third-party administrator. This can reveal when a fund is hiding exposures to hard-to-price securities. Many of the major MBS and ABS arbitrage funds were exposed to significant liquidity risk when those markets became extraordinarily illiquid. There were simply no buyers and no market for the securities, and accordingly, valuations continue to be highly problematic, with major investment houses taking radically different views of the value of securities. The abuses of inaccurate or improper valuations have occurred and will continue if the hedge fund manager does not have an independent valuation process.[17]

[16] See The Capital Markets Company, 2003.

[17] See the case of Beacon Hill in SEC v. Beacon Hill Asset Management, LLC et al. (Amended Complaint), 2004.

Investments can be made outside the stated fund strategy without the investors' knowledge or approval. Some experts suggest that the hedge fund's positions, trades, and cash balances should be reconciled daily with the manager and verified with prime brokers or administrators. Risk guidelines need to be enforced regularly. However, a universal requirement for daily reconciliations may not be a realistic requirement for many funds. The prime broker has no relationship with the investors and will not provide information to investors unless required by court order or under the direction and consent of the prime broker's client, the hedge fund, as directed by the hedge fund manager. This scenario is precisely when a fraudulent or misrepresenting manager would refuse consent. Also, given the use of multiple prime brokers, the stated strategy may be effected with multiple prime brokers, each with only a partial view into the hedge fund's activities. In such a case, where there are several prime brokers, an individual prime broker will not be able to confirm that the trading complies with the stated strategy as the entire portfolio of the hedge fund is unknown. Only the manager (or administrator) would know where a manager claims to be market neutral, but is, in fact, unhedged.

Outright Theft and Fraud

Removal of money from a fund may either be outright theft or to obscure trading losses. To address this risk, some have suggested a trust account structure. This structure is designed to provide a closed system where custody, control, and valuation of assets are separated from the hedge fund manager. However, the model has not been implemented in most cases and would result in significant changes to the current model.

Manager Fraud: Madoff

The scandal and Ponzi scheme of Bernard L. Madoff has tarnished the hedge fund community, broker-dealers, and the SEC. It has impacted trust and credibility for both hedge fund managers, broker-dealers, and secondary hedge fund advisers. It is strange that the most egregious and largest hedge fund fraud was not really a hedge fund at all. Madoff Investment Securities LLC (Madoff Securities) was a regulated broker-dealer. There were a number of failures in due diligence, which some advisers noted while others omitted. Significant questions remain about the review by some secondary investment advisers and the SEC.

In 1999, years prior to the public allegations against Madoff, Harry Markopolos, a derivatives expert, contacted SEC staff to alert them to his concerns.[18] Finally in 2005, Markopolos sent a letter to the SEC advising of the problems with Madoff's firm and presented two possible scenarios, one that he was front-running clients, and the other "highly likely" possibility that Madoff was running a Ponzi scheme, which stated:

> Madoff Securities is the world's largest Ponzi scheme.
>
> In this case there is no SEC reward payment due to the whistle-blower so basically I'm turning this case in because it's the right thing to do. Far better that the SEC is proactive in shutting down a Ponzi scheme of this size rather than reactive.[19]

There were both qualitative and quantitative reasons that made Madoff and his "fund" highly questionable. The structure, organization, secrecy, and financing were all highly unusual and suspect. Madoff Securities was not structured as a hedge fund in the traditional sense. He managed money and took investments in return for a tranche of securities in his broker-dealer. This is a particularly troublesome structure, as the financing is both unusually high and compromises the independence of the broker-dealer and the investment adviser.[20]

---

[18] See Lewis & Einhorn, 2009.

[19] Markopolos, 2005.

[20] This structure of hedge fund investments, directly in the broker-dealer, may allow for partial recovery of "lost" assets from the Securities Investor Protection Corporation, in the U.S. Securities Investor Protection regime; see www.sipc.org.

Madoff's list of clients was impressive, but largely avoided investments by professional counterparties. Similar to other hedge fund manager frauds, his clients relied upon his reputation and trust within the community.[21] It remains a contentious point of litigation what level of due diligence was conducted by investors and investment advisers. There were a number of glaring warning signs that were not recognized or addressed by investors, their advisers, or regulators.

Red Flags

In examining the structure, strategy, and results claimed, there were clear, unambiguous red flags. **Figure 5.3** is an example of some things that should have been obvious red flags in any examination of Bernie Madoff's hedge fund.

The structure of the hedge fund organization as a regulated broker-dealer and its extreme secrecy in investment strategy were unusual. The investment adviser and the broker-dealer arms allowed Madoff to act as a hedge fund manager, prime broker, and executing broker all at once. The lack of independence and separation between manager, investment vehicle, and the broker-dealer may have been challenged for some kind of independent confirmation or credible independent audit or administration.

In retrospect, there were many warning signals. The financing costs of the Madoff organization were unnecessarily high. Ultimately this was revealed to be in order to avoid public scrutiny. The index trading strategy, while common to other hedge funds, was held in total secrecy with family members only. The low-risk strategy was unrealistic for the alleged returns he was making when compared to other similar index hedge funds. Also, the size of Madoff's trading would have been multiples of the total exchange market for the derivatives he purportedly actively traded. The strategy lacked plausible credibility for the claimed returns. There were no external verifications with other market counterparties

---

[21] See Cass, 2008.

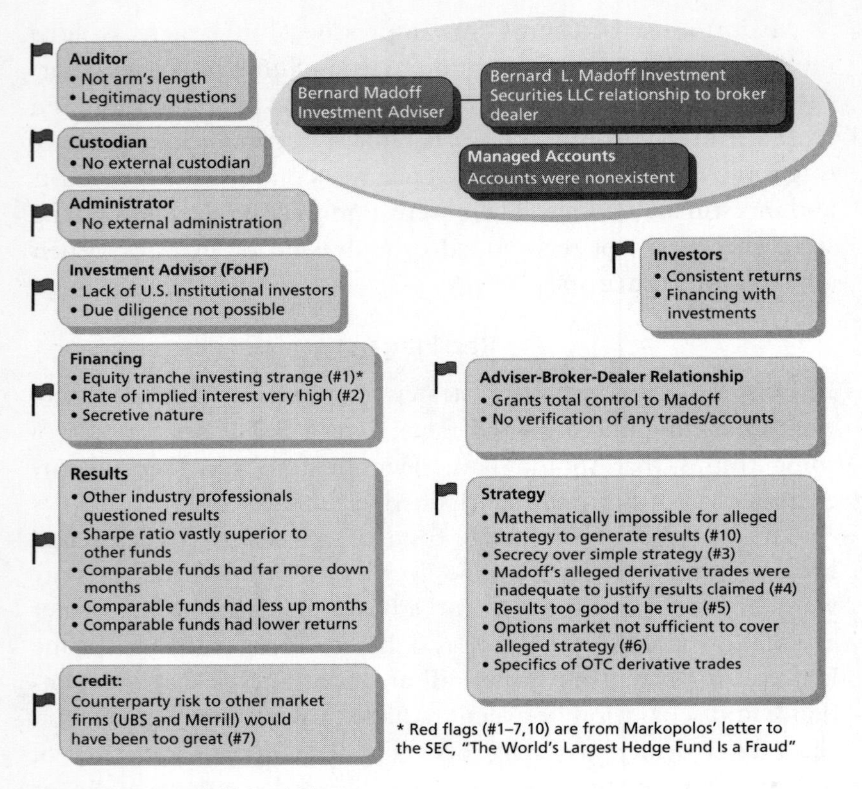

Figure 5.3 Madoff: Red Flags

or service providers. There was no external administrator or independent auditor.[22]

Madoff was not shut down proactively but only after $7 billion in redemptions from his fund exceeded his ability to redeem investor's capital. The fraud that continued for years and destroyed billions for investors resulted in convictions on just

[22] Madoff's auditor has been allegedly implicated in the fraud and faces related charges. It has been alleged that computer programmers and other service providers may have assisted with generating thousands of false trades and fraudulent reports.

eleven counts of securities fraud and other criminal conduct.[23] No new criminal sanctions were necessary to prevent or punish Madoff. What is now in question is how new regulations will detect and prevent frauds if the regulators are unable to understand or address such obvious frauds.

Madoff has done immeasurable damage to hedge fund managers' credibility and the integrity of the alternative investment industry.[24] Small investors, secondary investment advisers, and some large European banks were caught unawares in the fraud through FoHFs.[25] The repercussions will likely last for many years in civil litigation against the investment managers, investment consultants, and auditors, and between earlier and later investors. The unwinding of positions and calling back amounts paid to investors will no doubt continue for a lengthy period in protracted litigation.[26] Also, the strange imposition of the

---

[23] The securities fraud complaint against Madoff states:

> On December 11, 2008, I (an FBI special agent) spoke to Bernard L. Madoff, the defendant. After identifying myself, Madoff invited me, and the FBI agent who accompanied me, into his apartment. He acknowledged knowing why we were there. After I stated, "we're here to find out if there's an innocent explanation," Madoff stated, "There is no innocent explanation." Madoff stated, in substance, that he personally traded and lost money for institutional clients, and that it was all his fault. Madoff further stated, in substance, that he "paid investors with money that wasn't there." Madoff also said that he was "broke" and "insolvent." And that he had decided that "it could not go on," and that he expected to go to jail.

For more details see the information against Madoff (United States of America v. Bernard L. Madoff, 2008); also Madoff's and the FBI agent's personal statements upon sentencing are useful sources of information on his activities.

[24] See Scannell & Koppel, 2008.

[25] Reuters, 2008.

[26] See Reuters, 2008; litigation related to fraudulent conveyances is expected to continue to claim back against investors who withdrew funds before the collapse; see Reuters, 2008: where Connecticut hedge fund Bayou Group LLC collapsed in scandal, investors were required to return profits and part of the investors' principal.

broker-dealer has created a regulatory mechanism for investors to receive part of their investments back. Notwithstanding the uncomfortable revelations, questions will persist about how regulators were unable to detect such a massive and simple fraud. This is especially so in the face of multiple, repeated audits and whistleblowers' continued attempts to raise the alarm.[27] In the aftermath, calls for additional onerous regu-lation may not prove efficacious. The current criminal and civil laws appear sufficient to address such malfeasance. Regulation has a limited role in the prevention of overt manager fraud.[28] It may be more fruitful to focus on effective enforcement and proactive due diligence than on increasing the regulatory burden of an already overly complicated U.S. regulatory regime.

Conclusion

The hedge fund community faces a daunting, transitional market. Hedge fund managers require additional due diligence and will likely need to amend best practices to implement transparency spawned from increased regulation and investor oversight. The global equity markets have posted near historic losses in both developed and emerging markets, and hedge funds have not been immune to the volatility and, although some suffered losses, most have posted relatively positive results. The alternative investment industry has altered significantly with challenges to its core promise and the integrity of some managers. The market is changing and moving toward larger funds with longer track records and credible managers that can provide solid returns and transparency. Ultimately, assets will return to the hedge fund industry, provided managers can avoid the pitfalls.

There will undoubtedly be calls for greater transparency in the structure, function, and trading strategies of hedge fund managers to allay the concerns of distressed investors. Revelations

[27] See Reuters, 2008.
[28] See Kurdas, 2009 regarding the Manhattan Hedge Fund case.

about manager frauds have increased, and it is likely more will be discovered as managers take additional risk to make up for poor returns. Heightened due diligence will be required to detect and address potential fraud and generally oversee manager conduct, but the solutions will need to be sophisticated to balance the need for increased transparency without eliminating managers' coveted proprietary trading strategies and sources of alpha. Additional regulatory responses in the United States and internationally are underway to revamp and increase regulatory requirements, transparency, and investor protections.

6 Prime Brokerages

Prime brokers are important for a number of reasons. They are economically and strategically important parts of investment banks and the financial system. The market for prime brokerage services is estimated in the billions. The acquisition of Bear Stearns was effected in large part to acquire one of the leading prime brokerage businesses. Similarly, other investment banks have made investments to develop the prime brokerage business and others have pursued acquisitions to enter the prime brokerage businesses.[1]

There are two broad categories of prime brokers: standard prime brokerage and synthetic prime brokerage. The difference lies in the structure and nature of investments. Standard prime brokerage involves financing of standard market investments such as equities and bonds. The standard prime broker model works on securities in which the prime broker will provide financing for leveraged securities investments. **Figure 6.1** is a model of the prime broker relationship.

The developments in the derivatives market allowed leading prime brokers to develop both standard and synthetic offerings into universal prime brokerage. Synthetic prime brokerage

---

[1] UBS acquired ABN AMRO PB (2003); BNP Paribas acquired Bank of America Equities PB; Bear Stearns was acquired by JPMorgan Chase (2008).

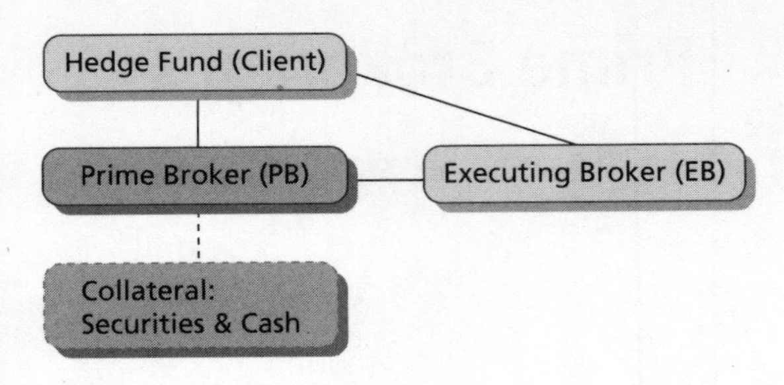

Figure 6.1 The Prime Broker Relationship

involves the use of derivatives to create similar economic effects to parallel standard prime brokerage.[2]

Synthetic Prime Brokerage

Many firms started by offering standard prime brokerage services and then developed into synthetic prime brokerage. The largest prime brokers offer full service prime brokerage across all types of securities and derivative classes, including equities, fixed income, commodities, forex, credit default swaps, and other unclassified derivatives.

The size of the derivatives market is truly colossal and vital to the international financial system. There are two broad categories of derivatives: exchange traded and over-the-counter derivatives. An important distinction between the two forms of contract is the ultimate counterparty. OTC contracts are normally bilateral and settled between the parties. Exchange traded derivatives have a central counterparty. For an exchange traded derivative, the ultimate counterparty is the relevant clearing house or exchange. The clearing house is a very large, regulated entity. Thus the exchange traded product has security in the counterparty risk since the clearing house will be the ultimate counterparty irrespective of whether one

[2] In many cases, the structure of the prime finance market is driven by the strategic investment needs of hedge funds, which may employ both long and short hedging strategies. Offering both standard prime brokerage and synthetic prime brokerage creates economies of scale and scope for the broker-dealers or banks that provide these services.

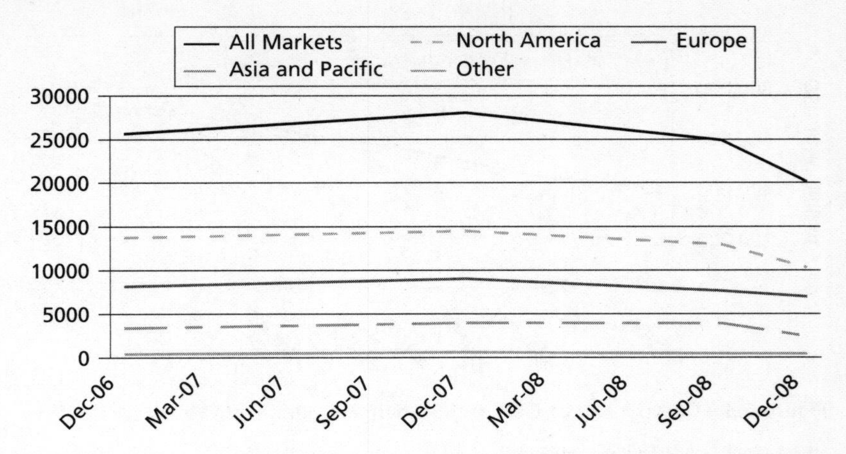

Figure 6.2 Exchange Traded Derivatives—Amounts Outstanding (in Billions)

is buying or selling a derivative. From a systemic risk perspective, many regulators have sided with the exchange traded model, as it provides transparency into the risks and size of the market. However, from a fundamental perspective, the development of large derivative exchanges and clearing houses may aggregate all risk into several titanic pots, contrary to the principles of risk diversification.

The exchange traded derivatives market is a complex group of large international markets. The total size of the exchange traded derivative markets stands at over $20 trillion dollars. The size of the exchange traded derivatives market has fallen significantly, as more and more derivatives contracts are executed off-exchange. While the combined markets are similar in size to the largest U.S. markets, they are dwarfed by the much larger OTC derivatives market.

The OTC derivatives market has grown to an enormous size. As of June 2008 the OTC derivatives contracts outstanding, simply for the G-10 and Switzerland, stood at an astounding estimated $683 trillion.[3] However, this is clearly only part of the actual market. Some financial professionals have estimated that the OTC derivatives market may now exceed $1 quadrillion.[4]

[3] Bank of International Settlements, 2008.
[4] Bank of International Settlements, 2008.

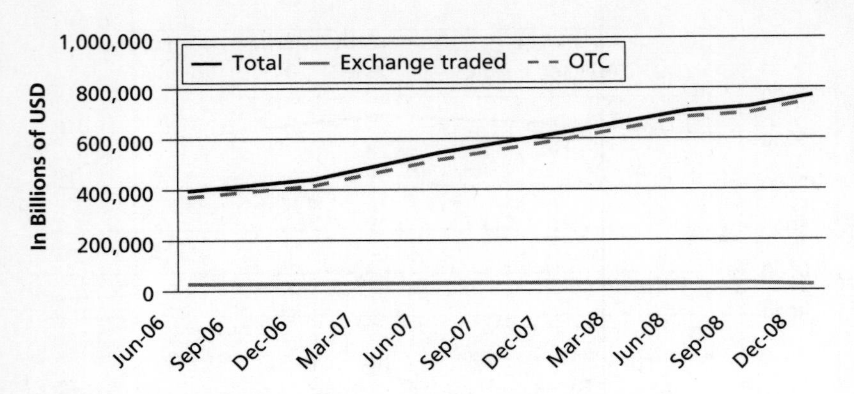

Figure 6.3 Comparison of OTC and Exchange Traded Derivatives

Source: Bank of International Settlements

This means that the largest exchange in the world, the NYSE, is a rounding error in the OTC derivatives market.

In the international sphere, the master derivatives contract is governed by the International Swaps and Derivatives Association (ISDA), which will have important ancillary annexes and definitions, depending upon the financial products traded. OTC derivatives contracts are private, bilateral contracts, which have a variety of different structures and purposes. Exchange traded derivatives, which are executed with a central counterparty or clearing house, account for less than 2.6 percent of the limited OTC derivatives market.[5]

OTC derivative contracts are settled between the counterparties on a standardized contract.[6] OTC contracts may be simple derivatives similar to plain vanilla swaps, but often have complicated bespoke triggers and financing requirements in structured products. The result has been increasingly complex contracts which defy traditional categories. The derivatives contracts referred to as

[5] There are more than twenty regulated derivatives exchanges in the world. In Europe, an important exchange is Euronext-LIFFE. The Chicago Mercantile Exchange (CME) is an important exchange in the United States. The Montreal Exchange (CMX) is an important market in Canada.

[6] See www.isda.org.

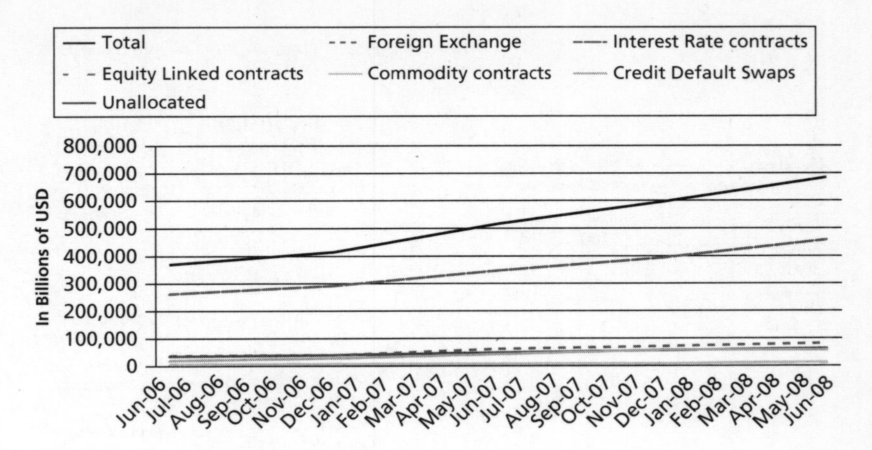

Figure 6.4 Amounts Outstanding of OTC Derivatives

Source: Bank of International Settlements, Quarterly Review Dec 2008

"unallocated" have a notional value of over $81 trillion and cannot be categorized in the normal taxonomy of derivatives. An OTC derivative product allows much greater flexibility and bespoke terms of the contract compared to standardized exchange traded versions.

Synthetic prime brokers offer derivatives to parallel the prime finance services on equity-linked products—interest rate derivatives—and many may offer foreign exchange, credit default, and other tailored derivatives.[7] Even without synthetic prime brokerage, derivatives are ancillary to standard prime brokerage services. Access to derivatives is an important part of many hedge fund strategies. Derivatives may be structured and arranged with the prime broker directly or with other executing brokers or market counterparties with the assistance of the prime broker.

Any derivative with a prime broker will require a hedged position on the underlying product for the contract. The result is that while the buyer of the derivative (hedge fund) has no actual security position, the prime broker or writer of the derivative may hold a significant position by writing the derivative contract. For example,

[7] Exotic derivatives may extend to highly structured derivatives, such as weather derivatives, which link financial payouts to various weather related events, such as how many times it rains in July in London.

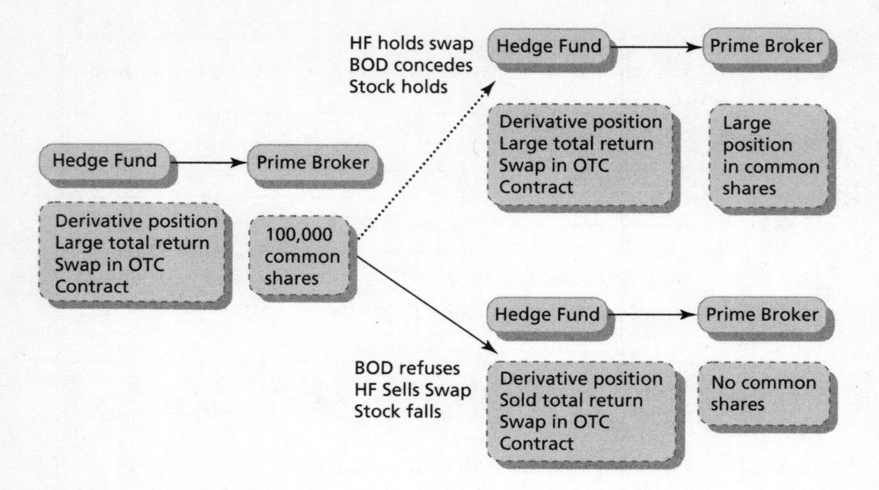

Figure 6.5 Derivative Examples–Hedge Fund and Prime Broker Positions

in a total return swap on a security, the hedge fund will have a derivative position, and the prime broker will have an underlying security interest to hedge the derivative position. This structure has led to issues about control and activism by hedge funds or investors, which may attempt to actively influence certain target companies' management through derivative positions.[8] While the hedge fund itself holds no securities, its actions to sell a derivative position will result in the prime broker selling the underlying stock.

It is particularly difficult for regulators to address, control, and assess the risks of derivatives, particularly OTC derivatives. The risk associated with these contracts may be complicated and particularly difficult to assess in complex products with limited or no transparency to foreign or domestic regulators. As a consequence, regulators and courts have had difficulties with understanding the implications of derivatives in both established and emerging markets.[9] The solution may appear to be to bring

[8] Consider the example set by Porsche when it disclosed that it held a large derivative position on Volkswagen, which effectively gave it indirect control over the company.

[9] For a broad derivatives review see Hull, 2006, and for a detailed examination of derivative products and applications see Taylor, 2007.

the large OTC derivatives markets, like credit default swaps, under domestic regulation; however, the international markets are portable and governed by private contracts between international entities and may be difficult, if not impossible, to incorporate. The effort to control the derivatives market as a part of the synthetic prime broker world will undoubtedly pose immense challenges in the future given its massive size and links to other markets and financial products.

Due Diligence on Prime Brokers

For hedge funds, their managers, and investors, prime brokers offer invaluable services and financing. Prime brokers are hedge funds' secondary source of financing. However, the financing relationship is not without risk. The risk of a prime broker default is clearly a primary concern for investment managers, who have fiduciary and statutory obligations to protect their clients' assets. Clearly, more due diligence on prime brokers is required.

Prior to Lehman Brothers, there had been a long history of bailing out systemically important hedge funds and prime brokers, from Long-Term Capital Management (LTCM) to Bear Stearns. Bear Stearns' bailout in the spring of 2008 may have created complacency that a leading prime broker would never be allowed to fail. However, observers and industry experts understood that Lehman Brothers was not an elite prime broker. Lehman Brothers was struggling to maintain its position among the leading prime brokers. Meanwhile, smaller prime brokers such as Refco were allowed to fail. A start-up prime broker failure had a limited impact and did not attract government attention, as it did not threaten to pose systemic failure, but rather limited counterparty risks. When Lehman Brothers failed, several funds were surprised to find their assets caught in a protracted bankruptcy proceeding in the United States, United Kingdom, and internationally.

The Lehman Brothers bankruptcy revealed several important questions about the structure of prime brokers, and the counterparty risk between broker-dealers and banks. There was a need to address specific concerns about the differentiation between broker-dealers and universal banks. If they were not already, many hedge fund managers became profoundly concerned about collateral assets posted with their prime brokers.

Eric Sprott, a leading hedge fund manager with Sprott Asset Management, successfully navigated financial crisis and the volatile markets after Lehman, but had advice for other managers and investors moving forward: "the viability of any prime broker has to be constantly questioned."[10] There are fundamental due diligence questions that need to be resolved by managers, and prime brokers should have specific answers related to their specific operation and location of accounts.

- What happens if a prime broker defaults or becomes bankrupt?
- What is the legal regime (locations and jurisdiction) that governs the bankruptcy?
- What level of recovery can be expected for the variety of different collateral assets held by the prime broker?
  a. Cash
  b. Fully paid securities
  c. Rehypothecated securities
  d. Securities held as security (or pledged) for loans

Lehman Brothers' failure clearly pointed out the counterparty default risk that prime brokers posed to hedge funds and hedge fund investors. Over one hundred notable funds had collateral assets frozen in the Lehman Brothers bankruptcy. Ultimately the return of collateral assets may take years if it is possible at all.

So how do prime brokers interconnect with hedge funds? There are a variety of service providers that service hedge funds. Hedge funds are designed to be streamlined organizations with minimal human and other fixed cost resources. The hedge fund

---

[10] Sprott, 2009.

may outsource everything that is ancillary to actually managing the investment activities of the hedge fund. The relationship is limited in terms of the standard of care that may be expected between prime brokers and clients. There is a difference in the standard of care between English and American executing and prime brokers. Where the United States typically provides for a standard of gross negligence, the U.K. higher courts have yet to recognize the distinction between the standard of negligence and gross negligence, except that gross negligence is something more than mere negligence.[11]

Prime brokers play an important role in assisting hedge funds with:

- Custody
- Trade execution
- Trade reporting
- Trade settlement
- Access to financial markets
- Access to financial products
- Financing
- Corporate action processing
- Account administration
- Operations
- Accounting
- Trading software
- Risk software
- Office space
- Information
- Technology and other technology support
- Research

[11] The standard of care for prime brokers is a developing area of law. While U.S. cases recognize the distinction between negligence and gross negligence, there is limited case law from the international perspective, which notes a distinction between negligence and gross negligence to be "something more than mere negligence"; see Lord Beldran in Scottish Railways.

- Seed investments
- Capital introduction and raising

The services offered are limited and circumscribed by the law of the relevant jurisdiction, the relevant contractual agreements, regulatory regimes and applicable jurisprudence. As a result, there may be considerable disparity between various U.S. domestic and international prime brokers.

Custody

There are a number of services that prime brokers offer hedge funds. Prime brokers will often take direct custody of securities or cash from hedge funds. The prime broker will have a security interest or charge over the collateral assets for loans of cash or securities to the hedge fund. Also, the custody of the assets is subject to different rules and industry practices in various jurisdictions. The assets held may be segregated or pooled with other client's assets.[12]

The collateral (securities or cash) may be held by the prime broker directly or more rarely with a custodian. The chief difference in the custodian or prime broker model relates to how assets are held and risks associated with a default. The trade-off between prime brokers and custodians relates to the availability of financing and the security over assets. Financing is much more expensive and less available with custodians. Prime brokers will take assets of hedge funds and utilize them for their own financing activities and thereby increase the leverage, rates, and amounts of financing available to hedge funds. Whether a hedge fund utilizes a prime broker or custodian often relates to the hedge fund's financing needs and risk profile over their assets.

[12] The U.S. protections in 15c3-3 of the *Securities Act* provide for rules to protect clients' assets. However, the handling of collateral securities and assets in excess of amounts required to satisfy debts to the prime broker are not internationally recognized and may vary by jurisdiction and between international prime brokers' practices.

Collateral Holding

Fundamental to the relationship is understanding the structure of the prime broker and the accounts it holds. U.S. domestic prime brokers are required to segregate collateral assets and provide individualized accounts, whereas international prime brokers may pool client assets together in an unsegregated account. Complexities arise where prime brokers have operations in both the United States and internationally. As a consequence, the location of accounts and the prime broker counterparty may impact clients' rights where assets are transferred between affiliates internationally. There are a number of fundamental questions on the custody of collateral:

- How is collateral held?
- Where is collateral held?
- What accounts will it be held in and where is the account located?
- Are the accounts pooled with other client accounts or segregated for the individual client?
- What risks are there in holding collateral assets?
- What rights does the prime broker (or custodian) have over the collateral (hypothecation and rehypothecation limits)?
- What impact would the default or insolvency of the prime broker (or custodian) have on the client's right to access or return the collateral?

The consequences of pooling client assets are not normally felt by the hedge fund client. However, in the event a prime broker defaults, or becomes insolvent or bankrupt, the consequences for hedge funds may be catastrophic. Whereas in the event of the insolvency of a custodian the hedge fund's assets are individually segregated, it is a matter of identifying client accounts and returning collateral to the client accordingly. With complex pooled accounts, there may be delays in returning collateral to the hedge fund, if possible at all. The business and other risks associated with delays in receiving frozen positions are significant. Where the prime broker has pooled the hedge fund's accounts and the collateral has been rehypothecated by the prime broker, the problems become even greater. The legal status of the claim against a prime broker may be questionable. The hedge fund may stand as an unsecured creditor to a bankrupt prime broker. While certain programs in the United States exist to protect small investors from failing brokers, there are considerable limits on recovery for institutional counterparties.[13] In this case, the hedge fund may be unable to recover their collateral and receive only a pro-rata share of assets of the bankrupt. Thus, investors in the hedge fund may ultimately pay for the losses. In the international sphere, the risks may be even greater and protections nonexistent depending upon the exact jurisdiction.

Access to Markets and Products

Prime brokers supply access to a broad range of markets both domestically and internationally. The prime brokers associated with large multinational investment banks offer a broad range of access to services, products, and markets, including:

- Equities Markets
- Fixed Income Markets
- Money Markets
- Commodities and Futures Trading
- Foreign Exchange Trading
- Securitization
- Options and Derivatives Markets (CFD, warrants, etc.)
- Mergers and Acquisitions

Access to the various services, markets, and financial products for the hedge fund is a key consideration in selecting prime and executing brokers. The cross-selling opportunities are also a key consideration for the prime broker and the larger investment

[13] See SIPC, www.sipc.org, and the related provisions of the Securities Investors Protection Act of 1970 (SIPA). There are limits to the value that may be claimed. For amounts in excess of SIPA, which all large hedge funds will be, other sources of investor protection include purchasing insurance or derivative products, for example credit default swaps.

banking operations. The strategy of the hedge fund must be able to be addressed by the capabilities, offering, and services of the prime broker, and a related executing broker or larger investment bank.

Margin or Leverage

There are a number of services that prime brokers and larger investment banks offer. The primary relationship is lender (prime broker) and borrower (hedge fund). One of the principal benefits of the margin account is to provide increased leverage and access to markets and services for hedge funds. While there are strict and complex regulations on U.S. domestic prime brokers lending to clients on margin,[14] there are fewer restrictions for brokers in the international sphere.[15]

The structure of the arrangement is deceptively simple. In effect, the prime broker allows for an expanded loan to value (LTV) ratio for the hedge fund. In the international market, the LTV ratio for prime brokers will depend on the nature of the securities invested by the fund. The risk of the portfolio is a primary determining factor of the total LTV amounts, which may reach 98 percent but may range between 50 percent and 90 percent in the case of collateral deposited with a prime broker of $10 million. The actual potential for the fund may reach well over $100 million in market power. Where the hedge fund takes on additional liabilities or requires cash, a prime broker will lend amounts to the hedge fund and provide access to a variety of markets and counterparties to trade.

Corporate Action Processing

Corporate actions, including stock splits, dividends, and other rights, are often managed by the prime broker for the hedge fund. Corporate actions pose operational difficulties for many prime

[14] See Lofchie, 2005.

[15] See Applicable rules under Rule 15a(6) of the Securities Exchange Act. There are a variety of complex chaperoning and intermediation requirements for broker-dealers in facing U.S. clients.

brokers in such cases. Corporate actions take up significant operational resources. One of the complexities results from the prime broker rehypothecating securities and loaning them out. In the event of a corporate action, recalling loaned stock to allow hedge funds to vote in a particular manner or to effect management change may pose regulatory challenges or may not be possible.

Trading and Risk Software

One of the main differentiators between prime brokers is the level of technology utilized and offered to hedge fund clients. More investment banks are providing sophisticated platforms that allow netting of positions between prime brokers, and expanding the asset classes that are captured by software systems. Where a short is financed with one prime broker and a long position is held with another prime broker, the hedge fund can select best prices or execution and still have real-time (or daily) risk assessments of portfolio positions with various prime brokers. The result is a better understanding of risk allocation for hedge fund clients.

Consulting Services

There are prime brokers, and related consulting areas of investment banks, that are focused on providing operational and strategic consulting for hedge funds. The transition in the hedge fund industry and limited internal resources make these services critical for many hedge funds. For some successful hedge funds it can be difficult to transition to larger, more sophisticated operations. For other hedge funds, managing a portfolio with declining assets and increasing redemptions requires assistance to maximize opportunities with changing operational and business risks. Hedge fund consulting services may range from strategy to operational efficiency and market expansion. The consulting services ancillary to some prime brokers' offerings provide useful services for hedge funds. Prime brokers also act as marketers and direct investors to hedge funds.

Seed Investments

Seed investments may be offered by certain prime brokers. A seed investment may be to entice hedge funds to utilize the prime broker, or simply part of a strategy of a prime broker to invest in promising hedge funds. Industry experts warn against selecting a prime broker simply for this reason. The operational capabilities and risks associated with the prime broker should be assessed prior to and continuously after selecting a prime broker. The implications of having a prime broker in capacities as investor, financier, and service provider may blur the already complicated and conflicting relationship between prime brokers and hedge funds. Even with seed investments where the conflicts can be openly addressed, the hedge fund manager should ensure that the operational limitations and default risks of the prime broker do not impact the fund. Nonetheless, hedge funds have been greatly assisted in the start-up phase by prime brokers. The prime brokers have provided direct seed investments, capital introduction, and marketing expertise, which are critical to successful capital raising and fund establishment.

Capital Introduction

Many prime brokers are affiliated with investment banks, which have an asset management arm. There are many clients of the asset management or private wealth management divisions that may be interested in investing in promising hedge funds or for risk diversification. The result is a natural economy of scope where cross-selling is performed by the various areas of the investment bank. Capital introduction may also be available on a more limited basis by mini-primes for particular investment strategies and managers.

Capital Raising

Capital raising may be facilitated by the prime broker. This may take the form of introductions to the private wealth management arm of an investment bank or other clients. The prime broker will often be able to introduce clients to a variety of sources of capital and assist with marketing and initial capital raising. While this is convenient, the hedge fund should ensure the fees associated with such introductions are made transparent and disclosed.

The initial start-up and capital raising are critical periods for hedge funds. The prime broker can be instrumental in assisting with capital raising and lending credibility for finance entrepreneurs. Discussions with the prime broker sales directors should reveal if synergies exist and the fees associated with assistance with capital raising should be disclosed.

Office Space

Dealing with the technical details and operational aspects of starting and running a hedge fund is something that many managers wish to avoid or minimize. It is preferable for hedge fund managers and their investors to have managers focused on risk and returns rather than back office operations. As a result, prime brokers focused on this need to create one-stop shops for hedge funds.[16] So-called "hedge fund hotels" have historically been operated by large investment banks, offering office space to hedge funds to provide hedge fund managers with prestigious addresses and technical support. New independent start-up hedge fund hotel operators have emerged to service smaller start-ups.[17] The market opportunity for smaller firms has emerged as larger investment banks are moving away from such services or declining to offer office space to new hedge funds.

The recent market changes and reduction in large fund formations simply does not fit with the strategy of many large prime brokers. Many leading prime brokers have refocused their strategies away from servicing smaller hedge fund start-ups

[16] Adamson, 2008.

[17] For example, Shoreline Trading Group, a mini-prime with extensive technology services had high rankings in prime broker rankings; see Prime Broking Poll 2008.

and have withdrawn ancillary services and office space. There have been notable cases where hedge funds complained of exorbitant fees associated with ancillary services from prime brokers. This served to confuse the already complex, multi-faceted relationship between prime brokers and hedge funds.

The large prime brokers associated with full-service investment banks are largely focused on well-established hedge funds. These hedge funds have addressed the start-up challenges and avoided redemptions by investors. These hedge funds are focused on streamlining operations and maintaining critical human and other capital resources rather than addressing early start-up issues.

There remains a need for hedge fund hotels to incubate and foster new hedge funds and the financial entrepreneurs of the future. However, it is unclear if hedge fund hotels will be a permanent fixture in alternative investments or a historical footnote in the euphoria of the prime finance industry. This will depend on the success of new hedge fund entrepreneurs and the ability of hedge fund hotels to service their clients' growing needs as the hedge fund life cycle develops.[18]

[18] Examples of hedge fund hotels include New York's Tabb Group and Erze Castle; Florida's HedgeCo Networks; a hedge fund hotel and consulting company, Shoreline Trading Group; and Knowledge Suites in Toronto, Canada.

7 Prime Brokerage Business Model

The ambit of prime brokers is large and varies considerably between domestic and international venues. The standard prime broker business model continues to be secured financing. The principal risk rests with the hedge fund client, and the collateral provided is utilized to protect the risk to the prime broker's assets and loans. Part of the financing of hedge funds, however, involves the prime broker utilizing the assets of the hedge fund clients.

To this end, collateral is provided by hedge funds. The collateral may be cash, financial instruments, or securities. The collateral is subject to a claim by the prime broker in the event that the hedge fund's positions lead to trading losses, and is subject to the prime broker's utilization through rehypothecation. The prime broker will normally not take steps to liquidate a portfolio until there is a default, or failure to provide sufficient margin for the hedge fund's loans. The most obvious default is a failure to provide additional collateral to meet a margin call.

The prime broker will not suffer any direct losses until the collateral provided has been exhausted. The hedge fund has principal risk in the event the market moves against their positions and leads to the loss of the collateral. The primary risk of the prime broker is the loss of the portfolio in excess of the

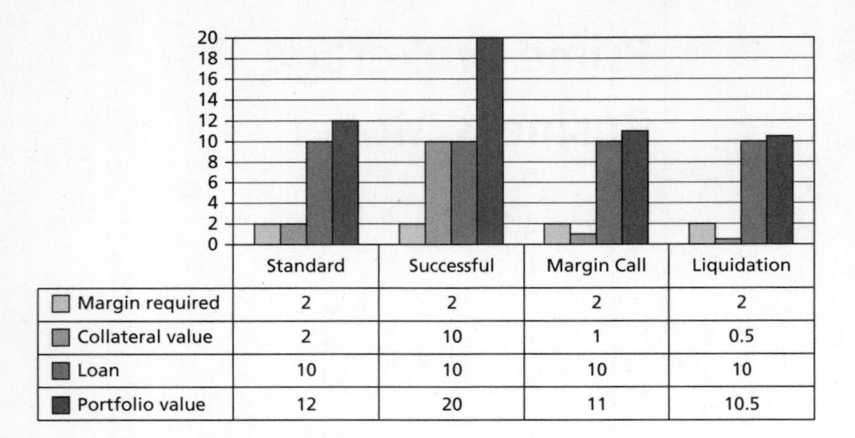

	Standard	Successful	Margin Call	Liquidation
Margin required	2	2	2	2
Collateral value	2	10	1	0.5
Loan	10	10	10	10
Portfolio value	12	20	11	10.5

Figure 7.1 Prime Broker Model—Scenarios

collateral provided. In practice a prime broker will not normally wait until all collateral is exhausted prior to demanding further collateral or defaulting the hedge fund client; see **Figure 7.1**.

The prime broker will facilitate the hedge fund's position with a loan, but the principal risk rests with the fund to the extent of the collateral, and in certain scenarios the liability may exceed the value of the collateral. Thus the prime broker model is elegant and provides protection to the prime broker while it offers a variety of loans, services, and fees. The hedge fund is granted loans to build a portfolio to amplify returns or effect strategies with leverage.

The prime broker services are often divided into various areas. The internal infrastructure of prime brokers varies greatly, yet shares certain characteristics; see **Figure 7.2**.

Figure 7.2 Prime Broker Departments and Structure

The various areas of a prime brokerage work together to provide full service, including capital introduction, financing and servicing hedge funds trading activities, and monitoring risk. There are a host of complex compliance, regulatory, and legal issues that arise in the relationship between prime brokers and hedge funds. The prime broker relationship is governed by the contractual terms in the Prime Brokerage Agreement (PBA) or Institutional Client Account Agreement (ICAA) and related ancillary agreements.[1]

Prime Broker Agreement

For regulatory purposes, there are various distinctions between international PBA and U.S. PBA or ICAA. The prime broker agreements may cover both standard prime brokerage and, increasingly, synthetic prime brokerage.[2] Thus, prime brokers may offer leveraged financing on debt, equity, derivatives, commodities, forex and other products. Synthetic prime broker is based upon market standard derivative contracts that are modified to parallel the secured financing of a prime brokerage model. A key feature is cross-product margining, which allows for a single margin payment to be made on different product classes.

The prime brokerage agreement is the standard agreement that governs the relationship between hedge funds and prime brokers lending arrangements. The key commercial considerations of the prime broker and hedge fund relationship are:

- Rates
- Fees
- Leverage

[1] The ancillary agreements may include margin agreements, lock-up agreements, and other custody or account agreements.

[2] In the case of synthetic prime brokerage, derivatives are utilized to provide "synthetic" exposures with exchange traded derivatives or OTC contracts from ISDA agreements or other market standard agreements, including relevant annexes.

- Lending securities
- Other agreements
- Valuations
- Timing and grace periods
- Duty of care
- Representations and warranties
- Collateral
- Substitution and withdrawal of collateral
- Utilization of collateral and rehypothecation
- Liabilities, taxes, and expenses
- Power to refuse transactions
- Delegation of transactions
- Disclosures
- Corporate actions and voting
- Indemnities
- Lock-up periods
- Notices of change
- Limited recourse and affiliates
- Events of default
- Cross-default
- Termination
- Netting and set-off

Loan Rates

One of the key considerations for all borrowers is the rate of the loans and the amounts that may be borrowed. While there will be different rates for loans of securities, the basic lending of cash to effect transactions will be agreed upon from time to time between the prime broker and the hedge fund. The greater the certainty over lending rates, the more stable access to capital is for the funds. This is why considerable time is often devoted to structuring lock-up agreements with prime brokers that effectively provide term financing and notice periods for any changes in margin rates. In light of the financial crisis, the cost of this kind of arrangement has become considerably more expensive and for shorter duration, if available at all.

Fees

Prime broker fees associated with servicing clients are comprehensive and substantial. The prime broker will make the client responsible for all fees and expenses associated with effecting, settling, reporting trades, and servicing the client's needs. Careful consideration must be given in negotiations over fees that may not be shared proportionately among clients. While fees are unavoidable, they should be identifiable, attributable, and transparent. The common scenario where a prime broker stands between two clients, it may entail that expenses are not shared on a pro-rata or equal basis. In any event, hedge fund clients should have clarity and transparency on fees and expenses.

Leverage

U.S. regulators have maximum restrictions on initial and ongoing leverage requirements. The international prime finance market practice gives the prime broker the discretion to set maximum leverage levels, subject to applicable regulatory limits or regulatory capital requirements.

The leverage of hedge funds is a particular concern to managers, investors, prime brokers, and regulators. Managers of investment funds utilize leverage for a variety of reasons. The most common reason is to exploit perceived inefficiencies and maximize the alpha generated from small inefficiencies. For example, where a contract-for-difference (CFD) is valued at a premium and the underlying equity trades at a difference, the manager who recognizes this opportunity will likely want to maximize leverage to maximize their position. Another reason is that activist funds may want to impact a change in a board of directors or corporate strategy. Through the use of leverage, a hedge fund may effect a change in management or strategy to become a significant shareholder.[3]

[3] Prime brokers will be very sensitive to efforts to take controlling interests in companies on leverage, and will need to be aware of mandatory take-over provisions as they relate to large holdings, or the potential for market abuses.

Where margins on a trade are minimal, the prime broker will normally offer a significant amount of leverage depending upon the relevant restrictions. In the international sphere, the leverage offered to clients may range from minimal in illiquid positions to more than one hundred times the value collateral for highly liquid securities, currencies, or bonds, and depends largely on the availability of capital and the risk appetite of the prime broker.

Lending Securities

Securities lending is a particularly important part of the prime finance offering for both the hedge fund and the prime broker. A strong, developed stock loan desk can give hedge fund clients significant benefits. When the prime broker has relationships with a broad spectrum of asset managers and pension funds, the stock loan desk will be able to provide access to "hard to borrow" stocks and reduce the costs to the hedge fund to borrow such stocks.

It is critical to understand that the prime broker will access the hedge funds' collateral and lend such securities out to create more financing for long positions sought by the hedge fund. Restrictions on lending collateral to the prime broker may have a significant impact on the costs of lending.

Valuation

The terms of the PBA or ICAA set out the relevant valuation standards, which are subject to common law or statutory limitations. A variety of standards apply to the manner in which prime brokers value collateral. At its core, the hedge fund's collateral is central to the secured financing arrangement, and valuation of the collateral should be of utmost concern to both hedge funds and prime brokers.

How to value collateral is a critical consideration. The standard position is that the prime broker is the lender and exposed to significant risk for the leveraged positions of the hedge fund. At its most basic, the hedge fund will take principal risk for its trades and will receive principal rewards if the investments are profitable.

The prime broker in the normal course will only receive interest, fees, and expenses for financing and other services. The risk for the prime broker is the total value of the hedge fund's loans, whereas the hedge fund may only be limited to losing the value of the collateral. Therefore, the prime broker will not take on principal risk for fixed agency-based returns and will normally require broad discretion in the evaluation of collateral.

The prime broker may require absolute discretion to value collateral. The collateral may have some value, but the market value of the security may not reflect the value to the prime broker. In addition to covering the minimal margin requirements, certain securities are more valuable to a prime broker. This is reflected in the financing transactions that may be undertaken in either repo or stock loan transactions. If the collateral posted is not capable of being utilized for these ancillary transactions, then the value of the collateral for the prime broker will be significantly reduced. Similarly, in the event that securities become illiquid, the value of the securities for financing will fall, and prime brokers will value such securities accordingly.

There are several different positions on prime brokers' valuation of collateral securities, including:

- Sole and absolute discretion
- Sole discretion
- Reasonable discretion
- Commercially reasonable discretion
- Commercially reasonable discretion in good faith

Granting absolute and sole discretion to the prime broker over the collateral provided by the hedge fund may create the potential for a perverse scenario where the prime broker values the collateral securities at zero, requires additional margin, and when other collateral is not provided, liquidates the hedge fund's portfolio. The prime broker would then push the fund into default based upon its sole and absolute discretion. This scenario may be avoided by ensuring that the valuation is not done arbitrarily. Ultimately, a court will review such a scenario based upon the relevant legal and regulatory framework, and the specifics of the contractual terms.

A small hedge fund may not have the economic power in the relationship to require commercially reasonable valuations in good faith. Even if commercially reasonable valuations were available, it would make financing significantly more expensive. The financing arrangement requires the prime broker to value the collateral, and the prime broker will seek to utilize the securities provided as collateral. If the securities are not hard to borrow or valuable from a stock loan perspective, the value of the securities to the prime broker will be diminished.

Timing and Grace Periods

In the background of all finance, risk is the square root of time.[4] The longer it takes a secured lender to have access to collateral, the greater the risk. Timing and grace periods for payment can be very important for hedge funds and prime brokers alike. Certain prime brokers with up-to-date computer systems apply margining and have intra-day margin calls and payment requirements. There are also highly technical and automated responses to margin requirements. Other prime brokers may allow margin calls to follow the next day or later depending upon the negotiated rate. This delay will increase costs for borrowing and may reduce the amount of leverage that the prime broker will grant.

In the PBA or ICAA, the definitions of the relevant times are particularly important, including the jurisdiction of the business day. This may fall to the relevant market for the securities, but complexities arise where securities are traded on multiple exchanges and in different time zones. In the event of multiple jurisdictions there may be delays associated with enforcing rights in different time zones.

For the hedge fund, the timing of margin calls is critical. Where the operations are in different jurisdictions, it may be operationally impracticable for smaller firms to set up traders

[4] See Danielsson & Zigrand, 2005.

ready to trade or make transfers at any hour or in any jurisdiction. In the event that intra-day, or even following day, margining is required, additional financing pools or emergency backup scenarios may need to be put in place. In order to address this scenario, sophisticated hedge funds may establish a financing facility in the relevant jurisdiction. In the event that a margin call is made by a prime broker in a market disruption event or emergency, the availability of such a facility will ease prime brokers' concerns and may justify lower lending rates or increased maximum leverage.

Certain hedge funds request that when a margin call is not made due to an "administrative error," the prime broker must wait a certain period prior to calling an event of default. This is a provision that many prime brokers are loathe to grant, as it creates extended delays and increased risk where a default has occurred.

Duty of Care

The duty of care between a prime broker and the hedge fund client is an area of developing law and business practice. The standard of care varies in the international market, but the industry revolves around gross negligence or negligence.

The PBA or ICAA may explicitly deny any partnership, joint venture, or fiduciary obligations between the prime broker and hedge fund. This provision is to avoid the scenario of having to act in the best interest of the hedge fund, and vice versa, particularly in a default scenario. Fiduciary obligations are anathema to the prime broker, as they would significantly restrict the lender's rights in the event of the default. There would potentially be a requirement for the prime broker to terminate the relationship in an orderly manner and continue to hold securities and dispose of the collateral in a commercially reasonable manner. This would undoubtedly have the effect of extending the portfolio transition and would create significant delays and risks for the prime broker. This would transfer principal risk to the prime broker for the transition period and would ultimately delay or restrict their ability to liquidate the hedge fund's positions in an emergency scenario. Given the recent market events, many prime brokers have been expeditiously reducing risk and potential liability. The prime broker will strongly resist any provisions that would require them to effect a reasonable or orderly liquidation of the hedge fund's securities in a default scenario. Investors, on the other hand, should press hedge fund managers, who owe the investors fiduciary obligations, to negotiate for a more efficient liquidation similar to a transition from a portfolio of securities to the relevant currency.

Hedging against the Hedge Fund

As a matter of good risk management, prime brokers may pre-hedge where appropriate. Where it is apparent to the prime broker that market risk on the underlying portfolio is great or liquidity concerns are present, the prime broker may take steps to insulate itself. The prime broker will have the ability to mitigate its risk against the leveraged positions of the hedge fund. There is a risk that the prime broker's hedging activity may adversely impact the hedge fund's positions. Where there is a diminished liquidity on a particular stock, the act of hedging may push the fund into a short squeeze or cause losses.

Hedge funds may seek assurances that such derivative or hedging positions by the prime broker will be disclosed. Hedge funds may also be consulted in such extraordinary circumstances so that managers are given the opportunity to reduce leverage or be given notice that the prime broker intends to utilize other means to reduce its own exposure where practicable.

Collateral Holding

How, where, and with whom collateral is held are important considerations for the hedge fund. The prime brokerage agreement or ancillary documentation should disclose where collateral is or may be held. Certain securities accounts may need to be set up in local markets where there is international trading taking place. For example, in certain markets a global prime broker will allow access into local markets through affiliates or associated brokers.

In the event of a default or insolvency by the prime broker, the hedge fund's rights may be restricted in certain jurisdictions.[5] A hedge fund may stand as an unsecured creditor to a bankrupt broker and may face severe delays in accessing securities, if it is possible at all.[6] For hedge funds with certain emerging market strategies this will be a significant concern. Although the ultimate risk may not be mitigated, the risk may be reduced by utilizing a number of prime brokers or utilizing a single prime broker that is associated with a large full-service investment bank, or even a custodian bank if the risk is deemed significant.[7]

Substitution and Withdrawal of Collateral

The prime broker agreement should include a general right, or even a requirement, by the prime broker, for the withdrawal of certain collateral assets that are not used for margin requirements. Particularly with successful funds, the amount required for margin will diminish, and collateral assets may be withdrawn for a variety of purposes ranging from risk mitigation, diversification, and redemptions. Similarly, a prime broker will have a general right to value collateral in a manner consistent with the valuation methods agreed. In the event that the prime broker does not give a fair valuation of certain securities in the view of the fund, then the hedge fund should be able to withdraw such collateral securities and replace it with other acceptable collateral.

In the post-Lehman Brothers world, it is common for hedge fund advisers to suggest that funds have a primary prime broker,

---

[5] This is a particular concern in international jurisdictions under legal regimes that do not recognize the distinction between beneficial and legal ownership. Although this may seem to be remote, even in developing economies within the EU this can be an issue.

[6] See the problems associated with Lehman Brothers bankruptcy in Four Private Investment Funds v. Lomas et al., 2008.

[7] The hedge fund counterparty risk has created elevated concern that government will always bail out a failing broker dealer; Mackintosh, 2008, and Anonymous, 2008b.

and several secondary or tertiary prime brokers. This may have the beneficial effect of creating more efficiency and competitiveness between prime brokers. However, it also increases the operational and compliance burdens on the fund manager in tracking positions and reconciliations. The general concern is in the ability to monitor and identify counterparty risk, when prime brokers may be distressed or approaching insolvency. Thus the availability of alternatives may assist in removing collateral assets to transfer funds or securities to another prime broker.[8]

Utilization of Collateral, Hypothecation, and Rehypothecation

The collateral posted to a prime broker serves to guarantee the loaned amounts to the hedge fund. Hypothecation of securities is the client's pledge to allow collateral to be used to satisfy any outstanding debt.[9] The collateral also has a real value to the prime broker as it utilizes the collateral and lends these assets to itself and other borrowers. Allowing a right of rehypothecation simply means that the prime broker will be able to utilize the assets of the hedge fund for its own purposes and to pledge assets as collateral for its own transactions (**Figure 7.3**).

Accounts: Segregated and Pooled

There are a number of different accounts, particularly in international prime broker arrangements. Proprietary accounts are the accounts for the benefit of the prime broker. Client accounts have

---

[8] To remove assets from a prime broker, a hedge fund may be required to liquidate positions and transfer cash to another prime broker. This was the case in the market before and after the Lehman Brothers bankruptcy. Hedge funds were reportedly unable to transfer securities to other prime brokers, as the major prime brokers were undergoing a deleveraging process and would not increase their balance sheets to accommodate collateral from other prime brokers. The result was increased volatility in the markets as hedge funds liquidated positions to transfer collateral away from distressed prime brokers.

[9] Hypothecation is "the pledging of something as security without delivery of title or possession," in Garner, 1999, p. 759.

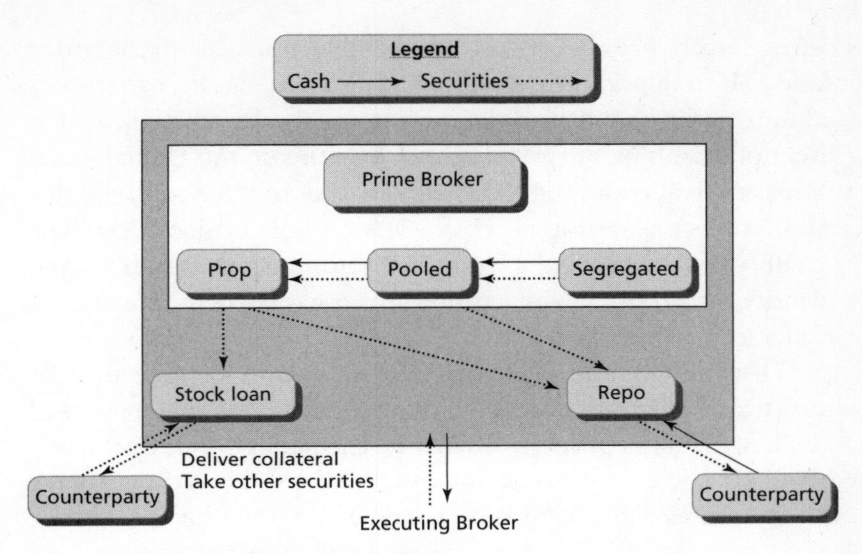

Figure 7.3 Rehypothecation Mechanics

various forms and may be either pooled accounts with other clients, pooled segregated accounts, or individually segregated accounts. The individually segregated accounts allow for discrete assessment of the individual hedge funds' holdings and provide greater transparency and identification of client assets. Pooled client accounts, although common, do not allow for immediate and simple identification of client assets and may result in delays in returning assets, particularly in the event of a prime broker default.[10]

Rehypothecation should be reflected with moving the assets from the segregated client account or pooled client account to the account of the prime broker. Limiting the financing abilities of the prime broker by restricting utilization will impact the prime broker's lending ability and raise the cost of borrowing to the hedge fund.

Segregated accounts provide the hedge fund with the comfort that the collateral is segregated from other assets and held in trust,

[10] This remains an issue in the Lehman Brothers default in the United Kingdom.

unencumbered by the prime broker, and identifi-able to the hedge fund. More importantly, there will be clarity for the bankruptcy administrator or judge, depending upon the jurisdiction, in the event of default by the prime broker. Whether in the United States or other jurisdiction, the ability of a creditor to trace collateral free from competing creditors' claims is a critical consideration. The inability of the client (or a bankruptcy administrator) to trace and identify assets posted with a prime broker has restricted the client's rights to their return.[11]

With individually segregated client accounts, there may be significant delays in accessing collateral, but the collateral will be identifiable as properly owned by the hedge fund, unencumbered by the prime broker or other claims. The counterparty risk increases significantly in a scenario with pooled accounts of client collateral. When prime brokers' infrastructure utilizes pooled accounts, several clients have their assets pooled into the same account. There will be a recording on the assets, related to which client owns what, but the lines of ownership and trust claims may blur when assets are rehypothecated and replaced with other assets, and as amounts are transferred between affiliates or street counterparties. The complexity of the prime brokers and the larger investment banking organizations, some of which have thousands of trading entities,[12] cannot be underestimated.

Consider the example of a client providing common shares as securities for collateral. The collateral is utilized by the prime broker, pursuant to the PBA, and loaned to a street counterparty. The prime broker receives other different common shares

---

[11] For an example of this in the United States, see MJK Clearing Inc., Debtor. Ferris, Baker Watts, Inc., Plaintiffs v. Stephenson, Trustee, 2002 and affirmed in all respects in In re MJK Clearing Inc., Debtor. Ferris, Baker Watts, Inc. v. Stephenson, Trustee for MJK Clearing Inc., 2003.

[12] For an idea of the staggering list of the entities and complexity of accounts for Lehman Brothers Holdings Inc., see In re Lehman Brothers Holdings Inc., et al., Debtors, 2008.

and then utilizes these shares for financing, receiving cash from another party in a repo transaction. The prime broker utilizes these funds to finance its operations and other business. The transactions are legal transfers of title of the securities. Now in the event of the bankruptcy of the prime broker, the prime broker does not have cash and the securities are legally transferred to other counterparties. The hedge fund requests the collateral assets held by the prime broker be returned. The prime broker is unable to do so because the assets are not held by the prime broker. In the absence of fraud, the result is the hedge funds may be left as common, unsecured creditors to the prime broker, which does not have the assets to pay back the collateral to the hedge funds. As an example of this, over one hundred hedge funds had assets frozen in Lehman Brothers' bankruptcy. The hedge funds were unable to get the full amount of collateral returned. The international prime broker simply does not have the collateral assets. The assets rehypothecated and loaned to other street counterparties are the property of the other counterparties in the event of default, and the cash generated has been utilized for continuing operations.

Hypothecation and Rehypothecation

There is a significant difference between domestic and international regulations relating to hypothecation and rehypothecation. The U.S. regulations provide for limits on custody and hypothecation of fully paid securities not used to cover margin requirements.[13] Hypothecation has been addressed specifically by U.S. domestic regulations.[14] International prime broker regulation and the practices of foreign broker dealers vary significantly.

[13] Rule 144 of the Securities Act of 1933 addresses issues related to handling of securities and security values in excess of the margin requirements. The fully paid securities are to be segregated by the broker-dealer.

[14] See Section 15c2-1(a)(1) of the Securities Exchange Act of 1934; for more information and detail on U.S. regulations, see Lofchie, 2005.

Lehman Brothers held the assets of clients, who allowed rehypothecation, as do all major prime brokers.[15] The collateral assets were then hypothecated (or borrowed) by Lehman Brothers for their own purposes and lent to the street. Clients viewed the collateral as the requirements of the prime broker to effect transactions, and it was used for this, but it was also used for financing other deals. The rehypothecated assets were used as collateral in other transactions for Lehman Brothers to raise cash and other collateral.

The rehypothecation clause is significant for hedge funds negotiating a prime broker relationship, as it poses significant counterparty risk for the hedge fund and is critical for the prime broker's financing operations. The trade-off for hedge funds is that the additional risk associated with utilization of their collateral allows for greater leverage to be provided. With the reduction in market leverage arising from extreme volatility, even funds with excellent strategies may result in unacceptable risk adjusted returns.[16] The key features for the hedge fund should be to have transparency and accurate, timely reporting of the level of utilization and rehypothecation by the prime broker.

Transparency

The prime broker should provide transparency on the collateral securities that have been utilized. The risk to the hedge fund is that the utilization levels are too high and the prime broker is moving toward insolvency or bankruptcy.

Transparency for prime brokers is particularly difficult. The operating vehicle of a prime broker is often a vehicle within a complex investment bank. There may be no transparency or

[15] There are certain prime brokers who offer custodial services and provide greater security for hedge funds, but with reduced availability of leverage and greater costs for holding the assets.

[16] The Sharpe ratio or Sortino ratio is a useful guide to the risk associated with daily volatility compared to results. The significant market volatility has a negative impact on risk adjusted performance.

professional rating agency with a view into the legal entity that one contracts with for prime brokerage services. If possible, transparency should be given into the prime broker legal entity, or a parental guarantee of the obligations of the prime broker which may allay concerns about a subsidiary bankruptcy or default. The availability of parental guarantees may be limited but would provide security in the event of a default by the prime broker, and where the parent or holding company remains solvent.

Power to Refuse Transactions

A prime broker will normally retain the right to effect or refuse transactions. While it may seem to be unfair, the prime broker often has significant operational and compliance issues owing to the complexity and number of transactions in which they are involved. In such circumstances, the broker-dealer will need the opportunity to refuse or take other action as it deems reasonably necessary. For example, a small equity position, under the required level for disclosure, may trigger disclosure requirements for the prime broker in the event that other clients have also taken on the same position. This leads the prime broker into a cumulative position that triggers either compliance and regulatory problems, mandatory takeover offer, or disclosure obligations in a foreign market. The disclosure obligation would potentially not be in the interest of the hedge funds holding the positions in the event that the disclosure revealed a weakness in their position. Prime brokers may refuse transactions for a variety of reasons ranging from risk and operational problems to legal or regulatory barriers.

Delegation of Transactions

In the normal course, domestic transactions will likely not be delegated to a variety of different entities and, if so, delegates may be specified. The U.S. market will not have to deal with the variety and breadth of international transactions in international markets, where the use of delegates is inevitable and consistently changing. Furthermore, the transactions will need to be effected by a variety of brokers, and advising clients of changes to brokers (or their delegates) prior to transactions is not practicable.

What should be discussed is who has the responsibility for trades executed by such delegates and who retains the responsibility to oversee such delegates and ensure they are solvent. The principal risk for transactions remains with the hedge fund, but there are circumstances where a prime broker has reason to question or becomes aware of the default, bankruptcy, or insolvency of a principal (or delegate). In such a scenario, there may be an argument for the prime broker to take some responsibility for monitoring the delegates used.

Large prime brokers should be able to advise which delegates are employed on a standard basis. If details of all of the broker links are requested, the prime broker will likely not want to provide full insight into the structure and function of all the related brokers and delegates in local markets. However, where the broker dealer has regulated affiliates, the entities should be disclosed and defined in the prime broker agreements. It is also important if an affiliate becomes insolvent or triggers a cross-default provision.

Manufactured Payments and Dividends

The PBA and ICAA will normally address the details of manufactured payments and dividends. There are a variety of concerns over the manufactured dividends, particularly around taxation issues. When stocks are lent, the borrower has an obligation to pass through dividends to the lender. As a result, litigation has arisen where counterparties and tax authorities disagree over the taxability of these payments.[17]

There may be differential treatments of dividends for different legal entities holding certain securities. For example, a hedge fund from an offshore jurisdiction (Cayman) may be subject to a withholding tax, whereas a U.S. entity is not subject to any withholding tax. The result is that a manufactured dividend

[17] DCC Holdings (UK) Ltd v. Revenue and Customs Commissioners, 2008.

of the value of the dividend that it would have received, had it been holding the security directly, will need to be transferred to the hedge fund client. There are opportunities for prime brokers to assist in the efficient management of manufactured dividends for funds.

Corporate Actions and Voting

Corporate actions are an area of considerable difficulty for investment banks and prime brokers. When the stocks are held in the legal name of the prime broker for the hedge fund (as beneficiary), corporate actions may be a simple matter of voting as directed by the client. When corporate actions occur in stocks that have been rehypothecated and utilized for securities lending, there may be considerable difficulty recalling stock and voting as directed in a timely manner. The difficulty arises where a series of loans are on-lent to various counterparties, which can create long chains of lending far beyond the initial counterparty.

Further complications arise when the hedge fund manager takes an activist role in a portfolio company whether with equity, debt securities, or derivative positions.[18] For example, certain hedge funds may take positions with struggling firms in order to effect strategy or management changes. These activist funds may target corporate structure, capital raising, debt reorganization, or general firm strategy.

When the manager wants to vote in a particular manner on a special election (such as a dividend or stock split) it is more of a matter of operational sufficiency for the prime broker. But when the hedge funds manager's goal is to seek concessions from

[18] Activist hedge funds require the ability to vote in particular ways to meet their specific objectives, which may be to change management (Reuters, 2009) or have access to records (Reuters, 2008), or change a target company's capital structure, or strategy. The U.S. regulatory complications on activist hedge funds' use of total return equity derivatives is examined in CSX Corporation v. The Children's Investment Fund Management (UK) LLP et al., 2008. The court deemed that the defendants were the beneficial owners of the underlying shares. However, this perplexing scenario has not been definitely addressed by appellate courts.

management, there are complex issues about effecting this goal and compliance with law. This is particularly complicated in the event that the manager arranges for a derivative position with the prime broker.

In one recent case, an activist hedge fund, The Children's Investment Fund, sought to make changes in the management of a railroad company, CSX. However, a company is only obligated to hear and address the concerns of stockholders. The Children's Investment Fund in this case held a large derivative position (total return equity swap) but had no legal right to make any demand on the company or to vote. Nonetheless, the hedge fund still has significant power over the target company through the derivative. The court deemed the hedge fund to be a beneficial owner of the underlying security and that it had violated securities laws.[19] Although the case was settled, the issue of derivatives and their alleged infractions will return for consideration by appellate courts.

It is important to note that the source of the power is in the hedge of the derivative position. If the derivative contract is with the prime or executing broker, then the broker in writing the contract will have a hedge in the underlying stock related to the derivative. In the event that the hedge fund sells the derivative position, the broker will sell the hedge. A prime broker may also be called upon to vote on the shares related to the hedge, yielding indirect control over the company to a hedge fund.[20] The links between the hedge fund and the prime broker may create indirect control over the securities or even an entire target company.

Indemnities

Prime brokers seek broad indemnities from the hedge fund in the normal course, similar to a normal borrower-lender scenario.

---

[19] CSX Corporation v. The Children's Investment Fund Management (UK) LLP et al., 2008.

[20] This scenario has been reviewed by regulators, and a variety of jurisdictions have stated they will address the disclosure and obligations on derivative positions.

Hedge funds will naturally attempt to restrict broad indemnities to the minimum required. Standard indemnifications for prime finance include:

- Acting on instructions
- Client's breach of agreement
- Performance of services under the agreement
- Failure by the customer to deliver equivalent securities
- Breach of law or regulation
- Acts or omissions of the executing broker
- Court proceedings

The indemnification will always be limited by the provision that the indemnity will not protect the prime broker from any action resulting from its own acts or omissions. In the normal course, this includes the prime broker's own negligence, wilful default, or fraud.

Lock-Up Agreements

Lock-up agreements are between the prime broker and the hedge fund and may include affiliates in different jurisdictions. The standard terms of the lock-up agreement include:

- Term of loan
- Rates of loan (variable or fixed)
- Amount of loan available
- Recall provisions
- Notices of changes to terms
- Timelines for return of capital

The terms of a lock-up agreement may extend several months or even years. Changes in the costs of financing have greatly increased the costs of borrowing for prime brokers. As a consequence, prime brokers may be reticent to provide long-term fixed financing terms. While variable rates may be agreed based upon LIBOR or another applicable rate, the increase in financing risk has reduced the availability of lock-up agreements and the terms that were previously common.

Limited Recourse and Affiliates

For a variety of reasons, hedge fund managers will not want the prime broker to have the ability to claim losses against different hedge funds, which may have different investors. To claim losses from unsuccessful funds against the profits made from successful funds defies the discrete nature of hedge fund investing and their respective investors. The reason for this is that many hedge funds are organized into several different legal entities (sub-funds) that may have been started at different times ("vintages") and may have different and distinct investors. Even where there are similar investors in the surviving fund, it defeats the purpose of a limited liability structure to allow for cross default among affiliates of the hedge fund. It is not unusual to have some form of limited recourse against master funds or the managers for the hedge fund, and to allow for claims by and against the prime broker's defined affiliates. This structure reflects the link between affiliates in different locations that would otherwise not have any contractual link to the fund and would be unable to make a claim directly.

However, the prime broker is often an arm of an investment bank, which may be a legal entity within a larger network of legal entities. The prime broker vehicles normally work in concert to provide comprehensive services to hedge funds, and accordingly the prime broker should take responsibility for certain concerted actions or related corporate vehicles.

Events of Default

One of the most important clauses of the prime brokerage agreement is the events of default. The events of default are particularly important for both hedge funds and prime brokers. There are a variety of events of default that arise in different scenarios ranging from business fundamentals to legal requirements. Standard events of default include:

- Failure to meet margin call
- Failure to perform

- Security compromised
- Insolvency of a party
- Admitting to being unable or unwilling to perform
- Breach of warranty
- Default of guarantor
- Cross-default
- Illegality

Failure to Pay Margin

The failure to pay or top-up margin is likely the most common reason for default. The requirement to provide collateral to justify the loans to the hedge fund is among the most fundamental tenets of the prime broker-hedge fund relationship.

When a hedge fund fails to meet a margin call, the hedge fund will have lost control over its collateral provided that default procedures are properly completed. The collateral and portfolio may be liquidated and the hedge fund will be paid out the residual amounts after liquidation, less any fees, costs, expenses, or other liabilities. In the event that there are trailing liabilities, the prime broker will usually wait until the liabilities are realized to return any residual collateral, which may delay the paying of amounts to the hedge fund in excess of the anticipated liabilities.

There is a concern that a minor default based upon valuation applied by the prime broker could force the hedge fund into default. The hedge fund would then be liquidated, expeditiously driving the value of the portfolio down considerably from normal trading volumes and reducing the collateral value. There is no general right to be liquidated in a reasonable manner, by slowly transitioning the portfolio in the course of a few days. The standard position has been for prime brokers to reserve their rights in extreme events, but the exercise of this right would have potentially dire reputational risks associated with abuse. Hedge funds often seek to limit unfettered discretion to liquidate an entire portfolio immediately. This may have a massive impact on the value of any residual collateral.

Failure to Perform

There may be a number of services where either the hedge fund or prime broker fails to perform. This may be used as a reason to terminate the relationship, but in most scenarios a failure to perform will result in covering losses to the other party as necessary.

If one of the parties fails to perform, it may justify an event of default. However, this is rarely invoked in the event of mistakes, as relationships are generally long-term and may normally be adequately addressed by payments rather than terminating the entire relationship.

Security Over Collateral Compromised

In the event that the prime broker's security over the collateral is no longer valid, an event of default may occur. This may occur in a particular jurisdiction as a result of a change of law, regulator, or government action or court decision. In any event, where the prime broker recognizes it is unable to enforce against the collateral provided, the prime broker will almost invariably take immediate steps to require other additional collateral. If security over collateral is compromised and not rectified, the prime broker may liquidate the portfolio to reduce its risk to the hedge fund client. The primary risk protection for the prime broker is the availability and security of the collateral. Where there are such secured claims on collateral, whether by way of pledge, secured interest, or direct transfer to the legal ownership of the prime broker, this security is of paramount concern to the prime broker.

Insolvency or Bankruptcy of a Party

In the past, hedge funds have been the party to suffer financial distress. Recent times have seen many funds become insolvent or bankrupt as a result of poor investment performance and redemptions by investors. The prime brokerage finance model is structured to tolerate and mitigate such distress. This is provided that in the event of liquidation of the hedge fund's portfolio, the residual collateral amounts exceed all liabilities owed to the prime broker.

Recently, much greater attention has been focused on the financial positions of prime brokers. A number of prime brokers have become bankrupt, insolvent, required government financing, or were acquired or rumored to be in financial distress. These included both mini-prime brokers and leading prime brokers. No U.S. or international prime brokers were immune from the financial crisis.

For many years, it was assumed that large international prime brokers were safe, as their secured financing models were sound, and their bankruptcy would have a contagion effect on the markets and pose systemic risk. Post-Lehman Brothers and Bear Stearns, it is now recognized that while many of the largest players are insulated with an elegant financing model, and backed by governmental guarantees, no prime broker is immune from distress from client withdrawals or the threat of bankruptcy.

The result is a new strategy for diversification of risk between prime brokers.[21] In the past, long-standing and close relationships were developed with a single prime broker. It is now a common risk management strategy to have second, third, or even more prime brokers for just such scenarios where one or more of the prime brokers become an unacceptable credit default risk. Some advisers recommend international diversification of risk with multiple prime brokers.

Many managers have been well advised to seek multiple, diversified prime brokers in multiple jurisdictions including North America, Europe, and Asia. As a result, the market shift has seen massive collateral assets move from the U.S.-dominated prime brokers to international prime brokers.[22]

Admitting to Being Unable or Unwilling to Perform

If a fund admits that it will not be able to meet requirements, or is unwilling to do so as a result of a dispute, the prime broker may

[21] Terzo, 2008b.

[22] Significant assets have moved to Deutsche Bank, Credit Suisse, BNP Paribas, and UBS as a diversification strategy for large funds.

declare an event of default and thereafter take steps to liquidate the portfolio or pay out the collateral. However, the prime broker must be careful not to accept the statement of just any person working with the hedge fund to declare a default. A hedge fund only speaks through certain individuals, who will normally be listed as "authorized persons" or directors, in the prime brokerage agreement. Whether a trader or transaction clerk's statement is sufficient to justify a default would depend on the specifics of the agreement and the context of the admission.

Breach of Representations or Warranties

A standard breach of representations or ongoing warranties is a common event of default. It is important to carefully consider the representations and warranties beyond standard provisions, as this may grant the prime broker an unexpected ability to default a struggling hedge fund. Contrastingly, a prime broker will have transparency over the positions and trades, financed, settled, and held with a particular prime broker, but may have no information on other matters related to other prime brokers. A standard provision is that the actions of the hedge fund manager will not breach a law or regulation. In the event a hedge fund utilizes multiple prime brokers to build a position in a target firm for a takeover, the hedge fund may breach a takeover regulation or mandatory offer requirement. In such circumstances, the prime broker may wish to detach itself from the hedge fund and avoid responsibility for aiding and abetting the misfeasance of the hedge fund.[23] Similarly, while a manager will have a comprehensive and complete view in the hedge fund's portfolio, the legal status of the fund may not be apparent to U.S. brokers if a problem has been created in another offshore jurisdiction. As such, a manager is normally required to provide such information on an ongoing basis.

---

[23] There are several examples of litigation that allege aiding and abetting responsibility to a prime broker for the conduct of the hedge fund, particularly where the hedge fund is bankrupt and plaintiffs attempt to recover damages from deep pockets.

Illegality

Illegality is a common provision that both prime brokers and hedge funds should be comfortable accepting. In the event that the relationship between a prime broker and a certain fund is deemed illegal by authorities in a relevant jurisdiction, one or both parties may wish to terminate the relationship.

Default of Guarantor

For both hedge funds and prime brokers, where a party has concerns about their counterparty's credit risk, it is common to request parental or affiliate guarantees. A default of the guarantor will become a direct event of default for the underlying fund. The request for a guarantee is typically made against the parental company or holding entity of a financial organization. The reason for the guarantee may be related to specific concerns about the credit of the counterparty, which may be a newly formed special purpose vehicle (SPV) with no discernible assets, or merely the lack of transparency to accurate credit ratings by ratings agencies. The parental company may be rated by a ratings agency such as Standard & Poor's, Reuters, or Moody's. Transparency into the parental company may be greater than into a special purpose vehicle that may be used for limited purposes with minimal assets. Similarly, with less established prime brokers, additional security may be gained from a parental guarantor.

Cross-Default

Cross-default is a particularly complex provision that may be global or have specific carve-outs for the prime brokerage relationship. The prime brokerage agreement may incorporate a variety of different products and purposes, including derivatives, commodities, foreign exchange, debt and equity securities, and other financial products. In effect, this provision allows for the default under one agreement to allow for the entire relationship to be closed, provided that the individual agreements allow for netting and set-off. The result gives counterparties the right to default all agreements based upon the default of one agreement. This may result in an unanticipated cascade of defaults in various agreements and among various counterparties.

Termination and Close Out

The prime broker agreement may be terminated by either party voluntarily under the terms of the agreement or may be terminated on an involuntary basis. There are several reasons why a fund would terminate a relationship with a particular prime broker. In the normal course, a fund will have several prime brokers, but these may be organized into primary, secondary, and tertiary. The order normally relates to the seniority of the prime broker and the related financing flows. More financing with a primary prime broker requires additional collateral to be placed with the prime broker, which in turn creates greater specific counterparty risk. Decisions to start new prime broker relationships are related to additional services, diversification of risk, or decreased costs of financing. In the context of competing prime brokers, funds may transfer funds to another prime broker with more suitable technology or services that focus on the fund's strategies or simply provide financing at better rates.

Termination for involuntary reasons occurs where an event of default has taken place. The close out mechanism varies considerably, but the discretion of the prime broker is central. The prime broker holds the client's assets and has control over the timing and close out of positions.

Netting and Set-Off

Netting and set-off within the hedge fund is a normal practice that allows for efficiency and scalability. Prime brokers' business is to lend margin on a variety of products, and their primary concern is risk management for the collateral. The secondary concern is the financial health of the hedge fund and its ability to provide additional collateral and income for the prime broker. Thus the prime broker that provides a variety of services outside of the standard prime brokerage agreement, such as derivatives, commodities, foreign exchange, and stock loan and repo transactions, will require netting and set-off.

Why is netting and set-off important? In the event that netting and set-off are not agreed, the prime broker will be required to discretely notify of margin calls and default notices under each agreement, which in many cases is operationally impracticable. The active margining of discrete positions is onerous and may create difficulties for risk management and allocation of resources for bank regulatory capital requirements. The netting and set-off provisions in the prime broker agreement may be the primary agreement for the prime finance relationship.

Law and Jurisdiction

The applicable law and jurisdiction of the prime brokerage agreement should be established in conjunction with legal due diligence over the entities involved, both client and prime broker. The choice of law appears to be a simple matter. However, in many legal cases, disputes over one agreement may spill into another, and changes in jurisdiction may bifurcate and extend proceedings.[24] The parties should be clear in complicated relationships with multiple agreements to select the applicable law and exclusive or nonexclusive jurisdiction of courts. The absence of consistent law and jurisdiction has caused confusion and delays in bifurcated proceedings, even where netting and set-off provisions apply.

---

[24] For example, in the case of UBS AG and another v. HSH Nordbank AG, 2008, concurrent proceedings were brought in England and New York. The claimants defaulted on assets and a dispute arose. The claimants commenced proceedings in English courts under an agreement with an exclusive English jurisdiction clause, and the defendants brought action in New York under a derivative agreement subject to a nonexclusive New York clause. The New York court held that in complicated relationships, the choice of law in different contracts govern complicated relationships and denied the declaratory relief that the proceedings should occur in England only.

The international PBA and U.S. ICAA are central agreements for prime finance. Their terms and function are critical components of the prime broker relationship. Other important agreements and transactions in prime finance interrelate and complement the prime broker services, including securities lending, repurchase (financing), and OTC derivatives agreements.

8 Securities Lending and Financing

Stock loan or securities lending is a critical part of both the financial services offered to hedge funds and the financing for the prime broker and investment banks. Stock loan or securities lending is important for the financing in both domestic and international markets. The standard U.S. stock lending agreement (SLA) and international standard agreements (GMSLA) share common aspects.[1]

So what does the stock loan desk do? Consider the example in which an asset manager is a long-term holder of securities. The asset manager may lend the securities to the prime broker to provide access to the securities for its clients, typically hedge funds or other broker dealers. The asset manager lends stock to generate additional fees for lending the stock. The stock will be returned at a later date.[2] The basic transaction is set out in **Figure 8.1** and may be repeated several times by the process of on-lending.

---

[1] The standard agreement in the international model is the Global Master Securities Lending Agreement (GMSLA), which is governed by English law and courts. For prior versions of the standard documents see www.isla.org. The Securities Lending Agreement (SLA) in the United States is typically subject to New York state law and courts. Either international or domestic agreements may be subject to binding arbitration.

[2] The return date may be fixed or remain open, and in general terms may be largely agreed between the parties.

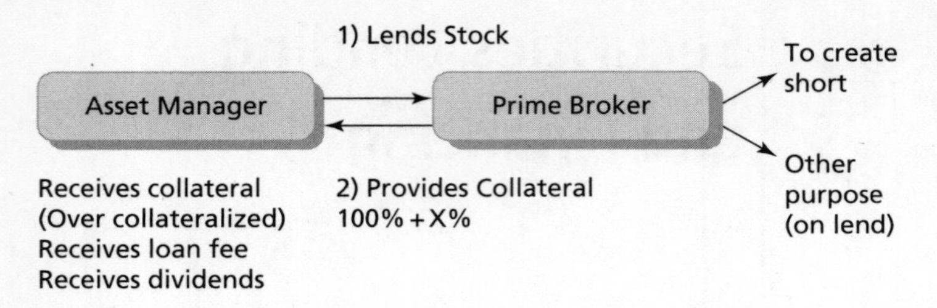

Figure 8.1 Stock Loan Basic Structure

Typically, the prime broker borrows "hard to borrow" securities and provides them to clients to short the stock or for other purposes. The result of selling the borrowed stock is a short position. This dual transaction of borrowing securities and selling them into the market is one way hedge funds create short positions. It is important to note that a short exposure to a security also raises cash for the hedge fund client.

Many strategies, including long/short, 130-30 funds, and statistical arbitrage, rely on both long and short positions to effect and finance their strategies. Similarly, the prime broker typically utilizes the collateral of the hedge fund through a stock loan arrangement. The prime broker utilizes collateral securities to raise capital in order to provide financial services and leverage through stock loan arrangements.

Stock Loan Economics

The basic economic transaction is a two stage transaction. First, the lender transfers securities to the borrower, in return for collateral and fees being paid on the borrowed securities (see **Figure 8.2**).

The second step is the return of collateral and margin to the borrower and the return of collateral and fees to the lender. The stock loan transaction is conducted on a standardized agreement for predictability and to benefit from improved regulatory capital requirements associated with secured transactions.[3]

[3] See Faulkner, 2004.

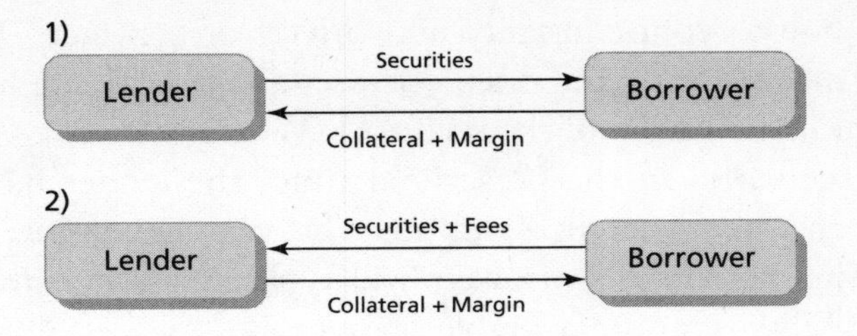

Figure 8.2 Stock Loan Transaction

A key feature of the stock loan transaction is that title over the securities moves from lender to borrower. In effect, it is a full sale, with a corresponding obligation to return the securities on a future date, which may be specified or unspecified. The lender is provided with collateral for the stock loan, which includes margin that acts as a buffer. Provided the lender has monitored the value of collateral, liquidity, and nature of securities provided, the lender often has limited concerns about the default of the borrower. In the event that the collateral provided drops in value significantly, the borrower may have greater concerns about the lender, especially where the stock borrowed has a significant "haircut" (also called margin) applied to it. Ironically, the borrower has greater concern about the counterparty risk of the lender due to the provision of additional margin.

In the normal course, the borrower may return stock at any time, or the lender has a right of recall of the securities depending upon the terms of the stock loan agreement and the specific terms of the trade confirmation. The borrower has the obligation to return the exact kind and amount of securities that were loaned. The driving force behind the stock loan transaction is either the need to borrow a specific security or the desire to create additional revenue from long-term holdings, particularly from hard-to-borrow securities.

The stock loan transaction is replicable, which leads to chains of stock loan transactions. The practice of on-loaning means that the ultimate location and owner of a specific security may not be known due to confidentiality and privity of contract.[4] When a recall is made, it may, and often does, set about a cascade of recalls to the ultimate holder of the securities. Where there is a failure to return securities in the prescribed time, the lender has rights to buy the borrower in. This may be very expensive for the defaulting borrower. Borrowers will typically attempt to reduce the possibility of an unfavorable "buy-in."

Restrictions on Stock Loan for Financial Stocks

In 2008, there was a focus on stock loan on financial stocks and some alleged abusive cases. In particular, where vulnerable stocks are heavily shorted to expose weakness, there were regulatory reactions.[5] These alleged abuses and systemic risks led the SEC and FSA, Australian, Canadian, EU, and other national or regional regulators to impose restrictions on short-selling their national or regional financial institutions' securities.

The temporary ban on short selling financials had overarching and unanticipated negative effects on legitimate financing arrangements.[6] In retrospect, the implementation was haphazard and lacked clarity in many instances. Many regulators appeared to enter their own short selling bans to keep up with their peers without substantial deliberation on the unanticipated consequences or even how to exit the ban. As a result, many market participants who sought short exposure to financial institutions were still able to get access without shorting securities directly, and the short bans had unintended negative implications for financing and legitimate investment strategies. The banks, mortgage companies, and financial firms that the short bans were intended to protect actually suffered due to their inability to lend many

[4] Confidentiality provisions are common in prime broker trading relationships with limited exceptions. The concept of privity of contract entails that those not party to a contract do not have the ability to enforce terms of the third party contract.

[5] Mehta, 2008.

[6] The short selling ban had negative implications on the profitability of prime brokers; see McIntosh, 2008.

stocks restricted by the short ban. The short ban further contracted and reduced liquidity and created financing problems for the very financial institutions that it was intended to protect. Legitimate trading and financing strategies were interrupted suddenly and repeatedly. Hedge funds and other market participants with hedged positions suddenly needed to alter their trading strategies and sell out of positions, which may have increased the volatility of certain stocks.[7]

Stock loan and the practice of shorting positions were reportedly considered to have a negative impact on the markets and particularly financial stocks. Further, short positions may have created additional volatility in the markets, arising from the placing and closing of short positions. Recent markets have seen an unprecedented amount of volatility, and regulators and other observers have pointed to short sellers as one of the causes of this volatility.

It is unlikely that volatility was generated by pernicious hedge funds hoping to force weak financials into default. There were abuses in naked shorting, but the markets in general had significant short interest. Short selling is a legitimate market practice that improves price discovery, liquidity, and is an important part of securities financing for hedge funds, prime brokers, banks and other financial institutions. Some academics have criticized the imposition of short selling restrictions as a consequence of its negligible impact on the financial stocks and negative impact on the efficiency of markets.[8] One recent study found no strong evidence that the imposition of restrictions on short selling in the United Kingdom or elsewhere changed the behavior of stock returns.[9] The expected impact across different countries failed to show systematic patterns consistent with the expected effect of the new regulations. However, the liquidity in the markets was

---

[7] Strasburg & Karmin, 2008 and Chung, Mackintosh, & Sender, 2008.

[8] For a brief review of the academic literature criticizing short restrictions, see Marsh & Neimer, 2008, p. 2.

[9] Marsh & Neimer, 2008; see the executive summary.

drained by the imposition of short selling restrictions. The various and sometimes erratic actions of governments clearly injected significant uncertainty into the financial markets.

The Benefits of Short Sellers

The practice of stock loan and ultimately short positions both perform a helpful price discovery function and create sources of liquidity for markets. In some cases, short selling may create volatility and expose the weakness of certain securities. When the fundamentals of a business model are poor or uneconomical, its management is not incentivized to maximize value; when financial reports are flawed, inaccurate, or fraudulent, short sellers are invaluable market participants. Short sellers test the integrity of firms in the capital markets. When the leading firms in the market are excessively overvalued, short sellers may expose weakness, fraud, and corruption.[10] Thus, puncturing manageable bubbles is vastly more preferable to allowing a bubble to expand until unsustainable, systemic losses result.

On a more fundamental market level, while the practice of stock loan and short selling is a valuable practice, the stock loan market itself suffers from a lack of clarity, transparency, and questionable practices around "best execution." The stock loan market is controlled by the broker-dealers who set the market for stock loan. There is limited transparency in the market for stock loan, especially where asset managers may loan stock to a number of broker-dealers. Each may provide a different valuation and haircut. The result is an inefficient market which will likely see additional regulation around pricing and disclosures.

These factors ultimately led to an equities stock loan market with decreased utilization rates which reportedly stand at $2 trillion. This is large, but only a fraction of the potential $17 trillion

[10] For example, if Bernard Madoff's firm had been a publicly traded security, it is possible, if not probable, that his fraud would have been revealed sooner if short sellers were allowed to short his securities.

market. Addressing the lack of transparency may result in an increase in liquidity in the financing markets.

Recent litigation has focused on alleged abuses related to stock lending fees,[11] and in particular naked short sales and increasing "fails to deliver." In one important case, related to Overstock.com, the litigants complained of a "massive, illegal stock market manipulation scheme."[12]

The naked short sales and "fail to deliver" are a product of the difference between trade date and settlement date for securities (which is typically T+3 in U.S. domestic markets). In effect, where a prime broker trades a stock, it will have three days to acquire the stock for settlement. Where the stock is not available or the counterparty fails to return a stock, the failed trade may impact the value of the security where the underlying stock price may be depressed by large short sales. The Overstock.com case is notable for its size; however, the litigation on this basis appears to lack a fundamental understanding of the prime brokerage business and will likely not alter the stock loan model.

U.S. Regulations on Short Selling

There are specific regulations on stock loan and short sales in the United States.[13] The uptick rule was removed in July 2007. Hedge funds and industry experts have both criticized this

[11] Current litigation is based upon phantom trades and excessive fees by a broker-dealer (Electronic Trading Group LLC v. Banc of America et al., 2007) and a hedge fund (Quark Fund LLC v. Banc of America et al.,), respectively.

[12] The California state complaint alleges 1) conversion, 2) trespass to chattels, 3) intentional interference with prospective economic advantage, 4) violations of California Corporations Codes. Sections 25400, and 5) unfair business practices subject to California law and seeks general damages of $3.48 billion, see Overstock.com, Inc. et al. v. Morgan Stanley & Co., Inc. et al., 2007, filed on February 2, 2007.

[13] See Rule 200 of Regulation SHO. U.S. regulations also place disclosure obligations on the broker-dealer to disclose whether a sell order was "long" or "short." The U.S. regulations dealing with stock loan and short sales depend upon the securities traded and whether the broker-dealer is regulated directly or indirectly under U.S. regulations.

deregulation. The recent reinstatement of the "uptick" rule may limit the ability of short sellers to continue to pound vulnerable stocks in falling markets.

Stock Loan Due Diligence

Primary stock loan due diligence requires an analysis of the legal entities involved and whether the local laws will accept, recognize and enforce the transaction, including important commercial terms, such as netting and set-off. Where, for example, an English firm and an Icelandic hedge fund wish to enter into a stock loan transaction, it will be critical to ensure that the transaction in both Iceland and England is legally binding, enforceable, and that netting and set-off apply to the transaction.

It is important to note that the securities transfer to the borrower and full title transfers with them. It is a full transfer of legal title with the right to sell to another party. The obligation of the borrower is to return equivalent securities, not the exact securities that were borrowed (**Figure 8.3**).

Rehypothecation

Stock lending is the manner by which collateral is transferred from the account of the hedge fund to the account of the prime broker. The prime broker will then utilize the securities for financing or other purposes. There is risk that where the prime broker hypothecates securities it will on-lend to another party (rehypothecate) and may not be able to return the borrowed securities. This is an issue for corporate actions and dividend payments in the case where the hedge fund receives dividends at a preferred rate; the prime broker will need to ensure that the rehypothecation does not create losses for the hedge fund when dividends are returned to the hedge fund. The term for such dividends transferred back to the hedge fund client is "manufactured dividends." It is common practice for many institutions to utilize the stock loan agreement to transfer securities to

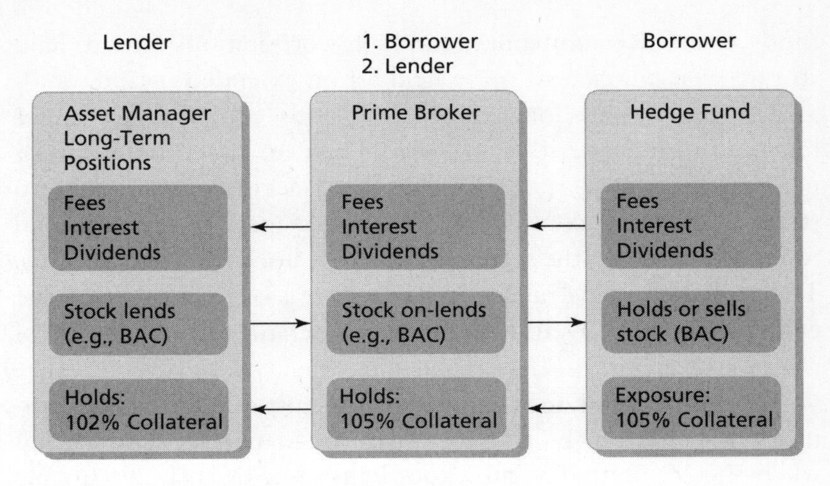

Figure 8.3 Stock Loan Transaction and Parties

jurisdictions that allow for the tax efficient transfer of dividends back to the lending hedge fund.

The stock loan agreement is the key to securities lending and the creation of short positions. While the prime broker agreement is bespoke and may vary considerably, the typical stock loan agreement and repurchase agreement are market standards.[14]

Why Lend Stocks?

The stock loan transaction is driven by the need to borrow a specific stock by the borrower, or the desire to lend stocks to increase returns by the lender. Prime brokers need to borrow stocks for hedge funds clients. Asset managers and pension funds lend stocks in return for increased fees when they understand that the stock will be held on a long-term basis. In practice, the prime brokers and investment banks tend to borrow stocks to meet the needs of their customers and asset managers; pension

[14] For the most recent version of the Global Master Stock Loan Agreement, see www.isla.org. The Global Master Repurchase Agreement is published by the International Capital Markets Association; see www.icma-group.org.

funds, insurance companies, and large corporations tend to lend stock that is anticipated to be held for an extended period.

The basic stock loan transaction adds additional revenues for long-term securities holders. Thus an asset manager or pension fund that is required to hold securities pursuant to statutory or other contractual obligations may create additional revenue by lending the securities through stock loan transactions. The nature of the transaction is secured by the value of the collateral posted, even in the event of default or bankruptcy of the borrower.

The primary risk for the lender of securities is that the counterparty will fail to be able to return the loaned securities. Even when the counterparty fails, goes bankrupt, or is simply unable to redeliver securities, the lender will still hold onto the collateral and margin. Provided the margin and collateral held is sufficient to cover the principal of the loaned securities, even in the event of a default or insolvency of the counterparty, the lender may actually not have any counterparty exposure.

Risks of Stock Loan

The stock loan transaction is based upon market standard agreements.[15] There is limited legal risk associated with relying upon standardized documents provided they are enforceable in the jurisdiction of both borrower and lender. The primary risk is the collateral position held by the lender or in the lender's account with a custodian. Provided the lender (or its agent) has been diligent in tracking its exposure to the borrower, there should be sufficient collateral and margin to cover the value of the loan in a default scenario. The secondary concern is ability of the borrower to provide additional margin and collateral when the collateral provided is not sufficient to justify the loan. The primary

[15] Market standards for stock lending are published by the International Securities Lending Association, including the current market standard GMSLA, and other market standards, which have been amended and expanded in line with market activities.

issue is sufficient collateral and where this is not sufficient, the next step is to assess the creditworthiness of the borrower.

Even if the counterparty fails, or becomes bankrupt, the ultimate risk for the lender is that the collateral provided will not be sufficient to claim the value of the loaned securities.[16] In practice there is a margin above the amount of the loan, which is varied for various kinds of securities. For lenders, such as asset managers and pension funds that hold significant portfolios, the focus should be on the credit of the counterparty and the characteristics of the securities provided as collateral. The considerations for the collateral include:

- Margin on the collateral
- Kinds and quality of acceptable collateral (such as S&P 500 stocks, bonds, MBS, ABS, and derivatives with a certain credit ranking)
- Liquidity of collateral
- Legal risk of collateral
- National risk of collateral
- Market risk

In the financial crisis, the margin required on collateral increased dramatically with market volatility and collapsing global markets. In normal markets, standard S&P 500 index securities utilized as collateral may require minimal margin of 2 percent in addition to the value of the loaned securities. However, given recent market events where volatility indexes have risen to historical highs, intraday margins in excess of 50 percent were not unknown. This increase in required margin resulted in the contracting liquidity. Similarly, the quality and kinds of acceptable collateral are critical determinants to risk. While the prime broker may seek to allow for broad definitions of acceptable collateral, there is a

[16] For limitation on the quantum of relief available under a GMSLA see Savings Bank of the Russian Federation v. Refco Securities LLC, 2006. Also, the industry practice of a run-through or "pass-through" loan was considered under an MSLA in Nomura Securities International, Inc. v. E*Trade Securities, Inc., 2003.

significant risk in broad definitions which may allow a party to provide illiquid, "toxic waste" as collateral. In the event of a default, the illiquid and hard to value securities may not cover the amount of the loaned securities.

The risks associated with the volatility of the collateral are primary in ongoing maintenance of sufficient collateral. However, in practice, margining and additional securities are required on a following day basis.[17] In the event of a default, the lender or borrower may take possession of the collateral or loaned securities, respectively, to return to a parity position.

Stock Loan Custodians

There are alternative structures for the stock loan transaction to further reduce counterparty and collateral risk and operational burdens (**Figure 8.4**). Triparty stock loan agreements utilize a triparty agent to minimize transactions by providing for netting and set-off, thus providing further assurances regarding collateral holding.

Increasingly after Lehman Brothers' bankruptcy, stock loan transactions are conducted with third party custodians. This can

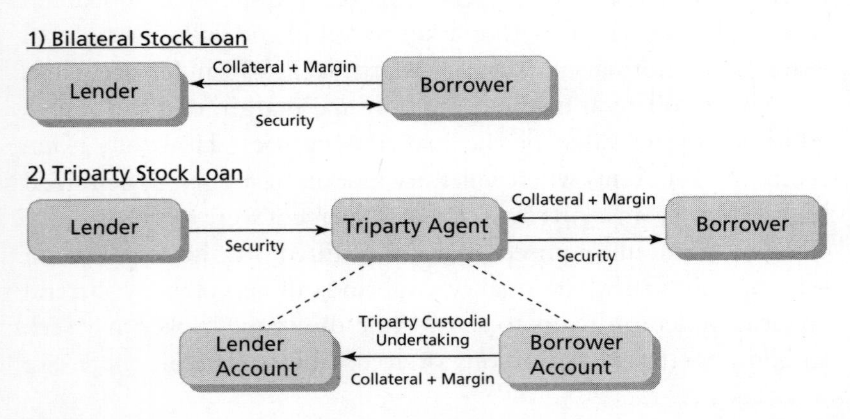

Figure 8.4 Stock Loan Alternative Transaction Structures

[17] See GMSLA, MIFSLA, MSLA, or applicable stock loan agreement for details.

either be two separate custodians or, more commonly, one large custodian acting as agent for both lender and borrower under a triparty contract amending the underlying standard stock lending agreement.

The fundamental nature of the transactions is a full transfer of legal title. Ironically, the borrower of the stock is not really a borrower, but a full owner. The transaction entails a full transfer of title to the borrower from the lender, and is a legal and enforceable contract even in bankruptcy.[18] In return the lender takes collateral from the borrower and an agreed margin rate and provides different securities or other financial instruments.[19] In a case where a trustee pledged shares to a third party and the third party exercised its right of power of sale, the beneficiary was unable to sue the pledgee for conversion of assets.[20] There has been a variety of litigation related to alleged schemes and frauds associated with stock lending.[21]

The key considerations for the parties in utilizing alternative structures are operational efficiency and risk mitigation. Principal to the various transactions is that netting and set-off apply. Another very similar transaction is the repurchase transaction.

Repurchase (Repo) and Financing Transactions

There are two critical sources of short-term financing for prime brokers and investment banks: the interbank lending

---

[18] See In the Matter of A. G. Becker & Company, Inc., 1982.

[19] The borrower may provide cash in return for securities, but this is normally conducted under a GMRA. There is nothing fundamental that would prevent this transaction, but normally the stock loan utilizes other securities as collateral. One reason for this is that financial institutions and broker-dealers require cash in the current market. Thus, it would be contrary to their monetary interest to finance stock loan transactions with cash except in the most aberrant scenarios.

[20] MCC Proceeds Inc. v. Lehman Brothers International (Europe), 1997.

[21] See Edwards & Hanley v. Wells Fargo Securities Clearance Corporation, 1979.

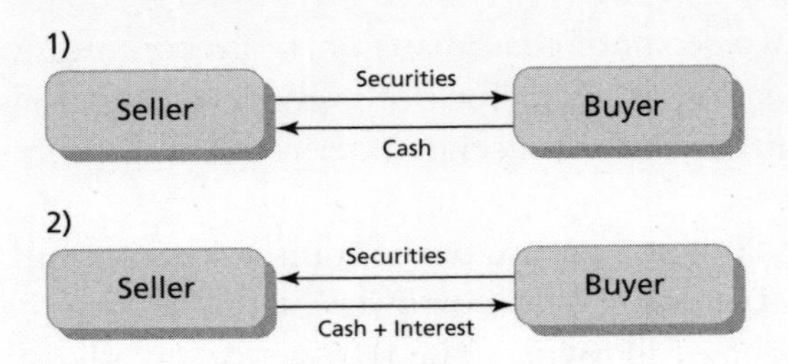

Figure 8.5 Repo Transactions—Two Leg Transactions

market and the repo market.[22] The repo market is estimated at approximately $5 trillion.

A repurchase (or "repo") transaction is similar to a stock loan transaction in many ways. The repo transaction is conducted on a standard agreement.[23] There are two legs of the transaction and four discrete movements of securities and cash (**Figure 8.5**). The two legs of the repo are commonly referred to as 1) the purchase price and 2) the repurchase price.

The first transaction includes the value of the securities, plus any haircut. The "haircut," or "initial margin," is the amount of extra collateral that is required to be posted to reflect the seller's risk for lending cash. The repo transaction is primarily guided by financing, and the terms are determined with respect to the amount of cash.

The repo is regarded as a secured financing operation, as entities with significant cash want to lend in a secured manner. The buyer of securities provides the cash to the seller of securities. The rates of the repo transaction are determined by a variety of factors including:

- Currency
- Duration of loan

[22] Others include the interbank deposit market. The collapse of Lehman Brothers and other factors exposed a vulnerability in the investment banking financing model; see Mackenzie, 2008.

[23] See www.icma-group.org for the up to date list of market standard repurchase agreements (GMRA) and applicable annexes.

- Repo rate
- Collateral

The second leg of the transaction occurs at maturity of the repo for a fixed repo, or when the parties terminate the repo for an open repo.[24] The seller repays cash borrowed with interest calculated at the repo rate. The collateral is returned and the full economic benefit of the collateral should remain with the seller.

The collateral and initial margin are to ensure that if the collateral provided reduced in value, the buyer would be covered by the margin. In the recent extreme markets, the initial margin rose from a traditional market standard of 2 percent to more than 25 percent in the throes of the crisis in October 2008. This increase in margin dramatically impacted the cost of financing. The repo market effectively seized with massive increases in margin requirements.

In the event that the collateral plus initial margin is reduced in value, buyers would be able to claim more margin to cover their exposure by making a margin call. This is typically done on a day after close basis on standard agreements but may be agreed otherwise. In the event of a failure to pay margin, buyers would be able to close out their position with the collateral provided and claim any additional amounts under the contract.[25]

The repo transaction is very similar to a stock loan transaction, but the purposes of the transaction vary considerably. The major differences relate to cash being utilized, and the effect is that the primary purpose of the repo transaction is financing.[26] Securities are used as collateral for the lending or borrowing of cash, which is typically driven by a need of the seller of securities to raise cash or a desire of the buyer of securities to lend cash in a secure manner with minimal risks. The buyer of securities holds cash and

---

[24] For more detail on the financial calculations involved in repo transactions see Steiner, 2007, pp. 166–169.

[25] See the underlying GMRA or other repo documents, which address this scenario.

[26] The stock loan transaction can be structured to produce a financial effect identical to the repo transaction.

wishes to generate income from the cash, which has preferential rates to other transactions for regulatory capital purposes.

The purpose of the repo transaction is financing (or raising cash) based upon securities. In practice, it is a secured loan based upon securities as collateral. In times of stress, hedge fund clients may have significant cash holdings when market volatility makes certain positions unattractive. As a result, hedge funds with large cash holdings may look to enhance returns by entering repo transactions. Repo trades are particularly important in financing for prime brokers and banks. The prime broker uses repo transactions to turn securities into cash.

There are a variety of different structures for repo transactions which may include reverse-repos, "holder in custody" transactions (termed "HIC repos"), and triparty repos. HIC repos are performed by the prime brokers (typically seller) with hedge funds (typically a buyer) who lend cash in return for securities. There is a fundamental difference between a standard bilateral repo and a HIC repo. Rather than having securities transferred to the buyer outright, the securities are transferred internally and assigned to a discrete account for the buyer. In the normal course, a repo transaction is a common method for lending cash at agreed rates secured by collateral. The standard structures for repo transactions are set out in **Figure 8.6**.

There are also various other similar transactions including buy/sell-back, or sell/buy-back, and reverse repos.[27] Our focus is on the first three kinds, which involve deviations from the standard bilateral two-step repo transaction.

A triparty repo is a development to further reduce counterparty default risk. The imposition of a triparty agent is done for three main reasons:

- To increase operational efficiency
- To allow for netting of collateral obligations
- To allow the triparty agent to optimize collateral attribution within the available collateral portfolio

[27] For a detailed explanation and worked examples of the transactions with a financial focus see Steiner, 2007, pp. 163–206.

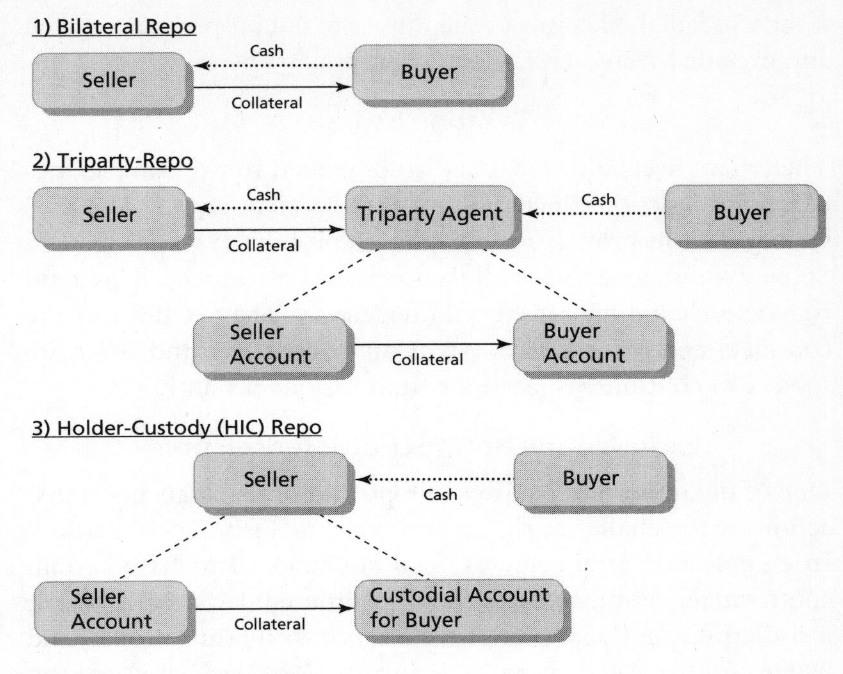

Figure 8.6 Repo Structures

The triparty agent will regularly review the collateral obligations of the seller and will allocate collateral according to the settlement directions and optimization requests of the seller. The complexity of a triparty arrangement lies in the details of the arrangements surrounding holding collateral and removal from the custodian. The seller will deposit collateral to its account with the triparty agent, which is normally a large custodian bank.

HIC Repo

In a HIC repo, the custodial function is taken on by the seller of the securities. The seller will act as counterparty and custodian for the securities. The benefits of structuring this arrangement are increased efficiency and lower borrowing rates. However, this efficiency is countered by increased legal risk in a default scenario if the Custodial Accounts of the Buyer are not properly segregated and excluded from other client or proprietary assets.

Taxation Issues

There have been additional tax issues related to the complexities of repo transactions, including manufactured interest.[28] The U.S. tax regulations provide for taxation on prohibited transactions.[29] Some English courts have taken a hands-off approach to repo transactions and manufactured dividends.[30] The taxability of the contracts and intricacies of payments from buyer and seller are subject to continuing questions from various tax authorities.

Exclusive and Non-Exclusive Jurisdiction

One of the important features of repo and other financing transactions is the challenge that arises from the jurisdiction clause.[31] In complicated arrangements, it is not unusual to have certain contractual relationships governed by different laws and different jurisdictions. In the area of prime finance with prime brokers and hedge funds located in multiple jurisdictions, lack of clarity on the jurisdiction may lead to unexpected and protracted litigation in multiple jurisdictions.[32] Many of the difficult cases for repo transactions involved the failure of Russian bonds, or GKOs, and the protracted litigation that resulted.[33]

---

[28] The U.K. revenue has focused on repo transactions, which have recently been decided in favor of the tax-efficiency of the transaction; see Revenue and Custom Commissioners v. D'Arcy, 2007.

[29] See section 4975 of the Internal Revenue Code, which provides for tax on prohibited transactions.

[30] See DCC Holdings (UK) Ltd v. Revenue and Customs Commissioners, 2008.

[31] For examples of the quagmire of litigation that may arise with a nonexclusive jurisdiction clause, see Credit Suisse First Boston (Europe) Ltd v. Seagate Trading Co Ltd, 1999.

[32] Credit Suisse First Boston (Europe) Ltd v. Seagate Trading Co Ltd, 1999.

[33] JPMorgan Chase Bank (formerly known as Chase Manhattan Bank) et al. v. Springwell Navigation Corp., 2008.

Also, while the contractual relationship may be appropriately dealt with under the *lex situs* of the contract, ancillary issues surrounding alleged fraud or breach of fiduciary duties may bifurcate and protract litigation.[34] In the case of *MLC (Bermuda) Ltd v. Credit Suisse First Boston Corporation*, U.S. courts deferred to the jurisdiction of the English courts in a dispute for fraudulent inducement and wrongful liquidation, with the defendant's consent.[35] The court granted a motion to dismiss on grounds of deference to a pending foreign action due to similarity of parties, adequacy of the alternative forum, convenience, judicial efficiency, possibility of prejudice, and the sequence of filing. Similar factors need to be assessed in scenarios where hedge funds and prime brokers agree to nonexclusive jurisdiction clauses and seek to resolve disputes in different venues and jurisdictions.[36]

[34] The Jordan (Bermuda) Investment Co. v. Hunter Green Investments LLC et al., 2007.

[35] See the U.S. action MLC (Bermuda) Ltd v. Credit Suisse First Boston Corporation and Aaron Tighe, 1999 and the U.K. action Credit Suisse First Boston (Europe) Ltd v. MLC (Bermuda) Ltd, 1998.

[36] See both the U.S. case, Credit Suisse First Boston (Europe) Ltd. v. MLC (Bermuda) Ltd, 1999, and English decision, Credit Suisse First Boston (Europe) Ltd v. MLC (Bermuda) Ltd, 1998.

9 Executing Brokers

The prime finance model relies upon prime brokers, executing brokers, and hedge funds working in an interdependent and concerted manner. As demonstrated in **Figure 9.1**, the executing broker is the trading arm for a variety of products and arranges for the execution of trades from the client either directly or with an affiliate. The prime broker arranges to settle and report trades with the executing broker, and finances, settles, and reports transactions.

An executing broker offers execution of a variety of different financial products and markets. There is no single broker who is a member of each exchange and provides access to every conceivable

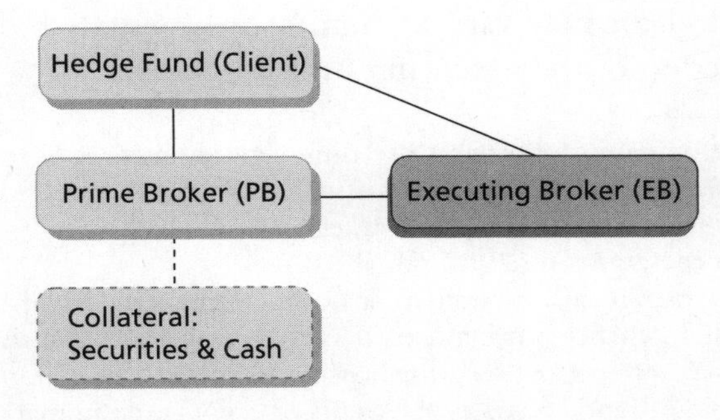

Figure 9.1 Executing Broker Relationship

financial product both domestically and internationally. As a result of the development of financial innovations in execution in the different markets, including regional and national differences, off-exchange markets, derivatives, and the development of dark pools (which are trading vehicles that allow for counterparty anonymity), electronic communication networks (ECNs), and multilateral trading facilities (MTFs), there are many players offering alternative execution services.[1] The executing broker may or may not offer margin lending or other services, but will not take on principal risk for trades, successful or failed. The client directs orders, and the executing broker executes them in the relevant market.

U.S. and Global Considerations

Executing brokers' obligations vary greatly between U.S. and international jurisdictions. The U.S. regulations mandate that certain procedures, communications, confirmations, and agreements are in place between the client, prime broker, and executing broker.[2] In the international sphere, the regulatory capital requirements for executing brokers, prime brokers, and customers may be limited or not exist at all. Similarly, record keeping, AML, KYC obligations, and required agreements may not be regulated, and settlement and clearing procedures and timelines vary substantially from jurisdiction to jurisdiction. Selling restrictions and the contractual terms and legal relationship between the prime broker and client may vary in significant ways depending upon the jurisdiction of the executing broker.[3]

---

[1] The development of alternative trading venues has greatly increased the number of execution platforms, with many new start-ups attracting more and more market share from traditional markets.

[2] McMilan & Bergmann, 2007, pp. 59–70.

[3] There are certain jurisdictions that do not recognize the distinction between legal and beneficial ownership. The result may be that in the event of a default or bankruptcy of an executing broker, the prime broker alone may make a claim that significantly restricts the rights of clients even in markets that are attempting harmonization.

Terms of Business

A key document for many executing brokers is the terms of business (TOB). The TOB applicable to the executing broker, if any, will set out the basic rights and recourse for clients. Generally, the TOB is limited to minimal legal mandates required by local law or is specifically designed to protect and limit liability for the executing broker. Executing brokers may not have agreements drafted, and any agreements may be aimed at reducing broker liability rather than articulating rights of the clients or prime brokers on their behalf. Fundamental to the variety of prime finance services is whether the TOB supersedes any of the prime finance agreements.[4] It is critical to establish whether the individual agreements take precedence over the TOB. The executing broker agreement or TOB may vary considerably in size and detail depending upon the local legal and market rules.

Executing Broker Market

In the United States and internationally, the market for execution is mature and highly competitive, with an increasing number of platforms for alternative execution. The market for execution services is largely focused on deal flow. The introduction of direct-market-access (DMA), electronic platforms such as Electronic Communications Networks in the United States, and Multilateral Trading Facilities, alternative execution venues have increased competition in the executing broker market. Economies of scale for executing brokers have risen considerably with technological advances. Hedge funds have focused on minimizing costs for execution and other transaction services. The result of the many new alternative execution forums is increased competition and reduced margins in certain business units. This fragmented the executing broker market with many new

[4] Prime finance agreements include the Prime Brokerage Agreement, Stock Loan Agreement, or any other ancillary agreements, including GMRA, ISDA, Repurchase Agreements, and Custodial Agreements.

entrants, focusing clients on reducing execution costs and improving ancillary services such as commission sharing and access to research.

Executing brokers in the United States and developed international markets are in a highly competitive market. There is increasing competition for market share. There has been continuing market fragmentation and decreased power for incumbent broker-dealers and increased competition in a diminishing market. The global financial crisis and global economic downturn is predicted to lead to reduced trade volumes on a broad variety of execution platforms.

The current U.S. domestic and EU market focus for executing brokers is to provide consistent long-term clients in return for deal flow. The attractive clients for executing brokers are large clients with actively traded portfolios. Clients with minimal trading do not generate significant returns for executing brokers. The objective is to establish and maintain deal flow for active traders. In order to attract deal flow, there are a variety of benefits that executing brokers are willing to provide to hedge funds. There are specific regulations in the United States and abroad governing the provision of services to hedge funds by executing brokers.

In more nascent markets, there are still rules that may limit the ability to utilize electronic execution, and alternative execution venues may not be available. Similarly, emerging markets may have significant barriers to multinational executing brokers competing with execution in their local markets for licenses, fees, residency, and other requirements. Emerging markets are struggling with the difficult tension between attracting international capital flows and having international executing brokers and financial institutions dominate inexperienced local brokers. The introduction of foreign capital may result in an increase in volatility related to capital inflows and outflows, making the developing markets less attractive on a risk-adjusted basis.

Executing brokers in the United States, EU, and elsewhere have utilized commission sharing to attract new customers and to encourage trading.[5] The calculation of commissions in the execution of trades for securities and derivatives is subject to regulation.[6]

Commission Sharing

Executing brokers offer ancillary benefits to hedge funds and other clients. Hedge funds, being highly outsourced organizations, have a variety of needs depending on their size, development, and strategy. For asset managers and hedge funds, access to research and ancillary services is vital. Executing brokers will offer access to research and other permitted services in many jurisdictions.[7] By directing deal flow with the executing broker, a percentage of the deal flow will be set aside for the benefit of the hedge fund to be utilized in a variety of permissible services, most commonly research.

One of the primary concerns for hedge fund managers is access to research and a variety of research providers. Research providers are important for hedge fund managers to be able to operate in multiple markets and to stay abreast of relevant market developments. Hedge fund managers utilize a significant amount of research to do so and either employ external or internal investment researchers.

In the United States, United Kingdom, and in many other jurisdictions, commission sharing is explicitly permitted by regulators or has developed as a tacit understanding in the securities industry. The United States provides for an additional focus on

---

[5] Previously, "soft dollars" were provided lump sum payments but these have now been restricted by regulators in the United Kingdom, EU, and United States.

[6] In the United States, FINRA has imposed sanctions for excessive commissions by executing brokers; see Investment Weekly News, 2008.

[7] In developed jurisdictions with advanced capital markets, commission sharing is normally explicitly allowed subject to local rules and regulations, or tacitly allowed with historical industry practice. However, in more nascent capital market there may be minimal due diligence possible where regulators have not addressed commission sharing and related issues.

the executing brokers to provide for a red flag review.[8] If the red flag review is required, there are additional restrictions on certain kinds of trades in the domestic U.S. and developed international markets. However, it should be noted that there are a number of restricted markets that do not allow commission sharing.[9]

What Is Commission Sharing?

Hedge funds, sovereign wealth funds, and asset managers of all descriptions utilize research from research providers to inform their trading decisions. The research providers range from research departments of large investment banks and research houses to small boutique research consultancies.

In the past, hedge fund clients paid commission to brokers for execution, research, and other ancillary services in a bundled package, expressed as a percentage of the total value of the trades.

---

[8] U.S. regulation of financial markets and investment managers is generally more onerous and rules-based than other jurisdictions. Companies situated and incorporated outside the United States may still be subject to U.S. financial regulation even if no trading or business takes place in the United States. Breaches of U.S. regulations can carry harsh penalties and a possibility of enforcement action by U.S. regulatory agencies, such as the SEC or CFTC.

U.S. securities regulation places some obligations on the executing broker in the context of commission sharing. The broker making the commission payment to the service provider must perform a review of the description of the services in order to ensure that there are no obvious "red flags" that indicate the services do not fall within the safe harbor of Section 28(e) of the Exchange Act. This is not a strict obligation on the broker making the payment to ensure that the services being paid for indeed fall within regulations, but merely that the broker must be alert to any obvious signs that the services being paid for are ineligible, for example, if the services are described as travel or entertainment expenses. It is important to note that the ultimate obligation for complying rests with the money manager client, not with the broker-dealer. The broker-dealers may incur "aiding and abetting liability" should they knowingly allow a money manager client to make payments outside of the safe harbor without a "red flag" review.

[9] Most jurisdictions either allow for, or are silent as to, commission sharing arrangements. There are several important exceptions: Korea, India, and Taiwan, and some other nations. Commission sharing has been prohibited in these jurisdictions.

This bundling process created apparent and real difficulties with transparency.

The industry in both the United Kingdom and United States has developed an unbundled model in which clients can choose to pay a portion of the commission relating to acceptable services to a service provider other than the executing broker. The executing broker is still entitled to the portion of the commission relating to execution services, but the client has a pool (termed the "CSA pot" or "research pot") from execution fees, which may be used to pay for research or other approved services.

Clients are usually investment managers who act on behalf of the underlying funds. Many international managers have a fiduciary relationship with their investors and have statutory obligations to disclose to them the details of any commission sharing arrangement they enter into.[10] Executing brokers are not under a direct obligation to police clients' compliance with these disclosure requirements, but there are concerns where obviously questionable payments are directed by the manager to research providers.

In egregious examples, payments have been made for a variety of inappropriate services and products, ranging from luxury goods to holidays for managers. The ethos of the market and of many regulators has been to clamp down on such abuses, to increase transparency, and to protect investors' interests.

Commission Sharing Basic Model

The Commission Sharing Agreement (CSA) is a bespoke document that sets out the general terms of the commission sharing operations, the legal status of the CSA pot, and the operational terms of the CSA (**Figure 9.2**).

The execution commission is fixed between the hedge funds and the executing broker, but the commission relating to research can be distributed to any number of research providers, according

[10] See FSA, English regulations on Commission Sharing, particularly COBS 11.6.12–11.6.19.

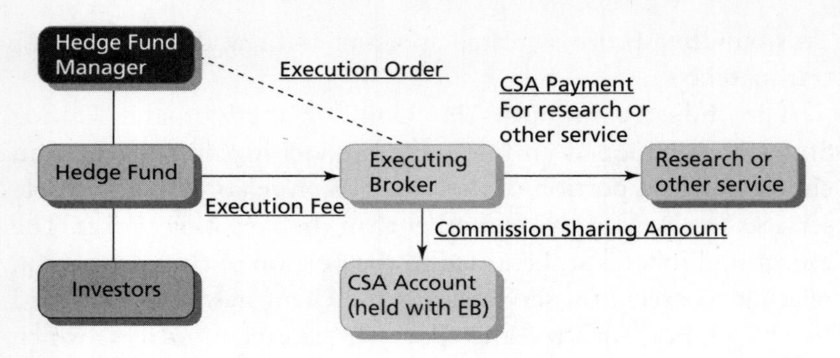

Figure 9.2 Commission Sharing Fundamentals

to the client's discretion. In practice, the investment manager or hedge fund manager will make the orders to the executing broker and direct allocations to certain research providers. For example, if the total commission rate charged by the executing broker is a certain standard amount in terms of basis points (bps), or as a fee (for example $0.001) per share in the American system, the executing broker retains its portion (bps or fees) for itself as execution commission, and the remainder is available for the hedge fund client from the research pot (or research pot). The research pot is then used to pay for research or other allowable products and services.[11] The service providers paid by the hedge fund from the research pot may include the executing broker in its alternative capacity as a research provider.

The executing broker pays the research provider directly from the research pot for the benefit of the fund. Due to the structure of the transaction between the research provider and the executing broker, it is common to have the research provider execute a

[11] What may be determined to be an allowable service will be dictated by the rules and regulations of the relevant regulator. The relevant FSA regulations are *New Conduct of Business Sourcebook* COBS Rule 11.6 (Use of dealing commission) and Rule 2.3 (Inducements). COBS 11.6 places obligations on the client as an investment manager. However, the rule on inducements in COBS 2.3 applies to brokers regardless of the client's regulatory status.

participation letter agreement, wherein it agrees that the payment for services complies with all applicable laws.[12]

The brokerage and research market has become more competitive due to these changes as the hedge funds or other clients can now choose to reward the best research instead of automatically paying executing brokers for research as part of their bundled services. There are also developments in the market to simplify and provide comprehensive services for hedge funds and their research services. Examples of these developments include aggregator models and reconciliation services. The reason for the development of these alternative structures is derived in part from the Lehman Brothers bankruptcy. Many funds found that their research pot with Lehman Brothers was vaporized in the bankruptcy. The result was a need for a different model to create operational efficiency and reduce counterparty risk to an executing broker for the amounts held with them under a commission sharing agreement.

Other CSA Models

Apart from the basic commission sharing arrangements, there are a variety of other CSA models, including aggregator and reconciliation agreements, that are used by executing brokers. The contractual agreements for each commission sharing arrangement vary depending upon the model employed and the associated risks. The different models give rise to different levels and types of risk.

Aggregator Model

A typical investment manager client uses multiple executing brokers and even more research service providers. On the basic model, this leads to increased administrative and operational costs for the hedge funds and the executing brokers (see **Figure 9.3**).

---

[12] The relationship between the hedge fund client and the executing broker is governed by a CSA and any applicable TOB. The executing broker will normally enter into participation letters with the service providers to which it will be making payments.

Some firms have developed an aggregator service for clients wishing to aggregate or centralize back office services in making payments to service providers in order to reduce administrative costs and time spent on these functions. Thus a single aggregator makes all the payments to each service provider instead of multiple brokers making payments to each service provider.

The client makes commission payments to each executing broker. Each broker retains the execution commission due to it and passes on the research commission to the aggregator. After the reconciliation process, the aggregator pays the service providers according to client's instructions.

Aggregator Business Model

An aggregator business model depends on retaining the interest earned on the amount of research commission held in the interim between receiving and paying out the research commission. A portion of the interest earned on the commission is usually paid to the funds managed by the client (not to the client investment manager itself). This increases the value of the funds, which provides a strong incentive for investment managers to make use of aggregator services.

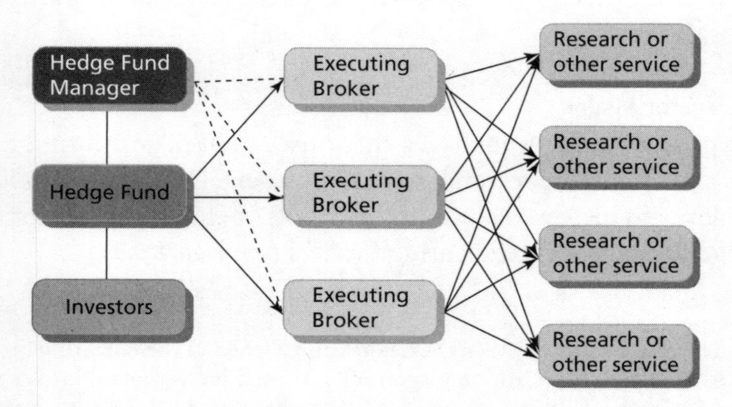

Figure 9.3 Commission Sharing Multiple Executing Broker Model

Aggregator Model Mechanics

The counterparty risk associated with an aggregator mode is simply that the research pot is held only by the aggregator, which may be a small SPV with minimal assets. In the event of a default by the aggregator vehicle, the hedge fund may stand as an unsecured creditor and receive limited recovery or a pro-rata share of the assets of the SPV or the parent organization, depending upon the terms and structure of the CSA (see **Figure 9.4**). Another model to address the complexities of CSAs is the reconciliation model.

Reconciliation Model

Reconciliation is a simple accounting process used to compare two sets of records to ensure that the figures match and are complete. In the context of a CSA on the basic model, the executing broker reconciles the transaction data provided by the client (contained in a trade file) with the data from its own records and accounts, before paying out to the service providers. On the aggregator model, reconciliation normally falls within the aggregator's services.

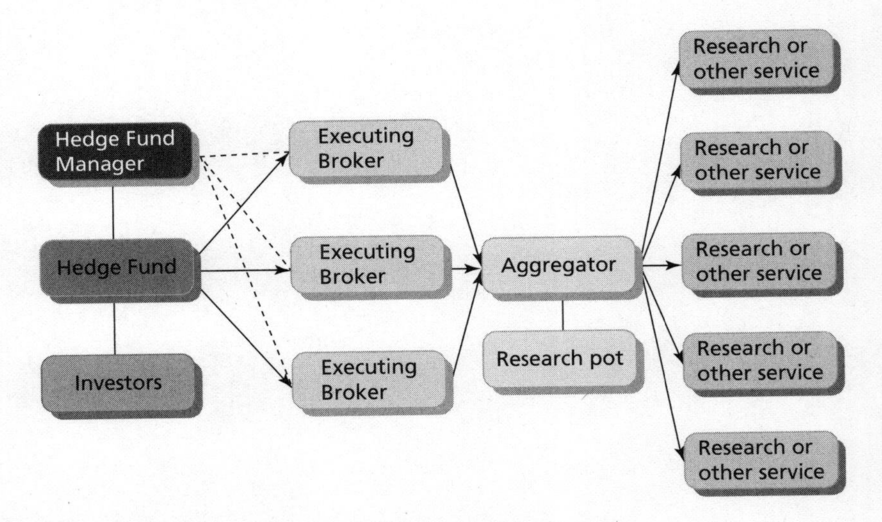

Figure 9.4 Commission Sharing Aggregator Model

Conclusion

The executing broker executes trades for hedge funds and other clients. In return for deal flow, the executing broker offers clients commission sharing, under the terms of a CSA. The CSA allows for a certain proportion of fees associated with trading to be allocated to the account of the client to pay for research and other services. The client may then direct the cash held for its benefit and its investors to be allocated to different service providers. There are a broad range of applicable services and regulatory issues surrounding commission sharing. The market practices and regulations vary in each international jurisdiction, which requires legal and operational due diligence. While this is primarily a due diligence and compliance task for the investment manager to comply with, there are obligations for the executing broker to avoid liability for aiding and abetting, or where there are strict U.S. regulations requiring a red flag review to comply with applicable regulations. New innovations to pool or aggregate resources may assist in operational efficiency and reduce counterparty risk with executing brokers. Each of these innovations present discrete counterparty risks, respectively.

PART III

The Risks and Rewards

10 Life Cycles

To understand the risks and potential rewards of prime finance at each stage of a hedge fund's development, the life cycle of that relationship must be examined.

The typical life cycle for hedge funds has six basic steps (see **Figure 10.1**). The life cycle is important because the relationship between the key service providers and the objectives of the hedge fund vary at each stage.[1] From initial planning, fund formation, and establishment, to capital raising, growth, and ultimately termination, prime finance has a role in each step of a fund's life cycle. The selection of a prime broker is the first step and one of the most important decisions of a hedge fund and its manager.

An investor may not consider which stage a particular fund is in as they may have a short investment horizon, but the development and growth of funds are impacted by service providers, and particularly the choice of prime brokers. Prime brokers are increasingly active in start-up assistance, distribution, and providing marketing assistance.[2] The stage of a hedge fund has important implications for the services provided by prime brokers and executing brokers.

---

[1] Other service providers also make important contributions to the life cycle of hedge funds, including administrators, lawyers, accountants, auditors, tax advisers, compliance officers, and other consultants.

[2] See Jaeger, 2002, p. 228.

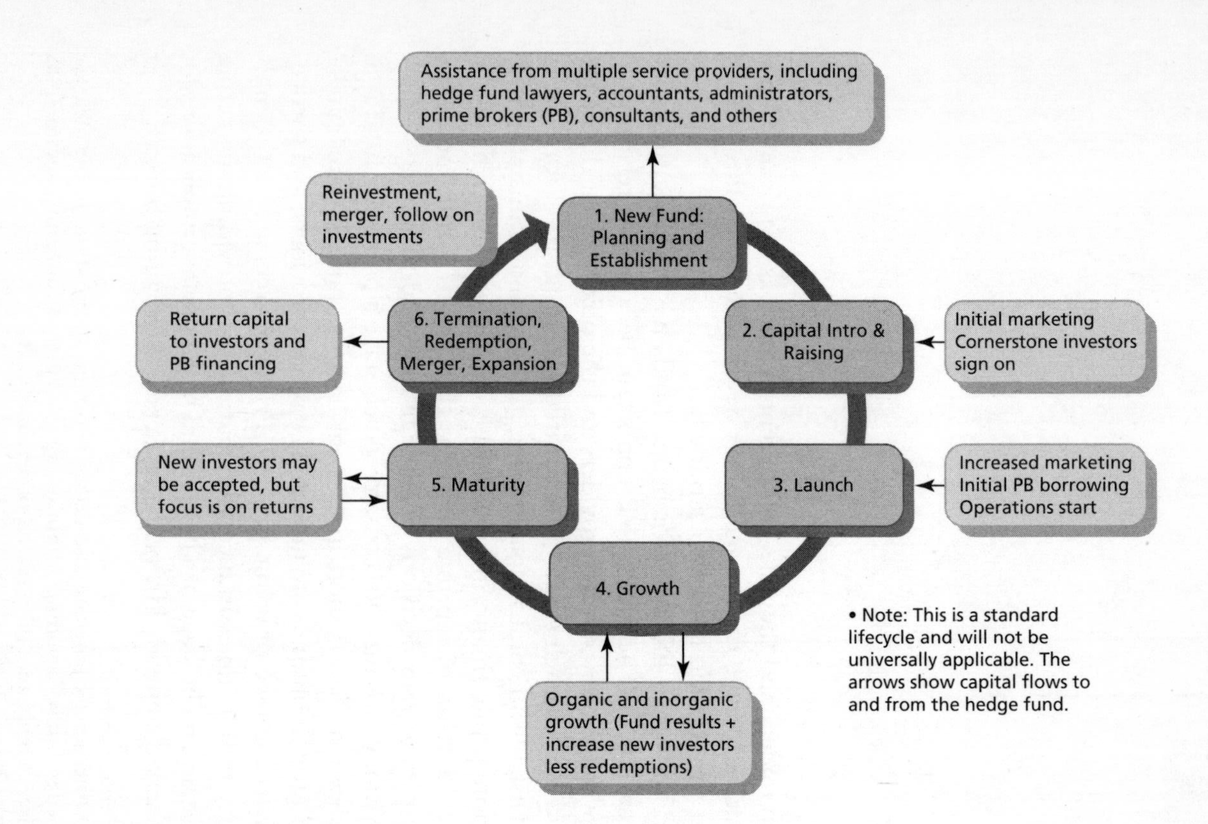

Figure 10.1 Life Cycle of a Hedge Fund

Planning and Establishment

The first step in the hedge fund life cycle is to develop both a plan of action for establishment and regulatory requirements of the hedge fund manager. The fund will need a strategy, brand, and team that is appealing to potential investors. Investors will require tax efficiency and some transparency on the strategies and investment history of the manager and structure and operations of the fund. A private placement memorandum (PPM) or offering memorandum will need to be prepared by the manager for the investors for marketing in the applicable jurisdictions. This is reviewed by legal counsel and subject to risk warnings and standard warnings regarding the limitations of the offering memorandum. The essential service providers for the hedge fund will need to be listed, including prime brokers, legal, accounting, administrators, auditors and other important service providers.

Legal counsel and tax advisers in all relevant jurisdictions will need to be convened to ensure that the fund is acceptable from a legal, compliance, and regulatory perspective for the hedge fund, the hedge fund manager, and anticipated investors. The hedge fund, including any feeder fund structure, will be addressed by local counsel in the relevant jurisdictions. Offshore hedge funds may be domiciled in a variety of jurisdictions, including the Cayman Islands, Bermuda, Barbados, the British Virgin Islands, Jersey, Guernsey, Mauritius, or others. The fund's legal counsel in the local jurisdiction of incorporation or establishment will address any necessary legal, compliance, or operational requirements in the local jurisdiction.

An early discussion with the prime broker can be a useful first step, as sales and marketing teams in prime finance are highly experienced with sophisticated fundraising and capital introduction. The prime finance sales team will be eager to plan marketing, distribution, and introductions for promising hedge fund managers. The prime broker may also have consulting services to assist the entrepreneur and capital introduction programs that may attract interest from investors.

Capital Introduction and Capital Raising

From the perspective of the fund, marketing the fund to potential investors is a particularly critical part of its development and establishment. The hedge fund management will need to review the marketing rules applicable to the investment and investors in the fund. Prime brokers will have considerable experience with marketing funds to investors. The prime broker will understand the marketability of a particular fund to investors and may assist with targeted suitable investors. Also, the prime broker may assist with finessing minimal regulatory requirements, assessing investor eligibility, fund domicile, disclosure obligations, and product regulation to providing a more sophisticated understanding of the market demand for particular alternative investments.[3]

Launch

Once an initial minimal level of capital, or a cornerstone investor, is secured, the operation of the hedge fund business begins. The launch phase requires a minimum target size of investor capital, but unlike closed funds, which are common to private equity funds, capital raising efforts for hedge funds may continue for the entire duration of the hedge fund's life.[4] Facilitating the launch of a hedge fund may require a variety of assistance from prime brokers ranging from selecting office space, trading platforms, risk management, information, research and other software.

Growth

Growth may derive from positive returns over time or additional investor capital. Many funds may grow and continue to market

[3] Marketing of hedge funds (particularly to retail customers) has been discussed and addressed in the United Kingdom by the FSA; see Kovas, 2005.

[4] From a practical perspective, finance entrepreneurs may not start a hedge fund without a minimum amount of capital to justify the infrastructure and other costs associated with running a hedge fund.

the hedge fund to new investors. Many institutional investors have investment due diligence programs that restrict investments with new managers and hedge funds. Once a successful track record has been demonstrated, funds may grow significantly from additional institutional asset allocation.

With successful returns and growing assets under management, a hedge fund will often outgrow limited office space, technologies, and human resources, and need to expand. This may involve seeking additional services from prime brokers to creating the hedge fund's own proprietary trading systems, while other strategies may involve changing or reprioritizing prime brokers to accommodate increasing trade volumes, financing, entering new markets, or other needs.

Maturity

Maturity may occur when a hedge fund has exploited the available market opportunities for their particular strategy. Sources of trading profits may change over time, and certain strategies may suffer from increased competition from other hedge funds or market participants. The prime finance area assists mature funds by providing access to additional financing, technology, or other resources to manage complex hedge fund organizations.

When the maximum hedge fund size relative to the fund is achieved, a fund may be closed to new investors. Mature funds may remain focused on core trading strategies or may branch out into new areas or markets. Successful hedge funds may create sub-funds with discrete mandates to tap into new trading strategies or sources of alpha.

Termination

Hedge funds terminate for a variety of reasons, both voluntary and involuntary. A hedge fund termination may be a voluntary decision by the hedge fund manager to discontinue operations if a strategy is unlikely to generate significant returns in the future, due to the departure or retirement of key personnel, poor performance, redemptions, mergers, or if the hedge fund defaults or blows up.

In almost all cases, the prime broker will be involved in the termination of the fund. However, there are obvious differences in the timing and planning for a hedge fund that is voluntarily winding down, compared to a hedge fund that has suddenly blown up. Hedge fund managers that have elected to terminate the fund, due to redemptions or a departing key man, may utilize risk management techniques to efficiently transition from the fund portfolio to cash for redemptions. For redemptions, transition management is an important consideration for the orderly liquidation of hedge funds. Large movements in illiquid positions may take a considerable period to transition without negatively impacting the fund's portfolio with market effects. As a result, the prime broker or related investment bank may have transition management services available to minimize the negative economic effects of large portfolio changes. The transition management service is common risk mitigation for a variety of hedge funds, asset managers, and pension funds that are transitioning a large portfolio. Hedge funds may take advantage of transition management services where prime brokers are associated with full-service investment banks to reduce the risk associated with transition or termination of the fund.

Prime finance assists in every aspect of the hedge fund life cycle. The hedge fund industry is currently changing in size and structure. The structuring and regulation of hedge funds and their interrelationships with prime brokers and investment banks are currently under increased regulatory and government scrutiny. The hedge fund industry, and hedge funds, have been quietly operating, but the international community is re-examining the relationship between investment banks, hedge funds, and the legal and regulatory framework of the international financial infrastructure. The complexity of legal and regulatory issues that prime brokers and hedge funds face currently are among the most complicated in finance. The anticipated changes to laws, regulations, and risk management regarding prime brokers and hedge funds promise an even more challenging future.

11 Risk Management

Historically, risk management has focused on risk on a firm-by-firm basis. In the international community, risk management is quickly moving to a more robust and holistic definition of risk.[1] After the cascade of collapsing financial firms, brokers, and banks commenced in 2008, systemic risk has been revealed. No longer is it sufficient to narrowly construe risk as it is limited to individual firms.

There are a variety of risks in the prime finance entities, the financial products they trade, and the relationships between the parties, including prime broker, hedge funds, managers, and investors. There are risks for each party, which may be partially measured on an individual firm basis. However, the more complex and less transparent risks are in the interlinkages between parties and when systems of leverage have been created. Further, some financial products lack transparency and have leverage financially engineered into them. Exotic OTC derivatives create a hybrid risk that combines individual firm risk with interlinkages and risk associated with the complex, misunderstood financial products.

---

[1] See the discussion of interlinkages in A World Economic Forum Report, in collaboration with Citigroup, Marsh & McLennan Companies (MMC), Swiss Re, Wharton School Risk Center, Zurich Financial Services, January 2009.

Hedge funds and prime brokers are subject to three primary risks: business, investment, and operational. However, these broad categories of risks are limited. Both hedge funds and prime brokers can and do blow up for a variety of reasons. It is critical to understand the respective risks to prime brokers and hedge funds, the financial products they trade, and the financial systems in which they operate. There are many risks in prime finance, including:

- Default risk
- Counterparty risk
- Currency risk
- National risk
- Liquidity risk
- Systemic risk
- Market risk
- Nonmarket risk
- Regulatory risk
- Legal risk
- Fraud risk
- Unknown risk

Prime Brokerage Risk

On an individual firm basis, the primary risks for the prime broker are the risks related to collateral and the positions for hedge funds, specifically the risk that the hedge fund's collateral will be insufficient to cover the total investment exposure. The posted collateral is the prime broker's primary concern. Provided that collateral is sufficient and monitored, well-managed prime brokers have limited exposure to hedge funds. Extreme scenarios may include the event that a hedge fund has built significant illiquid positions that are accepted as collateral or in the event that the entire market falls in a systemic crash. In these extraordinary scenarios, the prime broker may be exposed to proprietary risk.

Risk in Prime Finance

There are risks in the prime brokerage relationship for all parties involved. Hedge funds are concerned that they will be unable to access financing, invest in accordance with their strategies, have access to leverage, and borrow securities. Post-Lehman, hedge funds are acutely aware of the default risk posed by their prime broker and how liquidity and available leverage may change dramatically. The result has been a market shift to a multi-prime broker model away from reliance on just one prime broker.[2]

The prime broker has primary concerns over the revenues derived from servicing hedge funds and the concomitant risks or exposures posed by the hedge funds. The prime broker's primary risk is the risk that a fund will be unable to meet any margin calls with cash or securities in the event that collateral fails to cover exposures. In a highly leveraged scenario, the risk of the hedge fund is that the collateral pledged is lost,[3] leaving the prime broker exposed to principal risk for the hedge fund portfolio.

Individual investors, FoHF, institutional investors, and their advisers all should have concerns about prime finance, including transparency, accurate valuations, ancillary transactions, operational risks, redemptions, defaults, and counterparty risk. The key parties all have different concerns and interests in the prime finance world. The relationships of the past have changed significantly since 2008 with "unprecedented" market events.

---

[2] Terzo, 2008b.

[3] In certain cases, the hedge fund may lose all of its collateral held with the prime broker. In the event that the assets are not sufficient to cover the loans from the prime broker, an additional claim may be made against the hedge fund. This is a growing concern as more hedge funds allocate collateral to multiple prime brokers. Thus, a fund may blow up with one prime broker and still have significant assets with another prime broker. As such, the prime broker will make claims for restitution for losses suffered, although this may be subject to significant delays and difficulties owing to the nature and location of the hedge fund's assets.

Counterparty Risk

The collapse of Lehman Brothers has underlined the importance of assessing counterparty risk. It is a critical issue to which hedge funds are paying greater attention for obvious reasons. Many industry experts have noted that hedge funds have become more sophisticated in terms of discerning the layers in understanding counterparty risk.[4]

Risk mitigation and management techniques are now more commonly employed to reduce or diversify counterparty risk. The single prime broker model has been shaken, if not undermined entirely. Now hedge funds will take a diversified approach to prime brokers and examine the financial health of the individual prime broker. Limitations due to lack of transparency of a prime broker, which may be an arm of a large diversified investment bank, have caused hedge funds to pursue alternative structures. Parental, and in some cases independent, guarantees are sought to protect collateral assets. Some have moved to ultrasafe custodian banks to avoid the counterparty risk of prime brokers, content to significantly reduce leverage. However, even radical changes such as shifting collateral transfers to custodians may not protect hedge funds in all scenarios. In the event of systemic risk, or a total systemic failure, no bank or financial institution would be safe.

Systemic Risk

Systemic risk is a critical consideration. What are the risks that prime finance parties pose? There are a variety of hedge funds, investment funds, and sovereign wealth funds that may pose systemic risks to the international or U.S. financial system due to their immense size and the pervasive nature of their investments—these funds are thoroughly entrenched in the world financial structure. Their collapse could cause a domino-like effect, as we began to see in September 2008 with Lehman Brothers.

[4] David Gray, Head of Prime Services for UBS, Asia Pacific in Prime Broking Poll 2008.

Without immediate and extensive action by the United States and foreign governmental bodies, the systemic damage could have been irreparable.

A great deal of the policy to bail out broker-dealers is justified by concerns over the fear of systemic risk. But exactly what is systemic risk? The concept of systemic risk is nebulous at best and includes known and unknown risks, from both individual and collective factors.

There are fundamental tensions in the definition and assessment of systemic risk. The structure of the international markets breaks down into jurisdictions. Various English entities fall to the English regulator, the FSA or Bank of England, Treasury Department, or self-regulatory organizations (SROs) like ISLA or ICMA. U.S. entities fall to U.S. regulators: the SEC, Federal Reserve, CDIC, CFTC, Justice Department or state regulators, and SROs like NYSE, NASD, or FINRA. The relevant regulator only monitors aspects of those firms that relate to them. The inherent problem is that no single regulator has the power or jurisdiction to oversee an entire firm or the entire financial services market. Thus, the assessment of risk has been broken down to a discrete, activity-based, firm-by-firm risk analysis. Often multiple regulators and SROs examine small parts of gigantic organizations. The result is that they are unable to see the forest for the trees. This is a fundamentally incomplete approach to a comprehensive systemic risk management analysis. By specializing in our investment strategies, we have also mistakenly specialized our regulators along financial product lines (equities, bonds, commodities, foreign exchange) and thereby obscured the opportunity for analysis of the big picture, and hence the unheeded threat of systemic risk from their interlinkages.

Holistic Approaches to Risk

At present the question of which firms potentially pose systemic risk remains largely unknown. The unseen spectrum of banks, brokers, hedge funds, and investment funds cannot be monitored for interrelated systemic risks due to their lack of transparency and their international nature. Therefore, there remains an incomplete assessment of systemic risk that is limited to a small subset of the universe of domestic firms. The risk management paradigm must change to include individual firm assessments and their interrelationships to other national and international financial firms and markets.

The global financial crisis revealed, in its calamity, the glaring gaps and errors in risk management. Investment banks, for example, learned to their peril, that the underestimation of liquidity and access to financing had created severe systemic risk. Moreover, there was a significant lack of clarity about the extent of risk exposure in each part of the system, and financial firms and regulators were not proactive in seeking out that vital information. However, identifying and understating individual risks is not enough. Risk management must also account for market and firm interlinkages and remote but severe possibilities.[5]

While this paradigm shift to assess interlinkages is vital, it is necessarily incomplete. To understand the interlinkages there must be transparency in the universe of entities, banks, broker-dealers, hedge funds, and other investment funds that pose systemic risk. The necessary paradigm shift is to a holistic assessment of risk. By implementing transparency measures on some firms, our assessment of risk will be skewed to place a heavy regulatory burden on some domestic firms, while ignoring the others that are beyond the purview of domestic regulators. They are interconnected and inextricably intertwined problems. To address global risk in financial services in the future, each must be addressed including leverage, harnessing financial innovations, and transparency and monitoring of risk.

Banks and financial institutions are facing heightened domestic regulation; yet the international relationships are

[5] A World Economic Forum Report, in collaboration with Citigroup, Marsh & McLennan Companies (MMC), Swiss Re, Wharton School Risk Center, Zurich Financial Services, January 2009, p. 11.

largely ignored. This is the case even though actual risk to the United States may be greater from offshore entities than from the failure of a domestic U.S. broker, investment bank, or financial institution.

The public concern for domestic regulation is understandable, but necessarily incomplete. It misplaces attention from the "elephant in the room," which is the staggering size of unregulated entities, markets and jurisdictions, international sources of financing and competition, and unregulated innovations. The challenge for risk management in the future is to effectively manage risks without impeding domestic firms from competing in global markets.

12 Legal and Compliance Issues

The prime finance industry is regulated by a mosaic of international and U.S. regulations and laws. Hedge funds are commonly regarded as "light touch" onshore or unregulated offshore vehicles; however, indirectly there is a plethora of complex and interrelated regulations, laws, directives, and international conventions applicable to the prime broker, executing broker, and investment manager. Depending upon the trading strategies and securities traded, the relevant exchange, market, SRO, or regulator may also impact legal and compliance issues.

Prime Broker Regulation

There are multiple layers of legal and regulatory intervention that must be reviewed and their implications understood, particularly when trading is conducted, or collateral assets are held, outside the United States. The sphere of regulation includes international conventions, banking regulatory standards such as Basel I and II, regional EU directives, national or federal laws, provincial or state legislation and regulation, and the rules applicable to specific exchanges, clearing houses, and regulators. Within the United States, there are many different legal considerations (see **Figure 12.1**).

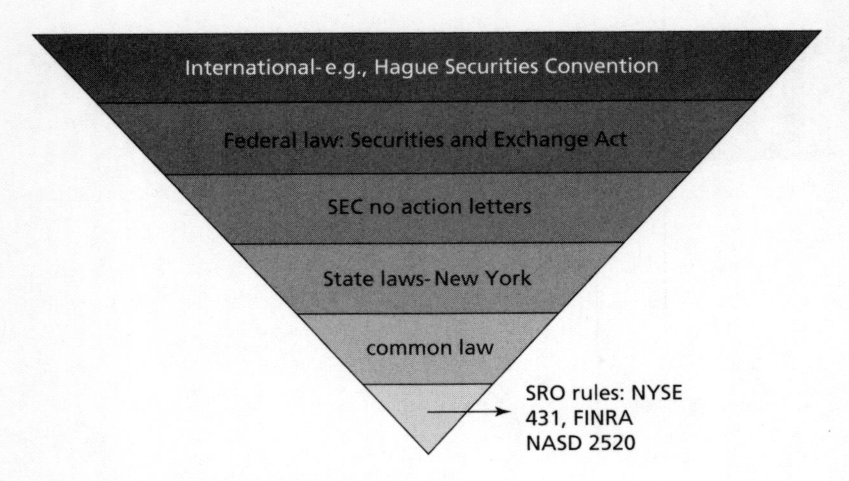

Figure 12.1 U.S. Regulation and Law

International treaties may play an important role in the future of prime finance, including the Convention on the Law Applicable to Certain Rights in Respect of Securities Held with an Intermediary (the "Hague Treaty") and various other European Community directives. However, at the international level there is a substantial divergence, and national standards largely prevail. International standards have not been accepted by most nations. In addition, there are important regional directives that impact aspects of international prime finance, such as the European Community directives. The prime broker and executing brokers are subject to complex and sometimes competing legal and regulatory requirements.

Broker-Dealers

There are a variety of complex regulations that apply to U.S. broker-dealers and to foreign broker-dealers. The major jurisdictions to consider are the onshore or U.S.-based firms, and the offshore entities that provide international prime brokerage services.

There are detailed bank regulations, securities regulations, and laws applicable to investment banks that act as broker-dealers.

The bank regulatory issues and capital requirements are particularly complex for U.S. broker-dealers related to a bank holding company.[1] The reason for the complexity of the regulation onshore is related to the origins of the securities legislation that stemmed from the market crashes of the Great Depression. However, many of the securities laws and regulations were operating in a much different financial world. Often the most important sources of U.S. securities law are currently derived from relevant no action letters issued by the SEC. In certain cases, innovations were developed in order to facilitate operational efficiency, as was the case with the emergence of the prime brokerage.

The First Prime Brokerage

The first U.S. prime brokerage was created as a consequence of the first hedge fund.[2] The development by Alfred Winslow Jones resulted in his broker, Neuberger Berman, structuring arrangements to allow for margin lending and consolidated accounts. The first prime broker arrangements were in place in the early 1950s. The industry developed quietly in parallel to the development of hedge funds. Prime brokerage was not officially addressed by U.S. regulators until 1994.

U.S. Prime Brokerage Model

The structure of the prime broker market developed informally in the United States. However, by 1994 it was directly addressed and shaped by the SEC no action letter issued by the Division of Market Regulation (1994 Letter).[3] The 1994 Letter prescribed the prime broker relationship and stated that the SEC would not recommend action under certain securities laws

[1] See a detailed examination of the U.S. Broker-Dealer regulations in Lofchie, 2005.

[2] Dailey, 1995.

[3] Securities Industry Association Prime Broker Committee, SEC No Action Letter (January 25, 1994). Subsequent letters extended the duration of the 1994 letter and it was made permanent on December 31, 1997.

provided the business was conducted in accordance with the 1994 Letter.[4]

1994 No Action Letter

The 1994 Letter provided that there are three critical parties in the prime brokerage system: clients, prime brokers, and executing brokers. Prime brokerage is a system developed by full-service firms to facilitate the clearance and settlement of securities trades for both retail and institutional investors that are active market participants. The prime broker clears, settles, and finances the trades that are executed by the executing broker. A single legal entity may act as both executing broker and prime broker. However, these two functions are segregated within investment banks to avoid conflicts of interest.

The primary obligation of the hedge fund client is to maintain collateral to satisfy its borrowing obligations. The client must maintain sufficient funds in a securities account with the prime broker. The orders that the client places with the executing broker are effected through an account in the name of the prime broker for the benefit of the client.

The client places a trade order with the executing broker and notifies the prime broker of the trade. The trade is then recorded in the cash or margin account with the prime broker. The prime broker executes and records the transaction in the appropriate account with the executing broker. The prime broker confirms the transaction with the executing broker and notifies the customer. The client's account with the prime broker is computed with applicable credit and Regulation T amounts. The trade then matches, clears, and settles in normal fashion. The prime broker regularly reports to the customer on at least a monthly basis. In practice this reporting is performed routinely as and when required by the hedge fund.

[4] The applicable legislation included sections 7, 10, 11(d), 15(c)(3) and 17 of the Securities and Exchange Act (Exchange Act), and Rules 10a-1, 10b-10, 11d1-1, 15c3-1 and 15c3-3 under the Exchange Act to prime broker arrangements.

PRIME BROKER BASIC STEPS

1. Collateral held with PB
2. Client trades with EB
3. EB effects trade with PB from account for benefits of client
4. EB advises PB of trade
5. Trades recorded in account of PB for client
6. PB records transaction in account with EB
7. PB confirms with client, complies with reg. requirements (Reg. T)
8. EB confirms with PB, then trade clears, settles in normal course
9. PB issues statement of account to customer on at least monthly basis

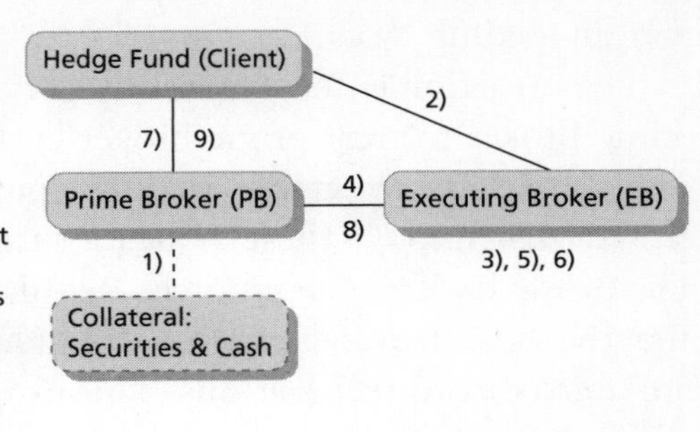

Figure 12.2 U.S. Prime Broker Mechanics

In addition to structuring business to comply with the 1994 no action letter, there are a variety of regulatory issues that the prime broker and executing broker need to address. The most important for many are the rules on margin lending. The margin rules are set by the Board of Governors of the Federal Reserve System.[5]

U.S. Regulation T Financing

In general, Regulation T governs the purchase of securities by a broker-dealer's customer by either a cash account or margin account. The initial margin is set at 50 percent, which drops to 25 percent thereafter.

The microstructure of this type of arrangement needs to be examined carefully. The initial transaction is between the client and the executing broker. The subsequent transfer is actually between the prime broker and the executing broker. It appears that, in effect, the executing broker has a relationship with the client and is extending margin loans for the purchase

[5] The authority for this sits in Section 7 of the Securities and Exchange Act ("Exchange Act").

of securities. This would obligate the executing broker to follow margin lending rules.

The no action letter structure allows the executing broker and prime broker to treat prime broker customer accounts as if they were broker-dealer credit accounts pursuant to Regulation T, rather than impose these obligations on the executing broker. The prime broker then enforces Regulation T against the client, and the broker-dealer credit account is used by the executing broker to record transactions. This position simplifies the complicated financing of trades that appeared to be between the executing broker and client, contrary to regulation. The 1994 no action letter resolved this issue. In effect, the executing broker does not have to collect margin in connection with trades, which reduces risk and increases operational efficiency. There are several conditions required in order to meet the Exchange Act and Regulation T requirements.[6]

There are restrictions on issuing credit while part of a selling syndicate, which entails a thirty-day delay.[7] The issuing securities confirmations are required by Rule 10b-10 of the Exchange Act. In practice, the customer makes the order through the executing broker, which sends a confirmation of trade to the prime broker. The prime broker then arranges for settlement with the executing broker.[8]

Self-Regulatory Organizations (SROs)

Other rules and regulations include those derived from important self-regulatory organizations. There are several critical SROs in the United States. Certain SROs have regulations that expand upon SEC regulation of the margin requirement and limits, including FINRA and the NASD.[9] Also, certain exchanges provide

[6] For further explanation see McMillan & Bergmann, 2007.

[7] See s.11(d)(1) of the Exchange Act.

[8] 17 CFR § 240.10a-1(a).

[9] FINRA has detailed margin and maintenance margin requirements in NASD 2520 (The National Association of Securities Dealers).

rules and regulations for members, such as the NYSE[10] and the CFTC. These additional margin rules impact on the various broker-dealers that are members.

SROs also have an important application to the resolution of disputes between prime brokers and clients. FINRA provides for arbitration of disputes between clients and prime brokers. There is the potential for hedge funds to bifurcate proceedings in both court and arbitration. In a recent case, the courts have granted injunctive relief where both court proceedings and arbitration were commenced.[11] In cases where arbitration has been commenced by SROs, courts have demonstrated deference to arbitral decisions.[12]

State versus Federal Laws

In the United States, securities have dual regulations with overarching federal regulations and limited state laws and regulations. State laws and regulations may be important for U.S.–based prime brokers.[13] Various applicable state laws may impact prime finance and related securities litigation. The Securities Litigation Uniform Standards Act, 1998 (SLUSA) was designed to replace the shortcomings of the Private Securities Litigation Reform Act of 1995 and to standardize litigation for nationally traded securities to avoid local rules creating bespoke state-by-state

[10] The NYSE has Rule 431, which impacts margin maintenance for equity futures to parallel rules of the CFTC commodity futures.

[11] Citigroup Global Markets Inc. v. VCG Special Opportunities Master Fund Limited f/k/a CDO Plus Master Fund Limited, 2008.

[12] Wedbush Morgan Securities, Inc. v. Robert W. Baird & Co., 2004.

[13] There are a variety of prime broker regulations, subject to specific state laws. However, New York remains the dominant state for prime brokerage domestically and often internationally. The prime brokerage agreement may require clients to waive rights under state legislation to avoid bifurcating legal processes and creating ambiguity in the relationship. For example, it is common for hedge fund clients of broker-dealers to waive rights under the New York Uniform Commercial Code.

litigation. Certain states have individual blue sky laws that should be noted by both managers and prime brokers.[14]

Investors who attempt to circumvent the federal securities regime to seek remedies from more favorable state courts have faced considerable resistance. In the case of *Anderson v. Merrill Lynch Pierce Fenner & Smith, Inc.*, the investors in a defunct New Mexico company, Solv-Ex, attempted to litigate when the majority shareholder of Solv-Ex started a margin account with a prime broker. The collateral posted was composed of Solv-Ex shares. The investor failed to meet a margin call on his account, which resulted in the prime broker liquidating a significant amount of Solv-Ex shares to cover the exposure. Not surprisingly, the exigent liquidation resulted in a dramatic reduction of the collateral securities value. The preclusion of this claim under the SLUSA resulted in the dismissal of the entire claim.[15] Similar unsuccessful attempts by plaintiffs to litigate claims against prime brokers have been made in state courts where federal courts have denied remedies.[16]

Common Law

The Common Law is an important source of law for both domestic and international prime brokers. The prime broker industry has seen growing emphasis and continued efforts by plaintiffs to develop and expand common law liability. The common causes

[14] There are a variety of states that have enacted important state securities laws. However, under New York law, specifically the Martin Act, N.Y. Gen. Bus. Law § 352, there is no implied private right of action for securities fraud. Under the Martin Act, the State Attorney General possesses the exclusive power to regulate the sale of securities. By contrast, for a review of complex transactions under Texas long arm statute, see Delta Products Company et al. v. Credit Commercial de France et al., 2004.

[15] The leading case was decided by the U.S. Supreme Court in Merrill Lynch, Pierce, Fenner & Smith Inc. v. Dabit, 2006.

[16] See current California litigation against the largest prime brokers in Overstock.com, Inc. et al. v. Morgan Stanley & Co., Inc. et al., 2007. While the Overstock.com case has not been resolved, another California case including claims by investors against a prime broker was reportedly resolved prior to an appeal for $2 million in Sam Bronstein et al. v. Crowell, Weedon & Co. et al., 2007.

of action against prime brokers include negligence, fraud, aiding and abetting fraud, breach of fiduciary duty, and aiding and abetting breach of fiduciary duty. Where investors have sought recovery for manager fraud against prime brokers, there have been significant barriers to recovery.[17] Recent cases, where investors have combined actions against other services providers, particularly administrators, have been more successful.[18]

Prime brokers have been accused of fraud, breach of fiduciary duty, and other common law and equitable claims. The number of such claims are increasing, but many clients have found such claims increasingly difficult to prosecute. With respect to fraud, the requisite *scienter*, or intent to defraud, has been difficult to establish. The required elements include knowledge, intent to defraud, and reasonable reliance by the plaintiff. The related claims of aiding and abetting fraud or breach of fiduciary duty have similarly been difficult to establish.[19]

The requisite knowledge of wrongdoing by a hedge fund or its investors is often vigorously disputed by prime brokers. When the hedge fund utilizes more than one prime broker, it has proven particularly challenging to establish the prime broker's knowledge.[20] Thus, the lack of transparency for prime brokers into the full portfolio of hedge funds has shielded them from certain liabilities, where knowledge of a hedge fund's misconduct cannot be imputed. Ironically, the risk diversification techniques of hedge funds, to set up multiple prime brokers, may also reduce potential

[17] The Court of Appeal of California, Second Appellate, District Two rejected claims of conspiracy between a local broker-dealer and a stockbroker to impugn liability to a prime broker. See Sam Bronstein et al. v. Crowell, Weedon & Co. et al., 2007.

[18] See The Pension Committee of the University of Montreal, et al. v. Banc of America Securities, LLC and Citco Fund Services (Curacao) N.V. et al., 2009.

[19] See the case of John Rusnak, a foreign exchange trader, who orchestrated a rogue-trading scheme that caused losses of approximately $691 million; Allied Irish Banks, P.L.C. v. Bank of America, N.A. and Citibank N.A., 2006 and Allied Irish Banks, P.L.C. v. Bank of America, N.A. and Citibank N.A., 2007.

[20] In re Manhattan Investment Fund Ltd. et al. v. Bear Stearns Securities Corp., 2007.

liability for prime brokers. Where knowledge of the wrongful trading or fraud is required to attribute liability to the prime broker, the prime broker's incomplete view into the hedge fund's portfolio may protect the prime broker. This risk mitigation technique may result in more prime brokers relying on their own ignorance, or willful blindness to the actions of hedge fund clients. However, a prime broker's liability may be distinguished from other service providers. For example, a recent focus on the role of the administrator and auditors has increased attention to liability for service providers. The administrator normally takes a broad view of the hedge fund's portfolio and trading activities. Accordingly, administrators may not escape liability for complicity in fraud or clear misrepresentations of a hedge fund's performance.[21]

U.S. Anti-Money Laundering

The U.S. Anti-Money Laundering provisions are set by a number of entities, regulators, and SROs. The federal government has broad restrictions on domestic and foreign broker-dealers and the entities that they may face in transactions, including AML and know-your-client requirements.[22] International governmental bodies such as the Financial Action Task Force also attempt to restrict money laundering. There are a limited number of participants in these organizations, and major offshore jurisdictions are not parties to it. The most significant regulations on AML, KYC, and money laundering stem from domestic U.S. nongovernmental organizations. FINRA is a prominent and important nongovernmental regulator with broad powers and rules for

[21] See Allied Irish Banks, P.L.C. v. Bank of America, N.A. and Citibank N.A., 2006 and Allied Irish Banks, P.L.C. v. Bank of America, N.A. and Citibank N.A., 2007.

[22] The U.S. Department of Treasury and the Office of Foreign Assets Control (OFAC) publish the Special Designated Nations List, which restricts international trade with these nations and related investment entities. See www .ustreas.gov/office/enforcement/ofac/index.shtml. Also, the USA PATRIOT Act provides for requirements related to avoidance of financing terrorism.

member firms to follow.[23] FINRA will likely play an increasingly important role in the new regime.

The typical hedge fund vehicle is located offshore in a tax haven (e.g., Cayman Islands) and is subject to nominal regulatory oversight and minimal AML and KYC requirements. The complexity of applicable law and regulation comes from the registration of the manager, the location of the prime broker, the administrator, and the contractual choice of law and jurisdiction of courts, SROs, and the relevant exchanges and clearing houses. Moving to the international market largely removes restrictions, but the complexity of operations, risks, and due diligence required expands exponentially.

International Prime Brokerage

There are important differences between the international and U.S. prime broker models. The capital requirements and regulations for investors, prime brokers, and executing brokers are different depending upon the respective regulators. Similarly, the clearing, settlement, and margining are different and more complex and varied in the international model. The clearing and settlement depend upon the regulations in place in the various markets and clearing houses. This may impact and extend the duration between trade, clearing, and settlement and associated risks. The U.S. model runs on a standard timetable with consistent trade, clearing, and settlement rules and timelines. In international or emerging markets there are massive discrepancies in market practices. As such, it is critical for hedge funds to understand the securities, idiosyncrasies, and infrastructure of the markets to have a complete view of legal, risk and compliance issues.

One of the fundamental issues for prime finance is which legal regime governs how an intermediary's securities, such as those of a prime broker, are held. There is broad difference between U.S. domestic markets, international conventions, and EU directives.

---

[23] For more information see www.finra.org.

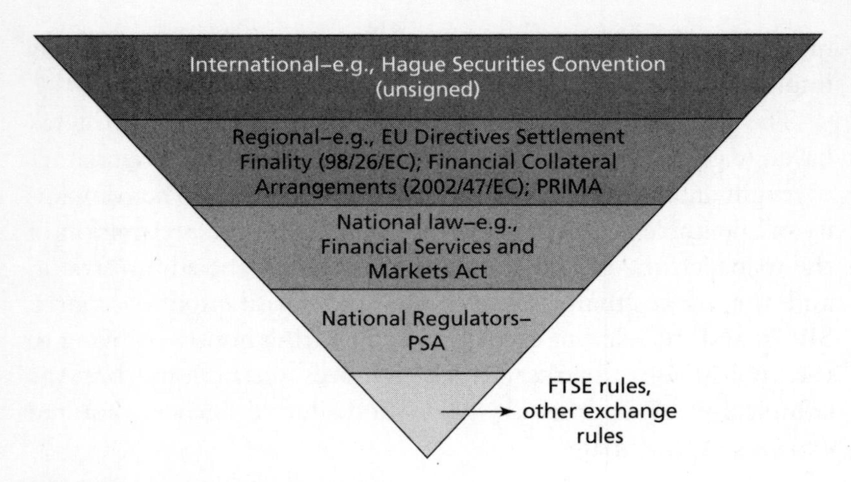

Figure 12.3 EU Regulation and Law

The U.S. domestic market and international treaties provide for the account agreement to determine the relevant jurisdiction. However, the EU region has a complex set of different national laws and overarching regional directives (see **Figure 12.3**).

Hague Securities Convention

The Hague Convention provides for a conflict of law regime applicable to securities holdings.[24] The relevant law and jurisdiction is named in the account agreement with the relevant intermediary. This differs considerably with the current European Community regime, which provides that the law applicable to securities holdings is determined by the location of the relevant account.[25]

---

[24] The limitations of the international treaty lie in its limited acceptance by only two nations. The United States and Switzerland have signed the Hague Securities Treaty.

[25] For more detail, see Article 9(2) of Directive 98/26/EC of the European Parliament and of the Council of 19 May 1998 on settlement finality in payment and securities settlement systems, and see Article 24 of the Directive 2001/24/EC of the European Parliament and of the Council of 4 April 2001 on the reorganization and winding up of credit institutions, and Article 9(1) of Directive 2002/47/EC regarding financial collateral arrangements.

In the European Community, there are a variety of national and regional directives that impact prime finance, particularly settlement and securities holdings by intermediaries, including prime brokers. Directive 98/26/EC on Settlement Finality in Payment and Securities Settlement Systems (Settlement Finality Directive),[26] Directive 2002/47/EC on Financial Collateral Arrangements (Financial Collateral Directive), and Directive 2001/24/EC on the winding up of credit institutions are the three main European Community instruments in the area of clearing and settlement and financial collateral. One of the most important of the directives for prime finance is the Settlement Finality Directive (SFD). The SFD was adopted in May 1998 to reduce the systemic risk associated with participants in payment and securities settlement systems.

PRIMA Rule

In the European Community, the effective rule is the "PRIMA Rule." Article 9 of the SFD provides that:

> Any question with respect to any of the matters specified in paragraph 2 arising in relation to book entry securities collateral shall be governed by the law of the country in which the relevant account is maintained. The reference to the law of a country is a reference to its domestic law, disregarding any rule under which, in deciding the relevant question, reference should be made to the law of another country.

The PRIMA Rule dictates that the applicable law for securities is derived from the location where the relevant account is maintained. The SFD intended to respect the different financial and legal regimes in the EU (as both Common Law and Civil Code govern in different regions) rather than harmonize and clarify the applicable law. This creates significant confusion and legal

[26] Recent challenges in the form of judicial review of the Financial Collateral Directive were denied; see R. (on the application of Cukurova Finance International Ltd. and another) v. HM Treasury, 2008.

uncertainty in the event of an international insolvency, which was the case with Lehman Brothers. The legal regime that applies to the securities will need to be identified, and the local law will dictate the court and legal regime for allocation of collateral. This may protract bankruptcy administration significantly and creates the strange scenario of litigation in unanticipated jurisdictions as a result of allocation to certain booking accounts. Securities are largely indirectly held, and the only indication that securities are held in one account or another may be a computerized book entry. There is growing justification to support broad and rapid adoption of the Hague Convention. The Hague Convention would reduce unnecessary legal uncertainty, risk and facilitate more open and transparent international securities markets. Other European community directives play a significant role in prime finance.

Markets in Financial Instruments Directive

The Markets in Financial Instruments Directive (MiFID) has further reduced barriers within the EU and has harmonized standards applicable to financial services for clients.[27] This directive provides for common standards among EU countries for financial services. MiFID has an impact on prime brokers and executing brokers. It is notable in execution and the requirement for "best execution," that is legally required for professional clients, including hedge funds.[28]

However, there is considerable difference between the Hague Convention and European Community directives. The Hague Convention attempts to provide for increased certainty over the law applicable to clearance, settlement, and secured credit transactions that cross national borders. The Hague Convention addresses applicable law, not substantive law to be applied. The

[27] The requirements under MiFID to provide for "best execution" which is not optional for professional clients.

[28] MiFID provides for categorization of clients, which includes 1) Eligible Counterparties, 2) Professional Clients, and 3) Retail Clients.

fundamental proposition is that the PRIMA Rule should be modified to allow that the law applicable to holdings of securities is the one named in the account agreement with the relevant intermediary. The parties would be able to dictate the applicable law irrespective of where certain securities may be held. In the event of insolvency, collateral assets may be transferred and held in a variety of other jurisdictions for commercial reasons. The result is a great deal of ambiguity and legal uncertainty over the applicable law to the securities transaction that may be held in the jurisdiction.

The Hague Convention was signed by the United States and Switzerland on July 5, 2006. Prior to the financial crisis, none of the European Community nations signed the Hague Convention, leaving substantial ambiguity over the governing law for securities settlement within the European Community. The G-30 has recommended that the Hague Convention be ratified as quickly as possible by as many nations as possible. However, the broad range of different holding systems and applicable legal regimes has created significant legal risk in international transactions.

Similarly, there are examples of operational and legal risk where investors in emerging markets have been surprised by closing markets and consequent delays in trading, clearing, and settlement with local executing brokers. The variety of different regulations, settlement systems, and legal regimes in place when moving to the international model impacts the prime broker, executing broker, and hedge funds.

The Regulatory Concerns

It has become apparent that the regulation of prime brokers, executing brokers, and their hedge fund clients will come under increasing regulatory scrutiny in the United States and internationally.[29] Former Federal Reserve Chairman Paul Volcker said,

[29] Calls for additional comprehensive regulation are continuing. Paul Volcker, who is chairman of the Trustees of the G-30, has called for greater financial services regulation (Fitzgerald, 2009).

"Our system is broken and it requires a thorough-going repair."[30] Volcker characterized the banking system using "a four-letter word: It's a mess."[31] The financial system failed on many levels. The financial system allowed irresponsible leverage to increase to dangerous levels for important firms and banks. The infrastructure of unregulated financial and insurance products resulted in cascading defaults. Like dominos, the defaults moved from insurance companies, mortgage companies, and investment banks, to hedge funds and other investment funds, to semigovernmental organizations, and ultimately to governments around the globe. The spiraling failures of the international financial system during the financial crisis were heading towards systemic liquidation. Systemic international failure was averted only by massive and repeated bailouts by the United States and governments around the world.

There are three broad concerns that regulators and governments now agree must be addressed: investor protection, market abuse prevention, and systemic risk.

Protecting Investors

The SEC and other regulators have repeatedly indicated their intention to protect small investors from the dangers of opaque hedge funds. But given that investors in hedge funds are rarely, if ever, small retail investors, the justification for additional regulation on the basis of investor protection seems hollow and misdirected. The typical investor in hedge funds or alternative investment vehicles is an institutional investor with significant expertise, assets, and income. Most alternative investments restrict small investors by setting minimal investor requirements. Such investors have the resources to acquire expert advice on their investments, or the skills, knowledge and abilities to conduct their own due diligence. However, the spectacular reverses of publicly traded banks, insurance companies, and financial firms

[30] Fitzgerald, 2009.
[31] Fitzgerald, 2009.

have impacted the investment portfolios of many individual investors. What should be of concern to the SEC, SROs, and other government regulators are the publicly traded financial institutions in which small investors actually invest their savings. Ultimately, hedge fund regulation is not needed to protect Main Street investors. Additional due diligence, transparency, and oversight on highly levered and opaque publicly traded financial institutions may more effectively protect vulnerable retail investors.

At present, this is by far the least important prerogative for prime finance and hedge funds.

Preventing Market Abuse

The second concern for regulators is market abuse. Market abuses may range from regulatory transgressions to criminal activities such as market manipulations (including pump-and-dump strategies or spreading false rumors of bankruptcy to create short pressure on a particular stock) and insider trading.

The restrictions on short-selling financial stocks stand as a flawed attempt by regulators to stop perceived market abuses. The stocks of financial institutions were under serious downward pressure from short sellers. To save the financial world, the United States initiated a short-selling ban on 900 securities, 799 of which were financial stocks. Many hedge funds and other investors had to adjust their trading strategies quickly when the second leg of many trades became illegal.[32] On September 17, 2008, Christopher Cox, the then SEC chairman, stated that the U.S. regulator was committed to "using every weapon in its arsenal to combat market manipulation that threatens investors and capital markets."[33] What remains unclear is who the enemy was and what the market manipulation actually consisted of. The markets and financial stocks were dropping in the shadow of Lehman Brothers' failure. But artificially propping them up with a crude short-selling ban was ill-considered and ultimately did

[32] Strasburg & Karmin, 2008.
[33] Statement of SEC Chairman, Christopher Cox, 2008.

not have the desired effect. In fact, a study of the short-selling ban found no strong evidence that the imposition of restrictions on short selling in the United Kingdom or elsewhere changed the behaviors of stock returns. Stocks subject to the restrictions behaved very similarly both to how they behaved before the imposition of restrictions and to how stocks not subject to the restrictions behaved.[34] The short-selling ban did not protect investors or prevent the financial stocks from falling. The SEC was focused on punishing the wrongdoers, but it failed because the financial crisis was not the result of market manipulation or unseen enemies at the gate. The crisis that resulted in financial securities depreciating from an accurate assessment of their value was precipitated by a broker-dealer failure, which created a cascade of defaults, and was fueled by fear and panic-stricken investors. The dramatic regulatory moves further crystallized already illiquid markets rather than lubricating them with much needed liquidity.

The intrusive regulatory measures did have an effect on market participants, as more and more investors were increasingly concerned about arbitrary market intervention by various regulators and governments. One hedge fund manager lamented with respect to the short-selling restrictions, "markets cannot withstand for long constantly changing rules in which each new regulation is announced in the middle of the night without any public comment or participation."[35] To establish efficient financial markets, the rules should be transparent, unambiguous, and predictable. The imposition of short-selling bans resulted in substantial confusion, dried up remaining liquidity, and had minimal if any benefits to financial firms struggling to finance themselves.[36] Also, the bans were largely poorly designed and

[34] For more details see Marsh & Neimer, 2008.

[35] Investment manager Jim Chanos in Chung, Mackintosh, & Sender, 2008.

[36] See the impact on hedge funds (Chung, Mackintosh, & Sender, 2008), a review of the market implications for the short bans and a statistical analysis of the short selling ban in Marsh & Neimer, 2008, and the unanticipated implications on the profitability of investment banks, Mackintosh, 2008.

failed to target alternative mechanisms (such as derivatives) for creating short positions.

As a consequence of one regulator moving to protect national financial stocks, many other national, regional, and state regulators initiated their own short-selling restrictions. Each regulator had a different position and sought to protect their particular interests and financial stocks. Although the bans were immediate and the markets reacted quickly, they lacked specific direction in many cases and had the added problem of preventing legitimate financing and trading strategies.[37] This had a catastrophic effect on proper and legitimate financing for certain hedge funds, prime brokers, and investment banks[38] and, in turn, further weakened the positions of the financial firms by not allowing certain trades; stock lending, financing (repo) and prime broker revenues all suffered. Ultimately, the weapons used to combat short pressure were turned against the firms that they sought to protect. The short bans needed to be expanded repeatedly as short pressure moved to other financial firms with exposure to the financial system and financing problems. Dramatic policy moves, with minimal industry input, failed to prevent the short pressure and increased more serious threats related to illiquidity and availability of financing for the financial firms.

Addressing Systemic Risk

The final and most critical factor in regulation for prime finance and hedge funds is the impact on systemic risk. Why is systemic risk important? When a prime broker fails, it has far reaching implications for many other entities and may pose risks to the underlying financial system. When a large hedge fund fails or a series of hedge funds fail, the theoretical implications may be extremely negative for the financial system. If the hedge fund is

[37] Mehta, 2008.

[38] For example, consider the mayhem that ensued for convertible arbitrage funds, which typically buy convertible bonds and short common equities, after the short selling ban. (See Vickers & Boyd, 2008.)

large enough, the blow-up may potentially pose systemic risk.[39] The Lehman Brothers bankruptcy had an unanticipated effect on the money market funds, hedge funds, investment banks, and derivative counterparties. The major counterparties to credit default swaps were severely impacted by Lehman's bankruptcy, which created large exposures.[40]

The consequences of Lehman Brothers' bankruptcy led governments to provide guarantees for banks to direct bailout funds, preferred and common equity investments and to provide access to indirect financing sources. The derivatives exposures for many financial institutions were massive and threatened to bankrupt major firms and banks. The exposures to money market mutual funds created a run on the funds which, if liquidated, would have seized liquidity further and dumped billions of short-term debt onto the international market at discount prices. The liquidation of many major hedge funds caught many sophisticated hedge funds, and their investors, off guard. The dramatic reduction in financing availability and the contraction of the repo and stock loan transactions, restricted normal financing. In general, the bankruptcy of a prime broker had massive, unanticipated effects that threatened to undermine the entire U.S. and international financial system.

Governments stepped in to avoid further prime broker and investment bank bankruptcies.[41] The totality of the interrelations and contracts between the prime brokers was not transparent or understood. The remaining major broker-dealers could not be allowed to fail because the implications were massive, broad,

---

[39] The concern for systemic risk was the thinking behind the LTCM bailout, which deferred systemic risk by passing the positions of the infamous hedge fund to the larger investment banks for $350 million each. See the great story of the rise and fall of Long-Term Capital Management in Lowenstein, 2002.

[40] AIG, Goldman Sachs, Morgan Stanley, and other major financial institutions were severely impacted by the Lehman bankruptcy.

[41] The United States, United Kingdom, Ireland, Germany, France, Belgium, the Netherlands, and other EU countries, Russia, and other countries provided both direct and indirect financing to their respective national financial firms to stabilize the financial system.

and largely unknown. If Lehman Brothers could precipitate such catastrophic effects, what would happen if an elite prime broker failed? The implications were unimaginable and the potential damages to the financial system terrible.

Leverage and Interconnections

Excessive leverage and cheap lending spawned from a long-standing government policy of low interest rates is one key factor in the systemic risk posed by prime brokers and the larger bank holding companies.[42] Prime finance involves provisions of leverage to hedge funds. The leverage offered to hedge funds may be regulated, as in the United States, or it may be left to the prime broker and hedge fund to decide acceptable levels of risk, leverage, and assessments of liquidity of the underlying portfolio in the international markets. The leverage for hedge funds ranges from modest or minimal leverage to extraordinary levels. Recent events have seen massive reductions in the availability and desire for leverage.[43] The international and U.S. prime finance markets work together as collateral, and funds flow internationally, allowing more aggressive leverage.

The impact of prime finance is not limited to securities markets alone. By combining services and asset classes, the old market distinctions between debt and equity securities, commodities, foreign exchange, and derivatives have collapsed. Whereas previously, the prime broker dealt exclusively with equities or debt products, there is a concerted industry move to provide hedge funds with a one-stop shop for all product classes. Thus, the prime broker is the conduit through which all banks, brokers, securities dealers, pension funds, mutual funds, and hedge funds pass. Efficient lending and access have been the paramount concerns. However, risk management is now at the forefront of investment managers and prime brokers concerns. The cross-product offering

---

[42] See Lord Turner in Turner, 2009 for conclusions as to the causes of the financial crisis.

[43] Terzo, 2008a.

and netting and set-off of the various areas of the prime finance theoretically reduces the cumulative risks within organizations. The effective leverage and liquidity of a complex portfolio may not be calculated accurately with standard models. Thus the development of netting and set-off may not mitigate risks in extreme markets but may give a false indication of risk between organizations.

Regulators need to balance the competing pressures in forging the new international financial system. Investor protections and methods of curbing market abuse may be implemented. But these provisions must be carefully assessed to avoid unintended negative consequences to the competitiveness of domestic financial firms and markets. The most daunting task will be to monitor and assess systemic risk in a financial world of large international parties whose strategies are necessarily private and lack public transparency without impacting domestic competitiveness in international markets.

13 What the Future Holds

The future for prime finance, hedge funds, and broker-dealers is uncertain. The current market transition and dislocation for prime finance has been profound and protracted. There is a global economic downturn coupled with near systemic failures in the financial system. But for massive multitrillion-dollar U.S. and international government bailouts, the international financial system faced systemic collapse and liquidation. The balance of power has shifted decidedly from industry to government. Now governments around the globe, particularly the G-20, are preparing regulations to prevent a recurrence. In addition, issues surrounding the gigantic OTC derivatives market and the international reserve currency loom in the background like the sword of Damocles. The size and depth of the problems for prime brokers, hedge funds, banks, and the larger financial industry are unprecedented. However, we have faced these challenges before.

September 15th is an important historic date. On September 15, legendary hedge fund manager George Soros was summoned before the U.S. House of Representatives Committee on Banking and Financial Services to explain the situation:

> This hearing is very timely because the global capitalist system which has been responsible for the remarkable

> prosperity of this country in the last decade is coming apart at the seams. The current decline in the U.S. stock market is only a symptom, and a belated symptom at that, of the more profound problems that are affecting the world economy.[1]

Soros continued to describe the dangers to the world economy: the defaulting international counterparties and an irresponsible overleveraged banking system that resulted in severe contractions in liquidity. Soros explained:

> These events led most market participants to reduce their exposure all round. Banks are frantically trying to limit their exposure, deleverage and reduce risk. Bank stocks have plummeted. A global credit crunch is in the making. It is already restricting the flow of funds to the periphery, but it has also begun to affect the availability of credit in the domestic economy . . .[2]

Furthermore, he pointed out the complexity of intertwined issues.[3] The complicated off-sheet OTC derivative trades formed a "daisy chain with many intermediaries and each intermediary has an obligation to his counterparties without knowing who else is involved."[4] Soros' testimony reflects clear insight into the current problems of hedge funds, prime brokers, and the financial industry.[5]

---

[1] Soros, Testimony to the U.S. House of Representatives: Committee on Banking and Financial Services, 1998.

[2] Ibid.

[3] For a contrasting view see the Testimony of Alan Greenspan, Chairman of the Federal Reserve Board, before the House Committee on Banking and Financial Services, October 1, 1998, and the Testimony of William McDonough, President of the New York Branch of the Federal Reserve, before the House Committee on Banking and Financial Services, October 1, 1998.

[4] Soros, Testimony to the U.S. House of Representatives: Committee on Banking and Financial Services, 1998.

[5] See also the testimony of Brooksley Born, Chairperson of the CFTC, before the House Committee on Banking and Financial Services, July 24, 1998, and Testimony of Brooksley Born, Chairperson of the CFTC, before the Subcommittee on Risk Management and Specialty Crops of the House Committee on Agriculture, June 10, 1998.

The irony is that Soros' testimony was not September 15, 2008, but rather September 15, 1998, exactly ten years to the day before Lehman Brothers' failure. In 1998, he was speaking of the Russian default and distress of hedge funds and its consequences rather than Lehman Brothers and the U.S. housing market failures. The same unaddressed problems and unheeded risks from the time of LTCM have returned today.[6] The present financial crisis is much like the past, yet vastly more expensive.

Long-Term Capital Management

In 1998, the diminishing returns of traditional strategies and no small amount of hubris led LTCM to enter into a variety of highly leveraged trades. This was no ordinary firm. LTCM included a group of leading investment bankers, revered traders, a former vic-chair of the Federal Reserve, and intelligentsia, including Nobel Laureates. With a few billion in investor capital, LTCM was able to expand its leverage to create a trillion-dollar footprint. Ultimately, LTCM expanded trading beyond the traditional scope and experience of its managers. Long-Term Capital Management was ironically neither in existence long-term nor effective in capital management. LTCM increased leverage substantially (either voluntarily or involuntarily) so that the fund was leveraged an astounding 300 to 400 times.[7]

In the fall of 1998, the perfect storm arrived on the doorstep of LTCM with the Russian government default. LTCM acted like an insurer buying risk from many different parties. The process of making small amounts from taking big but unlikely risks has often been likened to "picking up nickels in front of a steamroller." When Russia defaulted and credit spreads increased markedly around the globe in a variety of assets, LTCM's computer models failed, its diversified positions became illiquid, and the firm was devastated.

---

[6] For an interesting view of today's challenges see Soros, 2008.

[7] See Lowenstein, 2002.

All trades seemed to move against them as credit spreads widened and liquidity evaporated. LTCM's main prime broker, Bear Stearns, was preparing to liquidate the LTCM portfolio when the Federal Reserve and others became involved in the crisis.

The focus on LTCM has remained on its massive leverage and divergent positions. It was recognized that the LTCM liquidation would potentially have had catastrophic effects on a variety of markets, products, and counterparties. This ultimately led to the bailout by a range of U.S. investment banks, as indirectly guided, if not tacitly directed, by the Federal Reserve.[8] The price for each firm was approximately $350 million, a price that seems like a bargain by today's standards. Ironically, the LTCM trades that were assumed by the investment banks at a steep discount reportedly became profitable when liquidity returned and international markets resumed normal functioning.

In retrospect, the prime brokers who engineered and financed LTCM were not challenged for their role in creating systemic risk. The prime brokerage model and derivatives markets continued, and the threat of systemic risk was averted by an industry-financed bail out. Dispersing the risk posed by LTCM's failure now looks very much like a neglected opportunity to address more substantial concerns. The interrelationship between hedge funds and prime brokers, low interest rates, excessive leverage, multiple asset classes, including OTC derivatives, and how their interconnection of these posed systemic risk, was missed. LTCM is often remembered as a near miss that allowed the banking system, through the Fed and the financial assistance of investment banks, to bail out a distressed hedge fund. In retrospect, LTCM is reflective of the same problems facing hedge funds, prime finance, and the international financial industry today, only on a much more manageable scale. If LTCM had been allowed to fail, and Bear Stearns, their primary

[8] The Federal Reserve System is composed of twelve regional reserve banks governed by a Board of Governors. The most prominent is the Federal Reserve Bank of New York, which has most direct access to the markets. See www.fed.gov.

prime broker, had liquidated their positions, the fallout may have caused a small market crisis. The resulting focus on hedge funds and investment banks, excessive leverage, and derivatives may well have created a regulatory regime to address systemic risk and may have prevented the current, much larger financial crisis. Today we have devastated hedge funds, bankrupt prime brokers, and distressed investment banks, and yet the underlying issues and risks remain unaddressed.

Extinction and Resurrection

2008 saw the extinction of the last remaining free-standing investment banks, including some of the elite and leading prime brokers. The acquisitions of Bear Stearns and Merrill Lynch, the Lehman bankruptcy, and the registration of Goldman Sachs and Morgan Stanley as bank holding companies saw the end of an era. This was not by any means the end of investment banks or prime finance. The firms that were deeply affected by the financial crisis, including Goldman Sachs and Morgan Stanley, have made significant recoveries.

The prime broker market has seen massive changes, and undergone a paradigm shift. The structure of the prime finance market has changed. The prime brokers and their primary clients—hedge funds—have been challenged and humbled in some cases. In general, the majority of hedge funds suffered losses but far less than the equities markets. There were also notable exceptions of record gains by some hedge fund managers in the financial crisis. The leading and elite U.S. prime brokers saw massive moves in collateral assets, reductions in borrowing, and increasing importance of securities lending and repo financing. Other prime brokers and hedge funds have gained market share due to the volatility and market dislocation.

The future of prime finance will likely include greater emphasis on services provided to successful hedge funds. The market is not singular, and undoubtedly some prime brokers will compete on price while most will attempt to differentiate their services and offering. Prime finance products and services will need to embrace technological advances and accessible platforms that address heightened concerns about risk. Advanced risk analysis and transparency may prove to be a competitive advantage for firms that invest in the continuous development of new technologies.

This trend suggests continued development of consolidated prime finance services. This includes combining access to financing on multiple products and services from prime broker, synthetic prime broker, stock loan, repo, OTC derivatives, commodities, options, fund-linked products, equities and fixed-income products, and currencies. The elite and many leading prime brokers developed comprehensive services and technological advances to assist and facilitate hedge fund operations in order to develop their strategies. The prime brokerage areas provided economies of scale and scope for both the prime broker internally and synergies with other areas of the investment bank. The new entrants in prime finance will need to emulate and improve on the services and platforms developed by the leading prime brokers, or the surviving hedge funds may return to an elite few prime brokers. Indeed, the formidable innovations, top staff, and economic strength of elite U.S. firms will allow them to engage in international competition provided they are not restricted by regulation, if they are not hindered by punitive domestic regulation they may recapture international market dominance once again.

Hedge Funds

Alfred Winslow Jones' entrepreneurial idea that quietly started as a small, private limited partnership has spawned a multitrillion-dollar industry. That industry has now taken front stage for regulators, governments, and the media. Undoubtedly prime brokers and their investment banks and hedge funds will play major roles in determining the future of international finance. It seems increasingly probable that governments and regulations may alter the course and trajectory of the hedge fund and alternative investment industry.

Hedge fund oversight by governments and by their investors have increased in the wake of manager frauds, redemptions, and market volatility. Hedge fund indexes have experienced some of the worst performances in their history, yet performed very well compared to other markets and investments. The hedge fund redemptions and blow-ups occurred at record pace in the financial crisis. The hedge fund market continues to undergo a consolidation that industry experts estimate may eliminate anywhere from 10 percent to two-thirds of the hedge fund market.[9]

Litigation related to bankruptcies, hedge fund blow-ups, redemptions, and frauds is ramping up and may spread liability to other parties in prime finance. The complexities of contentious rehypothecation and the sensitivity of hedge fund managers to counterparty risk remain high. Litigation and conflicts arising from hedge funds and prime broker bankruptcies will take years to resolve. One particularly thorny area is the issue surrounding rehypothecation and international transfers in the final days before the Lehman Brothers' bankruptcy leading to a billion-dollar windfall for some banks, such as the reported multi-billion-dollar windfall in acquiring Lehman's U.S. brokerage operations.[10] The most notable litigation will continue as a result of blatant hedge fund manager frauds and the long unwinding of Lehman Brothers.

Trust and Fraud

The hedge fund community has been largely regulated on trust and reputation. There are few limited examples of overt fraud.

Nevertheless, there are notorious but rare examples of hedge fund managers and broker dealers engaging in fraud.[11] Managers have been incarcerated for a variety of frauds, Ponzi schemes, and other deceptions regarding their strategies and investment

[9] There have a been a number of high-profile blow-ups and speculation about the future of the industry; see Mackintosh, 2008.

[10] See MacIntosh, 2008 and Hughes, 2008.

[11] Wood River and Bayou scandals were notable fraud claims.

valuations. The notorious Madoff fraud may prove more important than all prior manager frauds in its duration, size, and implications for regulatory oversight and investor trust.

Bernard Madoff was a revered member of the investment community. The Ponzi scheme was a particularly massive and unsophisticated fraud involving both the Madoff investment management and broker-dealer arms. The numerous red flags were missed by investors and regulators. It is clear that additional operational due diligence is necessary for hedge funds, investment managers, broker-dealers, auditors, and even regulators. All parties to prime finance will be required to answer fundamental questions about transparency, operational due diligence, and counterparty risk. This will include increasing focus on transparency and security over collateral assets.

The titanic fraud of Bernard Madoff, the 71-year-old manager, will likely have far-reaching implications beyond his criminal convictions and extraordinary 150-year sentence. Many early investors who redeemed investments from the Madoff fund may have their transactions undone and clawed back by later investors. The concept of fraudulent conveyance allows for courts to effectively retroactively cancel out the redemptions and force prior investors to return capital. The Madoff scandal is a unique situation as it directly involves a domestically regulated broker-dealer. Normally when investors lose their investments with a hedge fund, there is no government support. In this case a restitution fund has paid some investors at least nominal amounts for their losses. The search for greater restitution has led investors to turn on each other and on administrators, auditors, secondary fund managers, and consultants to recover their massive losses. Notwithstanding the need to punish fraud and deter other managers from the same course of conduct, a balance must be struck between allowing managers to have private trading strategies and the need to prevent abuses. If we side too much with prevention and punishment, it may just stifle financial innovations and much needed entrepreneurship.

Financial Entrepreneurship

The World Economic Forum Report concluded that the tension between managers and investors can indeed be addressed. "Financial markets must always cope with imperfect information and moral hazard. Transparency is the antidote to remedy deficiencies arising from the asymmetric distribution of information."[12]

Financial innovations, such as the development of derivatives and securitized products, appeared to increase the efficiency of markets and allowed for a diversification of risk. However, the interconnectedness of markets and counterparties led to a cascade of effects. The unanticipated risks added together to cumulatively create a systemic threat.

There is a perceived need to revise the financial system, regulation of financial products, and the rules applicable to broker-dealers and hedge funds. The U.S. federal regulatory system is likely to change significantly. There are two overarching concerns. Firstly, the United States has lost some of the international leadership in financial services, and must move in concert with other nations. Altering rules radically to protect U.S. financial firms and investors may create uncertainty and volatility in the markets. The imposition of new rules and regulations on short selling exposed the unilateral steps the SEC and others were willing to take to defend the system from perceived attacks. However, there was no enemy at the gate, and their efforts to find one created uncertainty, volatility, and drained the remaining cash from already illiquid markets to the detriment of those financial firms they were seeking to protect.

Financial Innovations: Derivative Market and Securitization

Financial innovations, such as alternative investments, OTC derivatives, and securitization, have played an important role in the

[12] A World Economic Forum Report, in collaboration with Citigroup, Marsh & McLennan Companies (MMC), Swiss Re, Wharton School Risk Center, Zurich Financial Services, January 2009, p. 14.

development of U.S. and international financial markets. While there have been abuses and overleveraging of the system, these innovations have also been responsible for significant prosperity.[13] Now the size of the massive OTC derivatives markets may only be estimated, and dwarfs domestic markets. The volatility of the OTC derivatives market remains largely unknown. Given the unexpected surprise changes in the mortgage-backed securities and other AAA-rated securities, can other derivatives based on these be assumed to be non-volatile, without transparency, investigation, and active monitoring? This lack of knowledge and transparency should give us pause when considering making significant regulatory changes.

The OTC derivatives market was conservatively estimated at approximately $683 trillion for the G-10 and Switzerland alone. Consider simple volatility of 1 percent (less than many of the most stable equity markets).[14] This very small amount of volatility would result in transfers of over $6.8 trillion. The new proposed U.S. regulations of OTC derivatives may precipitate significant volatility in the markets. In an extreme scenario, where volatility reached 5 percent (or $34.2 trillion), the impact of the OTC derivatives market may constitute serious global systemic risk. And this time, the financial resources for another much larger bailout will be more difficult to raise, if it is possible at all.

The regulation of OTC derivatives in certain jurisdictions has moved to increasing the role of a central counterparty (CCP) which allows for transparency of the risks. The strategy to move to titanic clearing houses and giant exchanges has its own risks. The CCP model transfers and consolidates all counterparty risk to one or a few

---

[13] The Report of the President's Working Group on Financial Markets entitled *Over-the-Counter Derivatives Markets and the Commodity Exchange Act, 1999*, took a hands off approach to regulation. However, the CFTC, particularly former Chairperson, Brooksley Born, attempted to bring the OTC derivatives market under the purview of the *Commodities and Exchange Act*.

[14] Some proposed legislation, "*Over-the-Counter Derivatives Markets Act of 2009*," may divide enforcement between the CFTC and the SEC along financial product categories.

counter parties, which to be effective will need to be an organization greater in stature, expertise and financial strength than the DTCC, with access to trillions of dollars of assets. This strategy may increase transparency, but without additional supporting structures, expertise, and safeguards, it is incomplete and may only serve to focus all risk into a few gigantic entities. Rather than mitigating and diversifying risk, such an institution may increase systemic risk in the event of an operational failure.

Systemic Risk

Systemic risk is, and should be, the overarching concern for regulators and governments. Some European governments have lobbied for a comprehensive overview of the financial system, including hedge funds and other systemically important firms. The alternative is to prepare to provide bailouts for firms that pose systemic risk when they fail.

The proposed U.S. response has been a determination of systemic risk that is limited to the United States.[15] The problem with a narrow construction of systemic risk is that it fails to address the source of risk that may be external, or international. Systemic risk may be posed by non-U.S. entities, such as international arms of U.S. brokers or offshore investment funds. Even when U.S. entities have overseas operations, the risk and jurisdiction over foreign subsidiaries often falls to local law and regulation, such as in Lehman Brothers' European operations.

The default of international firms may also impact the U.S. financial market and economy. The bankruptcy regime in both the United States and internationally is fundamentally retrospective

[15] The *Resolution Authority for Systemically Significant Financial Companies Act of 2009* provides for a determination of systemic risk by the Federal Reserve Board and appropriate federal regulatory agency, including consultation with the President of the United States. Section 2(B) provides where "the failure of the financial company and its resolution under otherwise applicable Federal or State law would have serious adverse effects on financial stability or economic conditions in the United States," the FDIC may exercise resolution actions.

rather than forward thinking. The resolution authority over systemically important firms that default, such as the FDIC, or other regulatory bodies, creates profound philosophical and pragmatic issues around the purpose of the authority, monitoring, and avoiding future risks. To do so would require a paradigm shift from a retrospective regulatory power to a more forward thinking regulator that must constantly monitor the risks of firms and between firms, and the international markets. The significant difference is changing regulators from an ambulance driver to a coordinating air traffic controller. This is in order to monitor risk individually and between financial firms, and to understand the implications for the United States and between other nations.

The challenge is not simply to establish a regime for orderly liquidation of systemically important firms but that the new paradigm must identify interlinkages, and predict, and prepare for "low probability/high severity events."[16]

Enforcement and Authority Over Systemic Risk

Without an effective, powerful governing body, there are longstanding concerns regarding the establishment and enforcement of financial industry standards. Where one party may profit from the other's failure, it will be a continuing source of moral hazard that the failure of counterparties, and even nations, may be to the benefit of others, or a source of alpha.[17] While the dominant force in regulatory oversight resides with the U.S. federal government, there is no one body that may protect all international waters. Even with the tentative agreement of the G-20, there are still concerns that the limitations of the legal and regulatory framework will not extend far enough.[18]

---

[16] A World Economic Forum Report, in collaboration with Citigroup, Marsh & McLennan Companies (MMC), Swiss Re, Wharton School Risk Center, Zurich Financial Services, January 2009, p. 14.

[17] For example, Soros explicitly recognized that the Russian failure in 1998 benefited the United States economically.

[18] There are 194 countries in the world (or 195 countries depending upon views about Taiwan); CIA Handbook.

There is a need for a common power or regional enforcement of harmonized international standards to address the overarching concerns of systemic risk. However, the standards for the financial system will need to be agreed upon between nations, and not for nations. This is particularly so where the restructuring and regulation of the financial system is led by debtor nations rather than lender nations.

U.S. Leadership

The challenge is to forge a broad new regime to address risks in financial services and mainitaining competitive advantages. The President's Working Group on Financial Market Developments set out several important recommendations.

In general, the recommendations include measures to be implemented by government authorities or market participants that will:

- Reform key parts of the mortgage origination process in the United States
- Enhance disclosure and improve the practices of sponsors, underwriters, and investors with respect to securitized credits, thereby imposing more effective market discipline
- Reform the credit rating agencies' processes for and practices regarding rating structured credit products to ensure integrity and transparency
- Ensure that global financial institutions take appropriate steps to address the weaknesses in risk management and reporting practices that the market turmoil has exposed
- Ensure that prudential regulatory policies applicable to banks and securities firms, including capital and disclosure requirements, provide strong incentives for effective risk management practices[19]

Many have concluded that there was a major governance gap in the U.S. system, particularly between the resolution authority

[19] See Markets, 2008, Executive Summary, p. 3.

of the FDIC and other relevant federal authorities, over investment banks and bank holding companies.[20] At the foundation of prior justifications for intervention was the concept that risk may be contained provided there is orderly liquidation of systemically important firms, similar to failing banks. There remain additional questions about the current reach of the new regulatory regime, whether national or international:

> The global credit crisis demonstrated a major governance gap and the need to improve prudential oversight and regulation. Financial market stability is a public good, and global financial markets require a globally coordinated effort to create and maintain this public good. The financial architecture of the future must have an element that transcends national borders. To ensure success its institutions should include broad representation in rule-making bodies, macro prudential surveillance and have agreed procedures for systematic enforcement.[21]

The attempts by western nations, the G-20, and others to recreate financial services and amend lending practices will continue. The question is whether these efforts rely on the same pattern. What if the crackdown is too harsh? The hedge funds and associated investment funds of the world are global organizations. The availability of financing is international. Efforts to strictly regulate the U.S. and G-20 markets may only have a limited effect, and may ultimately lead to a "rush to the bottom" rather than establishing a gold standard that all must abide. In reality the interrelationship between U.S. financial regulations and foreign banks and brokers is complex and reflexive. The institutions and the international markets have been structured to finesse the dated U.S. regulations. Efforts to seize control

[20] The other relevant federal authorities include the Federal Reserve, U.S. Treasury, SEC, CFTC, NYSE, NASDAQ, and even the President.

[21] A World Economic Forum Report, in collaboration with Citigroup, Marsh & McLennan Companies (MMC), Swiss Re, Wharton School Risk Center, Zurich Financial Services, January 2009, p. 14.

of the international markets and dictate fundamental changes to the U.S. legal and regulatory regime may severely and negatively impact the U.S. markets and future competitiveness. The imposition of sweeping legislation that extends the U.S. reach to repudiate contracts, suspend debts, and cap liability may severely impair the perception of fairness, trust and undermine credibility. This would ultimately result in a change to the risk premium for U.S. investments similar to those of other markets, and force more financial innovations and opportunities offshore.

Transparency and Monitoring of Risk

The hedge fund industry is global, sophisticated, and mobile. The regulation of financial markets and products by individual states may not have the desired effect of reigning in risk. This may push financial innovations and hedge funds into more accommodating jurisdictions, actually increasing risk in the international financial system. The international efforts to create basic rules of transparency and risk must be dealt with on a collective basis, as individual and haphazard implementation of regulation will likely reorganize the global market and unintentionally create more risk. Having only a dozen nations may entail that new regulations create a Delaware Effect (a rush to the bottom), rather than the hoped for California Effect (where firms raise their standards to the highest standard). Also, while notable SROs have created laudable standards for hedge funds and other investment funds to comply with community standards, the authority and enforcement of these standards remains a critical question.[22]

Regulation

The significant regulatory efforts, and stated intentions, by various international governments, self-regulatory organizations, and international treaties will attempt to limit leverage regulate

[22] See www.aima.org.

financial innovations, such as OTC derivatives, and address systemic risk.[23] Further, the deleveraging process of the prime brokers, securities firms, banks, and the financial industry may lead to a reduction in leverage being offered to hedge funds. This may alter the availability and restrictions on financing for certain regulated or unregulated funds, but will likely be met with new strategies to finesse restrictions and new kinds of prime brokers to service the alternative investment market in developing jurisdictions.

Regulatory Reform

The stability of the markets and the underlying economy needs to be protected. There are some who wish to regulate the entire hedge fund industry, limit financial innovation, restrict leverage, and provide increased regulation. The international financial infrastructure and markets are complex, reflexive, and sensitive to intervention. The failure of the short sale restrictions should show that broad initiatives that are haphazardly and quickly implemented may cause great distress and confusion for the financial markets and the underlying economy. The impact of the financial crisis spread to the global economy and decreasing.

There must be greater emphasis on the limits of human knowledge and the corresponding epistemological limits of risk managers and the financial industry. The inductive models that were relied upon were poorly constructed, and profoundly flawed predictors of risk. Ultimately, the quantitative models were wrong and led to catastrophically misguided risk assessments in certain financial products, such as mortgage-backed securities.[24] The overreliance on historical models produced confidence for extreme leverage on deceptively labeled ("AAA") yet risky products.

---

[23] See for example, U.S. Secretary Geithner's Statement before the House Financial Services Committee, April 20, 2010.

[24] An example of this was the variance-at-risk (VAR) models used internationally. The model creator recognized and advised that the VAR model's usefulness was limited, but the statistical tool was adopted by regulators and used to justify large proprietary positions by many financial firms and banks.

Risk models are actually only able to model based upon past events and results. The risk models were in reality only inductive theories. The finance world is not detached from the rest of human understanding, but is just a subset of our knowledge.

The international regulatory system should address the challenges, including:

- Transparency of risks
- Monitoring risks
- Harmonization of international standards
- Effective local enforcement
- Orderly resolution

The financial products, entities, and interrelationships must have greater transparency. Individual regulators, SROs, securities associations, governments, and international institutions must work to reduce opaque structures, products, and contracts in prime brokers, banks, and hedge funds. The almost impenetrable complexity of international regulations of prime finance and the larger financial markets should be simplified and expanded to address obvious regulatory gaps.

With transparency there should be appropriate standards and monitoring of risks. The regulators have proved, with their failures to predict the implications of regulatory intervention, that discussion with the parties, including investment banks, prime brokers, and hedge funds is critical to determining the implications of regulatory actions. The effective international enforcement of international finance needs to be assessed. The U.S. led move toward regional enforcement by individual countries to assess and address systemic and individual firm transgressions will need to be followed with broad based international harmonization. The largest looming risks for the future are related to opaque financial innovations and offshore markets. Creating financial derivatives clearing houses, such as those proposed for the U.S. and European markets, may create transparency. However, this will consolidate all risk in a few, or possibly many, counterparties. Finally, orderly resolution authority of systemically important firms is important to address the complexities of the markets. As well, the limited nature of our understanding of the financial markets and players must be recognized and examined, this must be undertaken with the proviso that "our understanding is inherently imperfect because we are part of the world we seek to understand."[25]

The most prominent populist argument is that governments need to do something. It is unclear that the extinction of the investment banks was anything unusual or something that should not have been predicted. In an international financial world, the failures become part of history, but bailing out irresponsible, failing financial institutions may create additional "moral hazard" later. The assumption has been that we need to bail out the banks because the downside risk of not intervening would create systemic instability and negative impacts on the larger economy. The government policies, semi-governmental organizations and cheap credit that financed unsustainable development, perversely inflated housing prices, immense derivatives markets, and fueled egregious consumption levels are all unsustainable. While certain aspects of the markets are important to protect to avoid systemic failure, there are competing ethical considerations. The current financial crisis may have been contained at least temporarily. Yet, if the financial system and government policies continue as before it will undoubtedly create larger and larger bubbles. If the international standards cannot be harmonized, the future may hold more spectacular failures that threaten the international financial system. The challenge is to strike a balance between competing risks and rewards in an international market.

The prime finance model is an international business that has grown beyond limited U.S. and international regulation. Harsh or punitive regulatory responses may only serve to push managers and hedge funds and the OTC derivatives market to more hospitable jurisdictions. Leverage and financial innovations are useful tools

[25] See Soros, 2008, p. 3.

for developing business, diversifying, and mitigating risks. The current speculative market of unregulated derivatives dwarfs the major U.S. domestic and international equities markets and efforts to reign this in must be put in perspective. The reformation of the financial system should account for the realities of the international financial industry, the role of government policies in creating the financial crisis, and the inevitable forces of international competition at play. Simplistic politically motivated solutions to complex problems may only serve to impede domestic financial firms, increase ballooning government, and further fragment the competitive landscape. The lesson for the future is to require transparency, effectively monitor risks, and set international standards that are enforceable and reasonably enforced.

The financial crisis has led to a development of new knowledge only by destroying the old. The paradox of knowledge is that only when old assumptions are proven wrong is knowledge advanced. With the rediscovery and recognition of the unheeded risks of the past, we have another opportunity to address the challenges of tomorrow. One can rest assured that the problems of tomorrow will be born from the solutions of today.

Appendix A

Prime Broker List[1]

Alaris Trading Partners, LLC (www.alaristrading.com)
Albert Fried & Company, LLC (www.albertfried.com)
Assent, LLC (www.assent.com)
Banca IMI Securities Corporation
Bank of America Merrill Lynch (www.bankofamerica.com)
Barclays Capital (www.barcap.com)
Belzberg Technologies (www.belzberg.com)
BMO Capital Markets Corporation (www.bmocm.com)
BNP Paribas Prime Brokerage, Inc. (www.bnpparibas.com)
BNP Paribas Securities Corp. (securities.bnpparibas.com)
Calyon (www.calyon.com)
Calyon Securities (USA) (www.calyonamericas.com)
Cantor Fitzgerald (www.cantor.com)
Charles Schwab (www.schwab.com)
CIBC World Markets (www.cibcwm.com)
Citigroup Global Markets (www.citigroup.com)

[1] All lists, including the above, are limited reviews of U.S. and global service providers and are not complete or comprehensive. The inclusion in any listing is not a recommendation or endorsement, and individual due diligence should be conducted as a matter of standard business practice on any prime brokerage, executing brokerage, or other service provider.

Credit Suisse (www.credit-suisse.com)
Daiwa Securities (www.us.daiwacm.com)
Deutsche Bank (www.db.com)
E*TRADE Clearing (www.us.etrade.com)
First Southwest Company (www.firstsw.com)
Fortis Clearing Americas (www.us.fortisclearing.com)
Fortis Securities (www.holding.fortis.com)
Goldman, Sachs & Co. (www.goldmansachs.com)
HSBC (www.hsbc.com or www.hsbcusa.com)
ING Financial Markets (www.ingwholesalebanking.com)
Interactive Brokers (www.inactivebrokers.com)
Investment Technology Group (www.itg.com)
J.P. Morgan Chase (www.jpmorgan.com)
Jefferies & Company (www.jefferies.com)
Lazard Capital Markets (www.lazardcap.com)
Merlin Securities (www.merlinsecurities.com)
Merrill Lynch (www.ml.com)
MF Global (www.mfglobal.com)
Morgan Stanley Prime Brokerage (www.morganstanley.com)
National Bank Financial (www.nbf.ca)
National Financial Services (www.nationalfinancial.com)
Natixis (www.natixis.com)
Neuberger Berman (www.nb.com)
Newedge USA (www.newedgegroup.com)
Nomura (www.nomura.com)
Pershing (www.pershing.com)
RBC Capital Markets (www.rbccm.com)
RBS (www.rbs.com)
Scotia Capital (www.scotiacapital.com)
Societe Generale (www.sgcib.com)
Shoreline Trading Group (www.shorelinetrading.com)
TD Ameritrade Clearing (www.amtd.com)
Terra Nova Financial (www.tnfg.com)
TradeStation Securities (www.tradestation.com)
UBS (www.ibb.ubs.com)
Vision Financial Markets (www.visionfinancialmarkets.com)
Wedbush Morgan Securities, Inc. (www.wedbush.com)
Wells Fargo Investments (www.wellsfargo.com)

Appendix B

List of Securities Lenders[1]

Bank of America Merrill Lynch (www.bankofamerica.com)
Bank of New York Mellon (www.bnymellon.com)
Barclays Capital (www.barcap.com)
Brown Brothers Harriman (www.bbh.com)
Citigroup Global Markets (www.citigroup.com)
Charles Schwab Corporation (www.schwab.com)
Commerzbank (www.commerzbank.com)
Credit Suisse (www.credit-suisse.com)
Deutsche Bank (www.db.com)
eSecLending (www.eseclending.com)
Fidelity Prime (www.fidelityprime.com)
Goldman Sachs (www.goldmansachs.com)
HSBC (www.hsbc.com)
J.P. Morgan (www.jpmorgan.com)
Jefferies & Company (www.jefferies.com)

[1] Limited and abbreviated list of U.S. and global securities lenders and prime brokers focusing on securities lending.

RBC Dexia (www.rbcdexia.com)
Scotia Capital (www.scotiacapital.com)
Shoreline Trading (www.shorelinetrading.com)
State Street Corporation (www.statestreet.com)
UBS (www.ibb.ubs.com)
Wachovia Global Securities Lending (www.wgsl.com)

Appendix C
Prime Broker Due Diligence Questionnaire[1]

1. Basic Information

Prime Broker Name ______________________

Type of Legal Entity ______________________

Location of Incorporation ______________________

Registered Office Location ______________________

Satellite Offices ______________________

Ownership Structure ______________________

Registered Address ______________________

Phone Number ______________________

Facsimile ______________________

Email ______________________

Address for Service ______________________

Number of Prime Finance Employees ______________________

Market Capitalization ______________________

---

[1] The due diligence is a limited list of standard questions and issues that may be considered in selecting a prime broker. The individual requirements for institutional investors and hedge funds will vary considerably depending upon their risk profile, strategies, and leverage requirements. Individual due diligence on prime brokers is a necessary start to assess risks and advantages but may not be complete or comprehensive for individual requirements.

Assets under Management ______________________________
Years in Operation ______________________________
Regulatory Filings ______________________________
Registration Type ______________________________
Licenses ______________________________
Penalties/Fines/Restrictions Imposed in Last
Seven Years ______________________________
Auditor ______________________________
Legal Counsel ______________________________
Administrator ______________________________
Subsidiaries (list all relevant) ______________________________
Parent Company Name ______________________________
Parent Company Location ______________________________

2. Personnel

Chief Executive ______________________________
Prime Broker Chief ______________________________
Sales ______________________________
Operations ______________________________
Prime Broker Contact ______________________________
Stock Loan Contact ______________________________
Financing Contact ______________________________
Trading Contact ______________________________
Settlement Contact ______________________________
Corporate Actions Contact ______________________________
Emergency or After Hours Contact ______________________________

3. Services Offered

Custody ______________________________
Trade Execution ______________________________
Trade Reporting ______________________________
Trade Settlement ______________________________

Access to Financial Markets ____________________

North America ____________________

South America ____________________

EU Region ____________________

Middle East ____________________

Asia ____________________

Africa ____________________

Australia ____________________

Other Relevant Markets ____________________

Financial Products Offered ____________________

Equities ____________________

Debt and Bonds ____________________

Commodities ____________________

Foreign Exchange ____________________

Derivatives ____________________

Other Products ____________________

Margin Rates ____________________

Margin Amounts ____________________

Corporate Action Processing ____________________

Account Administration ____________________

Operations ____________________

Accounting ____________________

Trading Software ____________________

Risk Software ____________________

Office Space Available ____________________

Information Technology and Other Technology Support ____________________

Research ____________________

Consulting Services ____________________

Seed Investment ____________________

Capital Introduction ____________________

Capital Raising ____________________

Support for Activist Funds ____________________

4. Business Terms

Margin Rates ____________________

Fees (full details) ____________________

Expenses (full details) ____________________

Notification of Changes to Rates, Fees, and Expenses _____

Maximum Leverage Provided ____________________

Corporate Actions Management ____________________

Lock-Up Agreement ____________________

Rehypothecation Level ____________________

Minimum Required Rehypothecation Rights for the Prime Broker ____________________

Custodial Holding by Custodian Available ____________

Parental Guarantee over Assets of Hedge Fund __________

Assets Withdrawn from Prime Finance in Last Year _______

Minimum Collateral Posted ____________________

Netting and Set-Off Required ____________________

Cross-Default Provisions ____________________

5. Account Details

How Is Collateral Held? ____________________

Cash ____________________

Fully Paid Securities ____________________

Rehypothecated Securities ____________________

Securities Held as Security (or Pledged) for Loans _______

Segregated Account ____________________

Pooled Account ____________________

Custodial Account ____________________

Individual Account, Numerated ____________

Guarantees on Rehypothecation and Utilization Limits ____

Location and Use of Securities ____________________

Prime Broker Agreement Provides for Securities to
Be Held Where/How ______________________

Disaster Plan ______________________

What Happens in Prime Broker Defaults ______________________

What Level of Recovery Can Be Expected for the Variety of Different Collateral Assets Held by the Prime Broker ______

a. Cash ______________________
b. Fully Paid Securities ______________________
c. Rehypothecated Securities ______________________
d. Securities Held as Security (or Pledged) for Loans _____
e. Other ______________________

Position in Event of Default with Regard to Each ________

6. Strategy

Strategies Supported (or Specialties) ______________________

Maximum Number of Trades Per Day ______________________

Complicated Portfolio Management Available ______________________

Special Needs of the Hedge Fund ______________________

7. Securities and Instruments Available

Corporate Activist Support ______________________

Commodities ______________________

Debt ______________________

Equities ______________________

Derivatives ______________________

OTC ______________________

Other ______________________

8. Competitive Advantage of Prime Broker

Total Client Assets (Estimate) ______________________

Other Funds Types Managed ______________________

List Other Funds Supported ______________________

Compatibility with Current Portfolio ______________________

9. Prime Finance Related-Services Offered

Stock Loan ____________________

Financing ____________________

Technology Provided ____________________

Consulting Services ____________________

Risk Software ____________________

Technology Offered (Software, Hardware) ____________________

Research ____________________

Commission Sharing ____________________

Fundraising Support ____________________

Office Space ____________________

Staff Support ____________________

Technology Support ____________________

Accounting ____________________

Other ____________________

10. Risk

Time to Withdrawal from Assets under Management from Prime Brokers ____________________

Prime Finance Credit Risk ____________________

Rating Events Disclosures (S&P, Moody's, Fitch) ____________________

Prime Finance Monitor Executing Broker Default Risk ____________________

Civil, Regulatory, Actions, Fines Against Prime Broker (Employees or Directors) in Last Seven Years ____________________

Other ____________________

Appendix D

Useful Links—Prime Finance

Regulators
www.fed.gov
www.treasury.gov
www.fdic.gov
www.fsa.org.uk
www.sec.gov

SROs
www.finra.org
www.isla.com
www.icma-group.org
www.osfi-bsif.gc.ca
www.advocis.com

International Organizations
www.bankofcanada.ca
www.bis.org
www.cipf.ca
www.cds.ca
www.iosco.org
www.nasaa.org
www.world-exchanges.org

Hedge Fund Information

www.e-hedge.com
www.greenwichai.com
www.thehfa.org
www.hedgefundcenter.com
www.hedgefundintelligence.com
www.caia.org
www.aima.org

Prime Brokers

www.home.globalcustodian.com
www.primebrokerageguide.com
www.primefinanceguide.com

Securities Lending

www.paslaonline.com
www.asla.com.au
www.isla.org
www.rmahq.org/RMA/SecuritiesLending
www.icma-group.org

Investor Information

www.investment.com
www.ific.ca
www.adviceforinvestors.com
www.investorwords.com
www.investopedia.com
www.bloomberg.com

Bibliography

A World Economic Forum Report, in collaboration with Citigroup, Marsh & McLennan Companies (MMC), Swiss Re, Wharton School Risk Center, Zurich Financial Services. (2009, January). *Global Risks 2009: A Global Risk Network Report*. Geneva: World Economic Forum.

Adamson, L. (2008, October). Have Strategy, Need Space. *Institutional Investor.*

Allied Irish Banks, P.L.C. v. Bank of America, N.A. and Citibank N.A., U.S. Dist. Lexis 4247 (United States District Court for the Southern District of New York January 23, 2007).

Allied Irish Banks, P.L.C. v. Bank of America, N.A. and Citibank N.A., 03 Civ. 3748 (DAB) (United States District Court for the Southern District of New York February 2, 2006).

Alpha Magazine. (2009, April 1). The 25 Highest-Earning Hedge Fund Managers. *Institutional Investor Alpha Magazine*, p. 1.

American Home Mortgage, Inc. et al. v. Bear Stearns Mortgage Capital Corp. et al., 07-11047 (United States Bankruptcy Court for the District of Delaware October 30, 2008).

Anonymous. (2008a, December 27). All Fall Down. *Financial Times*, p. 18.

Anonymous. (2008b, September). Friction between Friends. *International Securities Finance.*

Anonymous. (2008c, December 18). Fund of Funds. *Financial Times*, p. 16.

Anonymous (2008d, October 11). Scramble to Deleverage Takes Heavy Toll on Stocks. *Financial Times*, p. 3.

Anson, M. J. (2006). *Handbook of Alternative Investments.* Hoboken, NJ: John Wiley & Sons.

Avery, H. (2008, December). All Change in Prime Brokerage. *Alternative Investments.*

Bank of International Settlements. (2008). *Quarterly Review December 2008.*

Baquero, G., & Verbeek, M. (2005). *A Portrait of Hedge Fund Investors: Flows, Performance and Smart Money.* Rotterdam: Erasmus Research Institute of Management (ERIM).

Beck, P., & Nagy, M. (2005). *Hedge Funds for Canadians: New Investment Strategies for Winning in any Market.* Mississauga: John Wiley & Sons Canada Ltd.

Benoit, B. (2007, February 14). No Regrets. *Financial Times*, 17:39.

Berman, M. (2007). *Hedge Funds and Prime Brokers.* London: Risk Books.

Billingsley, R. S. (2005). *Understanding Arbitrage: An Intuitive Approach to Financial Analysis.* Upper Saddle River, NJ: Wharton School Publishing.

Black, K. (2004). *Managing a Hedge Fund: A Complete Guide to Trading, Business Strategies, Operations and Regulations.* New York: McGraw-Hill.

Bluhm, C., Overbeck, L., & Wagner, C. (2003). *An Introduction to Credit Risk Modelling.* London: Chapman & Hall/CRC.

Boucher, M. (1998). *The Hedge Fund Edge: Maximum Profit/Minimum Risk Global Trend Trading Strategies.* New York: John Wiley & Sons.

Burton, K. (2007). *Hedge Hunters: Hedge Fund Masters on the Rewards, the Risk, and the Reckoning.* New York: Bloomberg Press.

Calamos, N. (2003). *Convertible Arbitrage.* Hoboken, NJ: John Wiley & Sons.

Cass, R. A. (2008, December 18). Madoff Exploited the Jews. *Wall Street Journal*, p. A.19.

Chandler, B. (2002). *Investing with the Hedge Fund Giants.* London: Pearson Education Limited.

Chatfeild-Roberts, J. (2006). *Fundology.* Hampshire: Harriman House Ltd.

Chung, J., Mackintosh, J., & Sender, H. (2008, September 20). Funds Scramble for Positions as Shorting Ban Hits. *Financial Times*, p. 4.

Citigroup Global Markets Inc. v. VCG Special Opportunities Master Fund Limited f/k/a CDO Plus Master Fund Limited, 08-CV-5520 (BSJ) (United States District Court for the Southern District of New York November 12, 2008).

Coggan, P. (2008). *Guide to Hedge Funds: What They Are, What They Do, Their Risks, Their Advantages.* London: Profile Books Ltd.

Collis, D. J., & Montgomery, C. A. (1998, May-June). How Can You Tell If Your Company Is Really More than the Sum of Its Parts: Creating Corporate Advantage. *Harvard Business Review*, pp. 71–83.

Credit Suisse First Boston (Europe) Ltd v. MLC (Bermuda) Ltd, [1999] All ER (D) 19 (Queen's Bench Division, Commercial Court December 21, 1998).

Credit Suisse First Boston (Europe) Ltd v. Seagate Trading Co Ltd, [1999] 1 Lloyd's Rep 784, [1999] 1 All ER (Comm) 261 (Queen's Bench Commercial Court January 15, 1999).

Credit Suisse First Boston (Europe) Ltd. v. MLC (Bermuda) Ltd, 46 F. Supp. 2d 249; 1999 U.S. Dist. Lexis 6031 (United States District Court for the Southern District of New York April 26, 1999).

CSX Corporation v. The Children's Investment Fund Management (UK) LLP et al., 08 Civ. 2764 (LAK) (United States District Court for the Southern District of New York June 11, 2008).

Dailey, G. C. (1995). Prime Brokerage. In J. Lederman & R. E. Klein, *Hedge Funds: Investment and Portfolio Strategies for the Institutional Investor* (pp. 233–243). New York: Irwin Professional Publishing.

Danielsson, J., & Zigrand, J.-P. (2005). *On Time-Scaling and the Square-Root-of-Time Rule**. London: London School of Economics.

Day, A. (2003). *Mastering Risk Modelling*. London: Pearson Education Limited.

DCC Holdings (UK) Ltd v. Revenue and Customs Commissioners, [2008] EWHC (Ch) 2429 (Chancery Division October 17, 2008).

Delta Products Company et al. v. Credit Commercial de France et al., SA-010CA-1194-XR, 2004 U.S. Dist. Lexis 22513 (United States District Court for the Western District of Texas, San Antonio Division October 6, 2004).

Diamond, B., & Kollar, M. (1989). *24 Hour Trading: The Global Network of Futures and Options Markets*. New York: John Wiley & Sons.

Downes, J., & Goodman, J. E. (2006). *Dictionary of Finance and Investment Terms*. Hauppauge, NY: Barron's Educational Series, Inc.

Edwards & Hanley v. Wells Fargo Securities Clearance Corporation, 602 F.2d 478 (United States Court of Appeals, Second Circuit June 27, 1979).

Ehrman, D. (2006). *The Handbook of Pairs Trading: Strategies Using Equities, Options, and Futures*. Hoboken, NJ: John Wiley & Sons.

Einhorn, D. (2008). *Fooling Some of the People All of the Time*. Hoboken, NJ: John Wiley & Sons.

Elder, D. A. (1993). *Trading for a Living*. New York: John Wiley & Sons.

Electronic Trading Group LLC v. Banc of America et al., Case No. 06 CV 2859 (United States District Court for the Southern District of New York 2007).

Eurycleia Partners LP et al. v. UBS Securities, LLC, 600874-07 (Supreme Court of the State of New York 2008).

Farber, M. (2005). *Why the Fed Has No Other Alternative but to Print Money!* Marc Farber Limited.

Faulkner, M. C. (2004). *An Introduction to Securities Lending © Mark C. Faulkner*. London: Securities Lending and Repo Committee, International Securities Lending Association, British Bankers' Association, London Investment Banking Association, London Stock Exchange.

Federated. (2008, September 16). *Federated Money Market Fund Update.*

FINRA. (2007, November). International Prime Brokerage Regulatory Notice 07–58.

Fitzgerald, A. (2009, January 15). *Group Led by Volcker Urges More Oversight of Banks, Hedge Funds.* Retrieved from www.bloomberg.com.

Fletcher, L., Dmitracova, O., & Dealtalks, R. (2009, January 9). Retrieved January 20, 2009, from www.Canadianhedgewatch.com: www.canadian hedgewatch.com/content/news/general/?id=3963

Four Private Investment Funds v. Lomas et al., [2008] EWHC 2869 (Ch) (Chancery Division, Companies Court November 24, 2008).

FSA. (2009). *DP09/02: A Regulatory Response to the Global Banking Crisis.* London: FSA.

FSA. (2006). *FS06/02.* London: FSA.

G-20. (2009a). *Working Group 1 Final Report: Enhancing Sound Regulation and Strengthening Transparency.* London: G-20.

G-20. (2009b). *Working Group 2 Final Report: Reinforcing International Cooperation and Promoting Integrity in Financial Markets.* London: G-20.

G-20. (2009c). *Working Group 3 Final Report: Reform of the IMF.* London: G-20.

G-20. (2009d). *Working Group 4 Final Report: The World Bank and other Multilateral Development Banks.* London: G-20.

Galbraith, J. K. (1993). *A Short History of Financial Euphoria.* Whittle Books in Association with Viking.

Galbraith, J. K. (1954). *The Great Crash 1929.* London: Penguin Books Limited.

Gangahar, A. (2008a, September 17). Hedge Fund Market's Growth Prospects Thrown into Doubt. *Financial Times*, p. 20.

Gangahar, A. (2008b, September 17). Hedge Funds' Growth Prospects Hit by Lehman Demise. *Financial Times*, p. 26.

Gardner, B. (2007). "Related Parties" and Their Role in the Relationship. In M. Berman, *Hedge Funds and Prime Brokers* (pp. 82–89). London: Risk Books.

Garner, B. A. (Ed.) (1999). *Black's Law Dictionary.* St. Paul, MN: West Group.

Giles, C., & Mackintosh, J. (2008, October 16). Hedge Funds Call for Intervention on Lehman. *Financial Times*, p. 15.

Goldstein v. SEC, No. 04-1434 (D.C. Cir. June 23, 2006).

Grant, R. M. (2005). *Contemporary Strategy Analysis.* London: Blackwell Publishing.

Grene, S. (2008, December 15). Lehman Venture Reborn as Ambix. *Financial Times*, p. 2.

Group, G. W. (2009). *Reinforcing International Cooperation and Promoting Integrity in Financial Markets.* London.

Hitchon, J. & Bausano, B. (2009, April 6). Global Heads of Prime Finance. (J. Aikman, Interviewer).

Hodson, J., & Lim, K. (2008, September 30). Hedge Funds Brace for Redemption Wave, Cash High. *Reuters Daily News*, p. 2008.

Horowitz, R. (2004). *Hedge Fund Risk Fundamentals.* New York: Bloomberg Press.

Hughes, J. (2008, November 7). Winding Up Lehman Brothers. *Financial Times.*

Hughes, J., Mackintosh, J., & Murphy, M. (2008, September 24). Funds in Battle to Recover Lehman Assets. *Financial Times*, p. 32.

Hull, J. C. (2006). *Options, Futures and Other Derivatives.* Upper Saddle River, NJ: Pearson Prentice Hall.

In re Lehman Brothers Holdings Inc., Debtors, 08-13555 (United States Bankruptcy Court, Southern District of New York November 5, 2008).

In re Lehman Brothers Holdings Inc. et al., Debtors, 08-13555 (United States Bankruptcy Court, Southern District of New York November 6, 2008).

In re Manhattan Investment Fund Ltd. et al. v. Bear Stearns Securities Corp., 397 B.R. 1; 2007 U.S. Dist. Lexis 92194 (United States District Court for the Southern District of New York December 17, 2007).

In re MJK Clearing Inc., Debtor. Ferris, Baker Watts, Inc. v. Stephenson, Trustee for MJK Clearing Inc., 2003 U.S. Dist. Lexis 5954; 49 Collier Bankr. Cas. 2d (MB) 1722 (United States District Court for the District of Minnesota April 7, 2003).

In the Matter of A. G. Becker & Company, Inc., Bankruptcy No. 75B1623-W-4; 18 B.R. 472; 1982 Bankr. Lexis 4738 (United States Bankruptcy Court for the Western District of Missouri, Western Division February 24, 1982).

Investment Weekly News. (2008, December 6). Financial Industry Regulatory Authority FINRA: Citigroup Global Markets Fined $300,000 for Failing to Supervise Commissions Charged to Customers on Stock and Options Trades. *Investment Weekly News*, p. 101.

Jaeger, D. L. (2002). *Managing Risk in Alternative Investment Strategies.* London: Pearson Education Limited.

Jenson, G., & Rotenberg, J. (February 13, 2004). *Hedge Funds Selling Beta as Alpha.* Bridgewater Associates, Inc.

Jones, H. (2008, December 4). Hedge Funds Will be Regulated. *Reuters.*

JPMorgan Chase Bank (formerly known as Chase Manhattan Bank) et al. v. Springwell Navigation Corp., [2008] EWHC 1186 (Comm) (Queen's Bench Division, Commercial Court May 27, 2008).

Khaner, L. (2008, October). Party's Over. *Institutional Investor.*

Kirschner, S., Mayer, E., & Kessler, L. (2006). *The Investor's Guide to Hedge Funds.* Hoboken, NJ: John Wiley & Sons.

Kovas, A. (2005). *Hedge Funds and U.K. Regulation.* London: Financial Services Authority.

Kurdas, C. (2009, Winter). Does Regulation Prevent Fraud? The Case of Manhattan Hedge Fund. *The Independent Review,* 13 (3), p. 325.

Larsen, P. T. (2008, October 1). Olivant Suffers Lehman Blow. *Financial Times,* p. 21.

Lederman, J. & Klein, R. A., Eds. (1995). *Hedge Funds: Investment and Portfolio Strategies for the Institutional Investor.* New York: Irwin Professional Publishing.

Levinson, M. (2006). *Guide to Financial Markets.* London: Profile Books Limited.

Lewis, M. (2008, December). The End. *Financial Times.*

Lewis, M., & Einhorn, D. (2009, January 3). The End of the Financial World as We Know It. *Financial Times.*

Lhabitant. (2002). *Hedge Funds: Myths and Limits.* Chichester: John Wiley & Sons Ltd.

Lhabitant. (2004). *Hedge Funds: Quantitative Insights.* Chichester: John Wiley & Sons Ltd.

Lofchie, S. (2005). *Lofchie's Guide to Broker-Dealer Regulation* (3rd ed.). Chicago: CCH Wall Street.

Lowenstein, R. (2002). *When Genius Failed.* London: Fourth Estate.

MacIntosh, J. (2008, December 19). Lehman Brother's Liquidation Turns to New Source of Funds. *Financial Times,* p. 15.

Mackenzie, M. (2008, December 18). Awaiting the Return of the Repo Market. *Financial Times,* p. 33.

Mackintosh, J. (2008a, September 25). Lehman Collapse Puts Prime Broker Model in Question. *Financial Times,* p. 47.

Mackintosh, J. (2008b, September 15). Hedge Funds Reassess Prime Broker Risk. *Financial Times.*

Mackintosh, J. (2008c, November 24). Hedge Funds Slash Leverage. *Financial Times,* p. 22.

Mackintosh, J. (2008d, September 27). MKM to Liquidate Its Flagship Fund. *Financial Times,* p. 22.

Management, U. G. (2008, September 16). Update: UBS Global AM US Money Market Funds. UBS website.

Markets, T. P. (2008). *Policy Statement on Financial Market Developments.*

Markopolos, H. (2005, November 7). The World's Largest Hedge Fund Is a Fraud: Submission to SEC.

Markowitz, H. (1959). *Portfolio Selection.* New Haven, CT: Yale University Press.

Marsh, I. W., & Neimer, N. (2008). *The Impact of Short Sales Restrictions.*

MCC Proceeds Inc. v. Lehman Brothers International (Europe), [1997] All ER (D) 132 (Court of Appeal, Civil Division December 19, 1997).

McIntosh, B. (2008, September 19). Short Selling Ban to Hit Investment Bank Profits. *Daily News.*

McMillan, K., & Bergmann, L. (2007). Hedge Funds and Prime Brokers: The Legal Relationship from the US Perspective. In M. Berman, *Hedge Funds and Prime Brokers.* London: Risk Books.

Mehta, N. (2008, September 1). In the Crosshairs. *Trader Magazine.*

Merrill Lynch, Pierce, Fenner & Smith Inc. v. Dabit, 547 U.S. 71, 81, 126 S. Ct. 1503, 164 L. Ed. 2d 179 (United States Supreme Court 2006).

MJK Clearing Inc., Debtor. Ferris, Baker Watts, Inc., Plaintiffs v. Stephenson, Trustee, 286 B.R. 109; 2002 Bankr. Lexis 1618; 49 U.C.C. rep. Serv. 2d (Callaghan) 11 (United States Bankruptcy Court for the District of Minnesota November 22, 2002).

MLC (Bermuda) Ltd v. Credit Suisse First Boston Corporation and Aaron Tighe, 98 Civ. 7585 (JSR) (United States District Court for the Southern District of New York April 26, 1999).

Molinski, D. (2008, December 26). Some Pension Funds Don't Flee—Managers Say They'll Keep Hedge Investments Despite the Madoff Scandal. *Wall Street Journal*, p. C.3.

Nicholas, J. (2005). *Investing in Hedge Funds, revised and updated edition.* New York: Bloomberg Press.

Nomura Securities International, Inc. v. E*Trade Securities, Inc., 280 F. Supp. 2d 184; 2003 U.S. Dist. Lexis 15253 (United States District Court for the Southern District of New York September 5, 2003).

Ontario (Securities Commission) v. Portus Alternative Asset Management Inc., [2006] O.J. No. 1121 (Ontario Superior Court of Justice, Commercial List March 21, 2006).

Overstock.com, Inc. et al. v. Morgan Stanley & Co., Inc. et al., CGC-07-460147 (Superior Court of the State of California, County of San Francisco February 2, 2007).

Pacek, N., & Thorniley, D. (2007). *Emerging Markets: Lessons for Business Success and the Outlook for Different Markets.* London: Profile Books Limited.

Perkins, T. (2009, March 14). G20 Urged to Target Toxic Assets. *Globe and Mail.*

Porter, M. E. (1980). *Competitive Strategy: Techniques for Analyzing Industries and Competitors.* New York: John Wiley & Sons.

Powell, T. C. (1995, January). Total Quality Management as Competitive Advantage: A Review and Empirical Study. *Strategic Management Journal*, pp. 15–37.

Prahalad, C., & Hamel, G. (1990, May-June). The Core Competances of the Corporation. *Harvard Business Review*, pp. 79–91.

Prime Broking Poll 2009. (2009).

Prime Broking Poll 2008. (2008).

Quark Fund LLC v. Banc of America et al., Case No. 06 CV 3933 (United States District Court Southern District of New York).

R. (on the application of Cukurova Finance International Ltd. and another) v. HM Treasury, [2008] EWHC 2567 (Admin), [2008] All ER (D) 02 (Nov). (Approved judgement) (Queen's Bench Division, Administrative Court September 29, 2008).

RAB Capital, P. L. C. v. Lehman Brothers International (Europe), 2008 WL 4657221 (Chancery Division, Companies Court September 22, 2008).

Reuters. (2009, January 13). *Reuters Daily News*, p. 1.

Reuters. (2009, December 9). Centarus Could Sell Atos Stake, but Not Now. *Reuters Daily News.*

Reuters. (2008, December 1). Deadline Extended for Rival Neuberger Bids. *Reuters Daily News.*

Reuters. (2008, December 8). Dillard's Shareholders Demand Access to Records. *Reuters Daily News.*

Reuters. (2008, December 17). European Banks Reel as Madoff Arrest Ordered. *Reuters Daily News.*

Reuters. (2008, September 30). Hedge Funds Brace for Redemption Wave, Cash High. *Reuters Daily News.*

Reuters. (2008, December 18). Lawyers, Others Line Up to Probe Madoff Scandal. *Reuters Daily News.*

Reuters. (2008, December 17). Liquidation Official Sees Madoff Case Taking Years. *Reuters Daily News.*

Reuters. (2008, December 17). Madoff Fraud Could Burn Those Who Pulled Out Early. *Reuters Daily News.*

Reuters. (2008, October 23). Morgan Stanley Prime Broker Woes Seen Lasting. *Reuters Daily News.*

Reuters. (2008, December 18). No Deluge of Lawsuits—Yet—Madoff Case. *Reuters Daily News.*

Reuters. (2008, December 17). No Proof of SEC Staff Wrongdoing in Madoff Case: Cox. *Reuters Daily News.*

Reuters. (2008, October 15). U.S. Funds Urge Freeing of Lehman Assets. *Reuters Daily News.*

Revenue and Custom Commissioners v. D'Arcy, [2007] EWHC 163 (Ch); [2008] STC 1329 (Chancery Division February 7, 2007).

Saltmarsh, M. (2009, March 14). Tax Havens Likely to Be Target of G-20. *New York Times.*

Sam Bronstein et al. v. Crowell, Weedon & Co. et al., B191738 (Unreported) (Courts of Appeal of California, Second Appellate District, Division Two April 3, 2007).

Savings Bank of the Russian Federation v. Refco Securities LLC, [2006] EWHC 857 (QB), [2006] 2 All ER (Comm) 722 (Queen's Bench Division, Commercial Court March 17, 2006).

Scannell, K., & Koppel, N. (2008, December 26). Crisis on Wall Street: Broad Probe into Hedge Fund—SEC Examines Whether Family, Associates Played Roles. *Wall Street Journal* (Eastern Edition), p. C.2.

SEC v. Beacon Hill Asset Management, LLC et al. (Amended Complaint), Civil Action 02-8855(LAK) (United States District Court for the Southern District of New York June 15, 2004).

SEC (1994, January 25). Prime Broker No Action Letter.

Sender, H. (2008, July 15). Relief for Big Two but Others Feel Trading Heat. *Financial Times*, p. 3.

Sender, H., Guerrera, F., Larsen, P. T., & Silverman, G. (2008, December 15). Brinkmanship Was Not Enough to Save Lehman. *Financial Times.*

Skinner, C., Ed. (2007). *The Future of Investing: In Europe's Markets after MiFID.* Chichester: John Wiley & Sons Ltd.

Soros, G. (2008). Testimony before the U.S. House of Representatives: Committee on Oversight and Government Reform. Washington, D.C.: U.S. House of Representatives p. 12.

Soros, G. (1998). Testimony to the U.S. House of Representatives: Committee on Banking and Financial Services. Washington, D.C.: U.S. House of Representatives, p. 4.

Soros, G. (2008). *The New Paradigm for Financial Markets: The Credit Crisis of 2008 and What It Means.* New York: Public Affairs.

Spangler, T. (2007). Hedge Funds: the Building Blocks. *PLC*, p. 21.

Speech. (2008, October 22). London.

Sprott, E. (2009, March 19). (J. Aikman, Interviewer).

Steiner, B. (2007). *Mastering Financial Calculations* (2nd ed.). Harlow, U.K.: Pearson Education Limited.

Stewart, J. (1991). *Den of Thieves.* New York: Simon & Schuster.

Strasburg, J., & Karmin, C. (2008, September 20). Market Rescue: Hedge Funds Adjust Their Trading Models. *Wall Street Journal*, p. B.3.

Surz, R. *Hedge Funds Have Alpha Is a Hypothesis Worth Testing.*

Taylor, F. (2007). *Mastering Derivatives Markets.* Harlow, U.K.: Pearson, Education Limited.

Terzo, G. (2008a, December 8). A Changing World for Hedge Funds; Days of Massive Leverage and Little Regulation Are Over; "Nobody Will Be Leveraged that Much Again" *The Investment Dealer's Digest*, p. 8.

Terzo, G. (2008b, October 20). Prime Time for Multi-Broker Model: As Fear Grips Wall Street, a Reality Emerges: the Single Prime Broker Model Is Dead. *The Investment Dealer's Digest.*

The Art of Speculation. (2006). New York: Cosimo Inc.

The Capital Markets Company. (2003). *Understanding and Mitigating Operational Risk in Hedge Fund Investments.*

The Jordan (Bermuda) Investment Co. v. Hunter Green Investments LLC et al., 00 Civ. 9214 (RWS) (United States District Court for the Southern District of New York October 9, 2007).

The Pension Committee of the University of Montreal et al. v. Bank of America Securities, LLC. and Citco Fund Services (Curacao) N.V. et al., 05 Civ. 9016 (SAS) (United States District Court for the Southern District of New York January 5, 2009).

Turner, Lord. (2009). *The Turner Review.* London.

UBS AG and another v. HSH Nordbank AG, [2008] EWHC 1529 (Comm), [2008] All ER (D) 70 (Jul), (Approved judgement) (Queen's Bench Division, Commercial Court July 4, 2008).

United States of America v. Bernard L. Madoff, 08 MAG 2735 (United States District Court for the Southern District of New York December 11, 2008).

Vereecken, M., & Nijenhuis, A., Eds. (2003). *Settlement Finality in the European Union: The EU Directive and Its Implementation in Selected Jurisdictions.* Kluwer Legal Publishers.

Vickers, M., & Boyd, R. (2008, December 22). Citadel Under Seige. *Fortune: Special Issue / Investor's Guide 2009*, p. 131.

Wall Street Newsletter. (2008, October 27). Top Prime Brokers Announced by Alpha Magazine. *Wall Street Newsletter.*

Wedbush Morgan Securities, Inc. v. Robert W. Baird & Co., 320 F. Supp. 2d 123; 2004 U.S. Dist. Lexis 10056 (United States District Court for the Sourthern District of New York June 3, 2004).

Weisenthal, J. (2009, February 27). Consulting Firms Failed Miserably on Westridge Fraud. *Wall Street Journal.*

Wyderko, S. F. (2006, May 16). Testimony Before the Subcommittee on Securities and Investment of the United States Senate Committee on Banking, Housing, and Urban Affairs. Washington, D.C.

Zola, A., & Finkel, A. (2008). *Getting a Job in Hedge Funds: An Inside Look at How Funds Hire.* Hoboken, NJ: John Wiley & Sons.

Glossary of Useful Terms

account opening: Standard process for evaluating clients and assessing KYC, AML, and other standard account opening forms and procedures, including basic fund documents, incorporations, tax certificates, relevant contracts, and articles of incorporation or partnership agreements.

alpha: Non-market risk attributable to the skill of a manager in selecting securities.

AML: Anti-money laundering.

AUM: Assets under management.

beta: Market risk. The beta of the market is the correlation coefficient of an asset to the performance of the overall market.

bottom-up analysis: Individual securities are evaluated for value, and then combined in a portfolio with macroeconomic or other factors being considered later.

CFD: Contract-for-difference; *see* (Downes & Goodman, 2006).

CFTC: Commodity Futures Trading Commission.

COB: Conduct of Business.

CTA: Commodity Trading Advisor; a person or entity that either directly or indirectly advises on futures contracts or options. In the United States, CTAs are required to register with the CFTC, and normally also register with the National Futures Association (NFA).

derivative: A contract whose value is based on an underlying asset, condition, event, financial product, or index; *see* (Downes & Goodman, 2006).

DMA: Direct Market Access.

EC: European Community.

EM: Emerging Market.

ETF: Exchange Traded Fund.

EU: European Union.

FASB: Financial Accounting Standards Board.

FINRA: An SRO for members in the securities industry in the United States and elsewhere.

FOHF: Fund of Hedge Funds.

free rider syndrome: The free rider syndrome occurs where an investor enjoys a benefit not applicable to prior investors. For example, where a fund has a high-water mark before the manager may receive performance fees, a late investor in a simple fund may not have to pay such fees even where the high-water mark does not reflect the losses of the late investor.

GMRA: Global Master Repurchase Agreement.

GMSLA: Global Master Securities Lending Agreement.

haircut: The haircut for a repo or stock loan transaction is the amount of margin required to be added to the collateral provided. The haircut is a critical consideration to the financing of securities lending and repo trades. Increasing haircuts decreases risk but also decreases the liquidity in the market.

hedge fund: No accepted definition, although Lhabitant provided a general definition, that "Hedge funds are privately organized, loosely regulated and professionally managed pools of capital not widely available to the public."

hedge fund manager: The manager of a hedge fund, who may be regulated or unregulated.

IAASB: International Auditing and Assurance Standards Board.

IADI: International Association of Deposit Insurers.

IAIS: International Association of Insurance Supervisors.

IASB: International Accounting Standards Board.

ICMA: International Capital Markets Association.

IMF: International Monetary Fund.

IOSCO: International Organization of Securities Commissions.

ISLA: International Securities Lending Association.

KYC: Know your client. Rules on disclosure of client information in certain jurisdictions related to anti-money laundering, and disclosure of basic information on clients.

long: To be long a stock is to profit from the increase in value of a security. A long position is normally created by simply purchasing securities on an exchange.

LTCM: Long-Term Capital Management.

LTV: Loan to value.

mega-hedge fund: A hedge fund with assets over $100M USD.

MFN: "Most-favored nation" provision grants investors similar rights to other investors in the event that an investor negotiates a specific concession from the manager. It allows the investor to rely on the provision negotiated by another investor and thereby avoid the situation where one investor is placed in a superior position to other investors.

MiFID: Markets in Financial Instruments Directive.

mini-primes: Prime broker not directly associated with a large investment or commercial bank.

OECD: Organization for Economic Cooperation and Development.

OEIC: Open Ended Investment Company.

OTC: Over-the-Counter.

PB: Prime broker.

PBA: Prime broker agreement.

prime broker: A prime broker is a broker-dealer who offers standard clearing, settlement, and leverage to clients.

repo: A repurchase transaction that is a form of secured financing. A repo is a financing transaction that includes a sale and a repurchase of securities; *see* the market standard Global Master Repurchase Agreement and relevant annexes at www.icma.org.

RM: Risk management.

short: An economic position that is inversely related to the long position in securities or derivatives. A short position in securities is typically created by borrowing securities and selling the borrowed securities to profit from the depreciating value of the securities. Short positions have come under increasing scrutiny as regulators have imposed short selling restrictions.

SRO: Self-regulating organization, such as FINRA or ISLA.

stress testing: A technique to determine the impact of potential risks on a portfolio, and to identify particular sensitivity to specific risk factors.

stock loan: A stock loan is a transaction where a specific security is loaned in return for collateral. Stock loans are often completed on standardized agreements, MSLA or GMSLA.

SWF: Sovereign wealth fund.

top-down analysis: A type of investment analysis where the analyst takes a global or national macroeconomic survey of industries, then sectors and then individual securities or financial instruments are considered for selection.

VAR: Value at risk. A statistical method for analyzing risk, useful for short-term inductive analysis of risk, but may yield incomplete and misleading assessments of total risk.

About the Author

J. S. Aikman advises managers and financial institutions in the areas of prime finance. He was previously VP and Counsel for an investment bank in London, England. He has broad international experience in alternative investments as a lawyer and management consultant. He completed an MBA from Oxford University and has advised on and led various successful entrepreneurial ventures.

Index